Japanese
American Women

JAPANESE AMERICAN WOMEN

THREE GENERATIONS 1890 - 1990

Mei T. Nakano

with **OKAASAN**

by   Grace Shibata

MINA PRESS PUBLISHING
Berkeley • Sebastopol
        and
NAT'L. JAPANESE AMERICAN HISTORICAL SOCIETY
San Francisco

Library of Congress Cataloging-in-Publication Data

Nakano, Mei (date)
    Japanese American Women: three generations
1890-1990.

    Includes bibliographical references.
    Includes Index.
    1. Japanese American women--History. I. Shibata,
Grace (date)   . II. Title
E184.J3N35   1990   973'.04956   89-91580
ISBN 0-942610-05-9
ISBN 0-942610-06-7 (pb)

Cover design by Janice Kawamoto

To you, Mama, who gave me a model

Contents

List of Photographs

Acknowledgments

First I want to thank my husband, friend and partner, Shiro Nakano, for unending patience and support and for that glass of wine delivered in the dead of night to remind me gently that there is a time for quitting.

A partnership with the National Japanese American Historical Society made the publication of this book possible. Special thanks to Rosalyn Tonai there, whose blend of professionalism and humanity manages to make sense out of chaos and keep everyone connected in a way quite beyond anyone's comprehension. Thanks to her and Grant Din, especially, for readying our photographs.

Valerie Nishimoto, Chizu Iiyama, and Clifford Uyeda provided invaluable editorial suggestions. I am deeply in their debt. Thanks too to Nik, Philip and Steven Omi, who gave up a weekend to comb the manuscript.

And how can I thank my good friend and editor, Adam David Miller, who prodded and guided and saw me through the wilderness of ideas and utterances, page by page, word by word.

Thanks too to those wonderful women of the Women's Exhibit Committee whose ideas and suggestions gave me a push. Interviewers for the Oral History Project, Chizu Iiyama, Rosalyn Tonai, Val Ito, Deki Seto, Kiku Funabiki, Yoji Ozaki and others, provided invaluable material for the book.

And I want to thank Suzanne and Vern Clark. Their love and encouragement, not to mention catered gourmet dinners, sustained me.

My deep respect and appreciation to all of those erudite folk whose works gave this one some solidity, especially Michi Weglyn, Harry Kitano, Bill Hosokawa, Evelyn Nakano Glenn and Yuji Ichioka.

Lastly, to all of those extraordinary Sansei women who took time out to share a chunk of their lives in the survey, also to those who wrote or telephoned, or contributed information in other ways, my profound thanks . This book would not have been given life without them.

Introduction

The imprisonment of Japanese Americans in camps during World War II so enraged a number of right-minded people that it moved them to produce a burst of literature. Yet, when one scans that literature, one finds that it is, to no one's surprise, a record almost exclusively about men. Never mind that they were the villains, never mind that some were even heroes, the record is skewed, imperfect, devoid of an account of half the people who lived it.

The history of women, told by women, is a recent phenomenon. It has called for a fundamental reevaluation of assumptions and principles that govern traditional history. It challenges us to have a more inclusive view of history, not merely the chronicling of events of the past, not dominated by the record of men marching forward through time, their paths strewn with the detritus of war and politics and industry and labor.

As writers, we are challenged to take into historical account ordinary people failing and succeeding, changes they undergo in the family, in the work place and in their attitudes. We are challenged to push the former boundaries of history and record not only the lives of the heroic, but that of the undervalued, of women as well as men. Above all, we need to think of history as primarily about people, not events, as an account of their states of mind as well as their actions.

Someone wisely said that you cannot presume to understand the history of a particular group unless you listen to what they have to say about it. If we consider it an important function of history to be that of understanding, then we would do well to listen to that sage.

Here, we present the history of a group, Japanese American women, never before presented. They have been largely invisible throughout the one hundred years of their lives in this country. Who are they? How did they spend their time while their male counterparts went off to war, or out to the vast fields to make their fortune or even into the halls of Congress? What kinds of cultural imperatives did they bear, and how did these help or hinder? How did they feel as they were making history? What, if anything did they contribute to this country?

To a large extent, we ask them to tell their history. They do so, eloquently, truthfully.

Because of the vagaries of immigration laws, it is possible to talk about Japanese American women in terms of three distinct generations: the Issei (first generation), the Nisei (second generation) and the Sansei (third generation). Non-Japanese sometimes find these terms confusing, but only if they are not acquainted with the history of Japanese in America. For those terms evolved out of that very history and are peculiar only to those Japanese who live in the United States.

Japanese women began trickling into this country around the turn of the century, then in sizable numbers around 1915. They came most frequently as picture brides, strangers to their husbands, strangers to the country. Then, in 1920, the immigration of brides was abruptly cut off, thus setting off the discrete generational pattern that was to distinguish the Japanese American population.

They came for a number of reasons, these brides, reasons that did not necessarily parallel those of their European counterparts. Some came to carry out the wishes of the parents, who had made the match. Others came because it presented a last hope for marriage. A few came for the adventure this country offered and bore dreams of an idyllic and romantic pioneer life.

Whatever their motives, the majority were disappointed. But they had committed themselves, and for that reason alone, most stayed. Never quite at home in this country in their early years, a country so alien to their own, they sacrificed their own aspirations and labored to give everything to their children.

The story of Issei women, is thus appealing, rife with privation and unremitting pioneer struggle. Because of this, a great deal has been written about them.

xiv

The major part of this work, therefore is given over to their daughters, the Nisei, for about them, almost nothing has been written.

Issei women were in a sense cushioned from the rabid racism that prevailed against the Japanese in the country before World War II. They retained their cultural values and were able to find meaning in their circumscribed lives. Thus their sense of selfhood remained for the most part intact amid the racist din. And while their marriages were not made in heaven, the unions did satisfy the Issei woman's concept of her ordained role in society.

The Nisei woman, on the other hand, had greater expectations. She was a citizen, after all, and when she encountered hate and humiliation because of her face, those things cut deep into her psyche. Moreover, she had to function out there--at school, at work at play--which made her extremely vulnerable.

Then her forced isolation in a concentration camp during the war became for her the perfect metaphor for how the society regarded her, a telling symbol of its disdain. How to deal with it? Change her face? Her values? Her lifestyle? In her youth and state of powerlessness and uncertainty, challenging the government was not a realistic option.

As for sexism, Nisei women long felt themselves in double jeopardy, objects of the sexism of the society-at-large as well as the deeply entrenched one of traditional Japanese society. The Nisei woman expected more of her spouse than did her mother, and for both partners to grow into an understanding of roles that satisfied, was difficult.

To a great degree, Nisei women functioned as bridges between the traditional culture and the new. They understood both languages and the underlying assumptions of both cultures. They passed on some valuable features of Japanese culture to their children, while struggling themselves to become fully "Americanized."

Their daughters the Sansei, born for the most part between 1940 and 1960, do not speak the language, as a rule. They enjoy options in their everyday lives, unprecedented in the history of Japanese Americans.

Sansei women marry non-Japanese upwards of 50% of the time.

And like their contemporaries, many set up households with male companions without formal marriage. Most are college graduates and work, whether or not they are married or have children.

The choice of careers for Sansei women is almost unlimited. From secretaries to attorneys to television reporters, they find little difficulty landing jobs. At the same time, many complain that few Japanese American women find themselves on the fast track to top-level executive positions in industry or government. The "glass ceiling" that bars women from such positions, they say, is doubly thick above them because they are perceived as passive and non-assertive. They strive to obliterate this stereotype, but in the process, they may be losing more than they are gaining.

One thing is certain. Sansei women recognize many positive Japanese cultural values that resonate in their thinking and actions. Not the least of these are the sense of the importance of family and a deeply infused sense of obligation and responsibility. And as they merge into the mainstream of American society, they worry that those and other values are being diluted. Will their children inevitably lose the legacy handed down them from three generations before?

A few are already recording the course of their lives in the form of literature, drama and films. They seem to be eminently aware that, in the making of history, females as well as males must be the measure of significance in order that the history be valid.

PART I

The Issei

Picture bride, just before leaving Japan for America, 1910. *Photo courtesy Marshall Sumida.*

Picture brides arriving at Angel Island, ca. 1920, San Francisco. *Photo courtesy Japanese American History Room, Japanese Cultural and Community Center, Northern California.*

Picture brides arriving at Angel Island immigration station, ca. 1912,
San Francisco. *National Archives.*

CHAPTER 1

Immigration - 1860-1924

If I had known more in detail beforehand, I would probably never have come.

---Sakiko Suyama

They came to the United States, as all immigrants did, nursing hopes for a better life than the one they had left. But Japanese women had emigrated under markedly different circumstances from those of their European counterparts, and the road they trod here in their lifetime had little semblance to the one on which the others made their way.

Between 1910 and 1920, when the majority of Japanese women emigrated, they could not make the independent decision to pack up their trunks and set sail. A Japanese woman could only emigrate to the United States provided that: she already had a spouse living here; an immigrant returned to Japan to marry her; or, she had married an immigrant by proxy. Thus whether she could even consider the choice depended on the vagaries of immigration laws and the will of a man.

And when she arrived in the new country, her life more or less followed that pattern. Severely bound by the prejudices of both race and gender, she took whatever options were available and struggled to fulfill what she deemed to be her destiny.

Partly because of a cultural bent, but also because of the chilly reception they received in the U.S., the Issei devoted themselves almost entirely toward the welfare of their citizen children. This often meant undue hardship for the women, for it was largely they who forged the bonds of family and kept it intact. They managed this by out-and-out sacrifice, subordinating their own needs and wants for the sake of the children and family. And they worked, no matter how hard and how long if it meant shoes, or food, or education, for the children.

If the story of Issei women seems all too saintly and noble in our time, one should note that in the context of the traditional Japanese society, the Issei woman took for granted her sharply defined role.

She did not go about her business burdened with a halo. Instead, she was more apt to perceive her life as ordained, the destiny of which she was working out. *"Shikata ga nai"* ("It can't be helped"), she would say, when things got particularly tough. Then, paradoxically-- and this was the crux of her survival and success--she would strive even harder.

This consciousness of destiny and purpose also gave the Issei woman her identity, her sense of self-worth. Like the heroine of *The Woman in the Dunes* (Kobo Abe, Alfred A Knopf, Inc. 1964), who found meaning in the endless round of clearing sand out of her living space, the Issei woman found meaning in the very process of her struggle. Years later, she would look back on her life in America and say, "Yes, it was good."

EARLY ARRIVALS 1868-1908

Japanese women arrived in the United States in considerably fewer numbers than men in the initial phase of immigration beginning in 1868. Out of a total of 27,440 Issei counted in the 1900 census, females numbered only about 1000, not all adults. Roughly half of these adults were listed as married.[1]

Little has been recorded about the lives of these pioneer married women but presumably they were, or had soon become, the wives of the immigrant laborers who had sent for them.

The experiences of the single women among these early arrivals are better known. But their stories emerge as anomalies, tiny ripples in the stream of Japanese American history.

"A Japanese Girl" Take, for instance, Okei Ito. Barely seventeen, she arrived in the United States in 1869 with the contingent of Japanese immigrants now known as the Wakamatsu Tea and Silk Colony.[2] Headed by John Henry Schnell, the group consisted of farmers and a few "political refugees," the latter, once loyalists of Lord Matsudaira, who had been crushed in a power struggle with the Emperor. The Colony settled in Gold Hill in El Dorado County, California, and immediately set about establishing a tea and silk enterprise on 600 acres of land they had purchased.

---

[1] Bill Hosokawa, *Nisei, the Quiet Americans* (William Morrow and Co., N.Y. 1969), p. 119.

[2] Henry Taketa, "Mayflower of the Pacific" *Pacific Citizen*, December 1966, Sec. 3-B. Taketa reports the story resulting from research done by Fern Sayre and Soichi Nakatani of Sacramento.

Okei, one of four women in the group, served as a nursemaid to the Schnell family. When the Colony failed miserably less than two years after its founding, Schnell left with his Japanese wife and two young daughters, never to return. Thus the settlers returned to Japan or went off to seek their livelihood elsewhere in the U.S. Only Okei and a samurai named Sakurai remained, subsequently becoming employed by the family of one Frances Veerkamp. Okei died not long afterwards. A simple gravestone marks her brief life: "IN MEMORY OF OKEI, DIED 1871, AGED 19 YEARS, A JAPANESE GIRL." The poignant story of this young woman became the subject of both a film and popular ballad in Japan.

Prostitutes   Equally marked by adversity, are the stories of prostitutes who made their appearance during the 1880s. By 1900, they comprised at least half of the few single Japanese women in the U.S.[3]

Many of these women were daughters of impoverished farm families in Japan who expected to do domestic work in the U.S. Most were brought over by Japanese men, procurers or agents of procurers, who lured them with promises of high wages in America. Once here, they were sold into prostitution. Male operators of brothels found the business lucrative:

> The most notorious procurer was Hasegawa Genji of San Francisco. Instead of going to Japan, he had women shipped regularly to him. In May 1890 he was sufficiently well-off to hire counsel when two women for whom he had sent were denied landing permission and detained by immigration officials. With writs of habeas corpus, he got them released and put them to work in his brothels.[4]

These women, unlike the spirited "saloon ladies" pictured in early western films, generally lived a life of pathos. Exploited by the men who brought them over, shunned by their own community, they also quickly became favorite targets of the American press and officials as an "immoral" influence on the domestic scene. Japanese officials, in both the United States and Japan, decried their activities as well, sensitive to the image they presented of Japan.

Details of these prostitutes' lives are not known, since few left memoirs. But a made-for-television film *Ameyuki San* (1979) illuminated the demeaning nature of this human trade in depicting

[3]Yuji Ichioka, *The Issei,* (The Free Press, Macmillan, N.Y. 1988), pp. 28-30.
[4]*Ibid.,* p. 31.

the story of Waka Yamada. Waka Yamada had been induced to come to the U.S. under false pretenses by an Issei man and forced into prostitution as soon as she landed in Seattle in 1902. Her tale of misery ended only when she managed to escape her bondage after several protracted attempts. She eventually returned to Japan to become a self-taught writer and noted critic.

The business of prostitution was lucrative for the men who ran it because single men outnumbered women so overwhelmingly. But it, along with the pimp-gamblers, all but disappeared with the arrival of thousands of brides from Japan, beginning in 1908.

Prototype   In stark contrast to Waka Yamada's story, another early immigrant woman's story stands out, luminous in content and promise. Shige Kushida, daughter of the co-founder of the Women's Christian Temperance Union in Japan, came to the U.S. in 1892 to study on a WCTU scholarship at the age of twenty-three. But the scholarship failed to materialize, and she was forced to take a job as a domestic in San Francisco. There she met Kikumatsu Togasaki. They married and formed a partnership of lifelong service to the community, offering advice, material help and moral guidance to newly-arrived immigrants as well as shelter to those in need. In the meantime, Mrs. Togasaki bore eight children. She scrimped, sacrificed and commanded forth her considerable resourcefulness to insure her children's education. They, in turn, would serve society: three daughters became nurses, three became doctors, among the first, and the few, Nisei (second generation) women to enter that latter profession.[5]

In an important sense, Shige Togasaki can be seen as the prototype of the Issei woman. Hard work and sacrifice for the sake of the family coupled with enormous resourcefulness were to be the Issei woman's enduring hallmark.

PICTURE BRIDES - 1908-1920

Shige Togasaki's early example of establishing a stable and permanent household in America became commonplace during the first two decades of the 1900s when more than 20,000 Japanese women arrived, more often than not as "picture brides." Most had been called here by laborers. And although these brides had no way of knowing it as they struggled against unremitting hardships, their unions would form the bedrock upon which future Japanese Americans would establish themselves and flourish.   The vast

---

[5]Interview with daughter Dr. Yoshiye Togasaki.

majority of the Japanese born in the U.S. trace their ancestry to a picture bride.

The picture bride phenomenon arose from the external realities the Issei faced in the U.S. as well as from the cultural practices of the Japanese. Issei males greatly outnumbered females at the outset of this period, having emigrated primarily as laborers. Because of the hostility they faced in this country and because of sentimental attachments to Japan, the majority had seen themselves as sojourners in America, intending to return to Japan as soon as they had made a "fortune." But when it became apparent that this elusive goal was not to be achieved overnight, they hastened to establish families. Too, many had squandered their hard-earned wages on gambling, women and drink, and now yearned for a more stable, anchored life. Some returned to Japan to marry; others married by proxy and went to Japan to fetch their brides or sent for them after having exchanged letters and photographs. These proxy marriages became known as *shashin kekkon* (literally, "photograph marriage") by the Issei, as "picture bride marriages" by others.

Process and Purpose   From the Western point of view, these so-called picture bride marriages might have seemed "quaint" at best and vaguely immoral at worst. But for the Japanese, they were not that far removed from traditional marriage practices. In Japan, as Yuji Ichioka notes, "marriage was never an individual matter, but always a family affair." He explains that, only after thoroughly investigating the backgrounds of the prospective partners through an intermediary, did the heads of households agree to a match.[6] Then if the principals agreed to marry, the name of the woman was placed in the man's family registry in order to formalize the marriage. Essentially the same process was completed in the picture marriages except that the intermediary often played a more prominent role.

Why did these brides make the radical decision to cross the Pacific on a grueling month-long voyage to an alien country? Surely, the prospect of marriage to a stranger and making a home in a land with alien customs must have given them pause. A variety of overriding motives impelled them. Some of the more prominent

---

[6]Ichioka, p. 165. The author notes additionally that, until 1915, all laborers were ineligible to summon wives because they did not command wages high enough to meet the standards set by Japanese consulates. After 1915, however, the ban was lifted, but laborers were still required to show proof of a bank account of at least $800 deposited for a period of 5 months prior to sending for their wives.

ones were set down in a journal by Shika Takaya, herself a bride, as she journeyed to America aboard the *Mexico Maru* in 1917.

> I believe we all go to America for one of the following reasons:
> 1. Hopes of becoming rich.
> 2. Curiosity of this civilized country called America.
> 3. Fear of mother-in-law in Japan.
> 4. Sexual anxiety in those who have passed marriage-age.
> 5. Dreams of an idyllic, romantic life in the new land.
> 6. Lack of ability to support self.
> 7. Filial obedience: sacrificing self to obey parents' wishes.[7]

Disillusionment and Trials   "Dreams of an idyllic, romantic life" soon vanished when new brides faced the realities that confronted them. To begin with, many felt a shock of disappointment upon meeting their husbands, who bore little resemblance to the handsome portraits they had submitted. Later, many brides were to discover that their husbands had exaggerated their talents and circumstances as well. "Men who claimed to be owners of large stores, turned out to be running small fruit stands," writes Mrs. Takaya. "'Big farmers' turned out to be share-croppers of five or six acres. And many of those men who had sent us splendid letters written in a fine hand, had had their letters written for them."[8]

Stories abound about the painful, sometimes comic, experiences these women underwent in adapting to the new culture. One, for example, tells of a newly-arrived bride who was so taken with the beauty and intricacy of a corset that she wore it over her new, long Western dress. Another bride remembers being served raw steak, sliced thin, by her husband, who offered it as "American sashimi."

Nor were these women prepared for the back-breaking labor, poverty, and loneliness they faced. Farm laborers' brides were apt to become ensconced in a two-room shack with a dirt floor, nothing but a wood stove, a bed and a table as furnishings. It was a far cry from the grand home they had envisioned.

Culture shock, too, was extraordinarily severe, for unlike European immigrants whose languages, food and clothing had some relationship to the new world, Japanese immigrants found nearly everything alien to their own culture. Most Issei women could not,

---

[7]Featured in *The Colorado Times*, November 1931.
[8]*Ibid.*

and never would, master the English language, a tongue which had no linguistic connection to their own.[9]

Riyo Orite tells of being advised to answer "no" from behind the locked door if anybody knocked. "I didn't even know how to say 'hello' or 'good-by' in English. My husband should have taught me to say a few words." Later, she did learn a few words, managing a "thank you" to a neighbor who had attempted to teach her English:

> The wife displayed a lot of canned food and taught me, "This is a can of tomatoes. This is a can of mushrooms." Since I couldn't speak English, I answered her in Japanese. . . . I repeated "Thank you," although I didn't understand her. I said, "Good-by," and came home. I didn't feel like visiting her again.[10]

Implicit in Mrs. Orite's narrative, too, is the suggestion that, apart from the language difficulty, the mode of social interaction of her neighbor--direct and friendly, but diametrically opposed to the polite, rather deferential, group-oriented mode of the Japanese-- tended to discourage communication between them. Most brides who were confronted with a communication style similar to Mrs. Orite's neighbor no doubt felt uncomfortable.

Good Neighbors   In spite of the general climate of hostility towards the Japanese, many Issei women, like Mrs. Orite, reported numerous instances of kindness and generosity on the part of white neighbors. Shiki Ito, for example, remembers some white people who became very friendly and brought trout and venison to her family in exchange for vegetables.[11] Shika Takaya's neighbor taught her how to bake bread, beans and tortillas, which were essential to the family's menu, since it was difficult and expensive to get Japanese ingredients in the remote country where they lived in Colorado.

Desertions   Notwithstanding the adjustment most Issei women made with the help of neighbors and a growing network of Japanese

---

[9]Notable exceptions were women who were educated in Japan by Christian missionaries and women who went to work outside the family enterprise, like those engaged in domestic work. Many of these women eventually grasped a functional speaking knowledge of English.

[10]Eileen Sunada Sarasohn, ed., *The Issei: Portrait of a Pioneer*, (Pacific Publishers, Palo Alto CA), p. 123.

[11]*East Bay Japanese for Action Presents "Our Recollections,"* (EBJA, Inc. 1986), p. 131.

friends, some wives could not brook the disappointment of the matches they had made, nor could they endure the unrelenting hardships of their lives. They left their husbands, often running away with lovers. Ads appeared regularly in the language press in which the deserted husbands offered a bounty of twenty-five dollars or thereabouts for information leading to the return of their wives. The newspapers also printed titillating stories about the desertions. The details differ, says Ichioka, depending upon the story:

> A picture bride deserts right after arriving; another deserts after living with her husband for a spell. An older married woman leaves her husband and children, while another takes her infant with her. A woman and her paramour plot to steal her husband's hidden money before absconding together. A women is caught and sent back to Japan, while another is placed in a church-operated women's home. The men with whom women run off range from young laborers to roving city salesman, to partners in their husbands' farms or businesses, and even to professional gamblers.[12]

Ichioka astutely observes that, in addition to attracting readers, publishing these stories of deserting wives was a means of social control. The publicity marked them as "adulteresses," who would be shunned and most likely be forced to move. In an insular society such as that of the Japanese immigrant society, those prospects caused the women to be very circumspect; they would have had to be desperate to even consider deserting.[13]

THE HUSBANDS

For their part, the men could hardly be blamed for overselling themselves to their prospective brides. They were in a sense desperate to find marriage partners.

Around the year 1910, most had not accumulated the fortune they had expected to carry back to Japan. Apart from labor contractors (middlemen between American employers and Japanese laborers), who commanded lucrative incomes, and others who had moved from wage labor to self-employment, immigrant men had struggled as common laborers at the lowest end of the wage scale. But the conviction that America still held greater promise for them than Japan, or pride that would not allow them to admit failure to those back home, persuaded them to stay.

---

[12]Ichioka, p. 170
[13]*Ibid.*

The majority of these bachelors were now between ages 29-45, past the average marrying age for males of that era. Anxious to start a family before it became too late, they looked to Japan for wives. Not only was this their preference, few single Issei women were available in the U.S., and they were prevented by anti-miscegenation laws from marrying Caucasians. Prof. Evelyn Nakano Glenn makes the additional point that "quite apart from any sentimental desire for family life, men had pragmatic reasons to send for wives. A wife would provide much-needed labor in the form of services in the home and income-producing activities outside it."[14]

And the men, too, had difficulties with their photo marriages. In more than one case, bridegrooms claimed that they had not received the gentle beauty they had been promised and rejected their brides practically at dockside. Some complained that their wives were too "high toned" to suit them or were not fit for the rigors of pioneer life.

Others, like Asahiko Sawada encountered daunting difficulties. Sawada had married for the first time in Japan. After having fathered a son, who died shortly after birth, he boarded a ship to San Francisco, promising his wife that he would return a wealthy man. But in America he had difficulty accumulating enough money to fulfill his promise. Finally, in 1910, after six years, he was able to send for his wife, only to find that she had divorced him and remarried. In the subsequent eight years, he spent a small fortune "investing" in three photo marriages, which, for one reason or another did not work out. Now forty-five, still determined, he married once again. His fifth bride came to him "blemished" by her own confession, having had a son out of wedlock. But he was satisfied. Writes daughter Noriko Sawada Bridges: "No matter what she had done in the past, Papa wanted to keep Mama and make the best of it. . . . He wanted to give her a chance. He wanted a chance himself."[15]

Indeed a mood of "no matter what" underscored the immigrants' outlook. They would *gaman* (be patient, persevere), no matter what, to survive.

END OF IMMIGRATION

Oral histories and memoirs of Issei women suggest that they were largely ignorant of the institutionalized policy of racial discrimination against the Japanese existent in the United States.

---

[14]*Issei, Nisei, War Bride*, (Temple University Press, Philadelphia 1986), p. 68.

[15]Noriko Sawada Bridges, "Papa Takes a Bride," *Harper's*, December 1980, pp. 58-64.

Years before the majority of them arrived on U.S. shores, rankling resentment on the West Coast against Japanese laborers had been a fact of life. By 1906, labor and agricultural interests, ambitious politicians, and exclusionist groups, abetted by the press, clamored for an end to Japanese immigration. In February of 1905, for example, the San Francisco *Chronicle*, one of the more influential West Coast newspapers at that time, trumpeted these headlines: THE JAPANESE INVASION, THE PROBLEM OF THE HOUR and CRIME AND POVERTY GO HAND IN HAND WITH ASIATIC LABOR.[16]

In rapid succession, measures such as those which ordered Japanese American children into segregated schools (San Francisco 1906), the executive order issued by Theodore Roosevelt, terminating migration through Hawaii, Canada and Mexico (1907), and the Gentlemen's Agreement (1907-08) collectively delivered a message that the Japanese were not wanted. Into this situation the brides arrived.

The Gentlemen's Agreement   The Gentlemen's Agreement, it should be noted, had been designed specifically to curb the entry of immigrants who would enter the labor market. Because of anti-Japanese agitation of Californians and resultant pressure from the U.S. government, Japan agreed not to issue any further passports to laborers, skilled or unskilled, in what was called The Gentlemen's Agreement. This measure, however, did not strictly prohibit the entry of certain other persons, among them parents, wives and children of established residents of the U.S. Thus in practice, while drastically cutting the flow of male immigration, the Agreement proved to be the benchmark for the greatest influx of Japanese brides to the United States.

U.S. Immigration Act of 1924   Even so, in 1920, Japanese female immigrants numbered 24,125 in total, constituting only 30 percent of the immigrant population.[17] And considering that the total number of Japanese in the U.S. amounted to no more than 0.10 percent of the population,[18] it is self-evident that racial bias underscored U.S. immigration policy.

---

[16]Hosokawa, pp. 82-83.

[17]Dorothy Swaine Thomas, *The Salvage*, (Univ. of California Press, 1952), p.576.

[18]Hosokawa, p. 98.

At the same time, alarmists persisted in arguing that the immigration of brides breached the spirit if not the letter of the Gentlemen's Agreement. The women were laborers, they charged, deviously making their way into the U.S. by way of the picture bride system. Moreover, they contended, the marriages were leading to a Japanese population boom, and immigrants, who had previously been prohibited from buying land, were now gobbling up acreage in the name of their citizen children.[19] Some, like Senator James D. Phelan of California, took to the pious, moral ground. The Senator, who had based his 1920 reelection campaign on the issue of keeping California "white," pronounced the picture bride practice an uncivilized "Asiatic" custom in which women were being married off without regard to love or morality.[20]

To attempt to quell this rising clamor, the Japanese government ceased issuing passports to picture brides altogether in 1920.

But far from mitigating the issue, the measure only presaged a harsher one, this one enacted by the United States. In 1924, the United States government passed the U.S. Immigration Act, which effectively slammed the door to any further immigration from Japan. The door would not be opened again until after World War II.

---

[19]The Alien Land Act of 1913 stipulated that those who were considered "ineligible for citizenship" could not purchase land. Since it had long been assumed that Japanese and Chinese immigrants were "ineligible," it is clear that they had been the targets of the measure. Nevertheless, the assumption of non-eligibility was tested in the 1922 U.S. Supreme Court case of Ozawa vs. U.S. The Court ruled that the law did indeed limit naturalization to free white persons, to aliens of African nativity and to persons of African descent, in effect, prohibiting Asians from owning land.

[20]Ichioka, p. 173.

Issei woman. Chicago, ca. 1915. *Photo courtesy Daisy Satoda.*

CHAPTER 2

The Family

As if he wished they were boys, for an instant
Sadness shades his face:
Our daughters bending in the fields
In their faded overalls.

---Shika Takaya (1934)

"In every society," writes Evelyn Nakano Glenn, "the family is the central institution defining women's place and social identity."[1] This was particularly true for Issei women, and to a large extent, their daughters, because the family was such a dominant force in Japanese society.

THE TRADITIONAL FAMILY SYSTEM

The Issei quite naturally brought to the new country, traditional family values extant in Meiji Japan.[2] An understanding of the traditional Japanese family, or *ie*, is therefore fundamental to our understanding of Issei women and to the immigrant society as a whole.

The *ie* referred to an extended family which typically included the head of the household, his wife, his married sons, their wives, his unmarried children and his sons' children. It could also include other family members such as siblings of the head of the house as well as non-relatives. As can be noted here, descent was traced through the male line, and the principle of primogeniture, that is, succession to the family headship and inheritance of the family property by the eldest son, prevailed.

Designed to perpetuate the family both as a kinship unit and a corporate unit, the system put primary emphasis on the family as a

---

[1]*Issei, Nisei, War Bride*, (Temple University Press, Philadelphia 1986), p. 201.

[2]"Meiji" refers to the period between 1868 and 1912, but the values of traditional family system had been well codified prior to that in feudal Japan. Interestingly enough, when Issei women spoke of their husbands' failure to share household chores or the care of the children, they often remarked matter-of-factly that he was, after all, a "Meiji man."

corporate group through its name and occupation.[3] Of less importance was preserving the patrilineal blood line. When, for example, the family lacked a male heir, they often adopted one as an expedient, even if he was not blood-related.

The all-encompassing nature of this family system is revealed in one Nisei informant's description of his father's household in a village in Fukuoka prefecture, where he spent a year before W. W. II:

> There were seventeen families involved in my father's ie. He was the head, although he didn't act like it. Whenever an issue came up, like a business matter or a wedding or a death, a lady would beat a drum, and everyone would gather at the village shrine, which was near my father's house. There the men, mostly fathers, would sit in a circle and discuss what should be done.
>
> They grew rice. There was a large storage house beside the shrine where they stored the surplus products. There was also a store. Each family had their own vegetable garden. Almost everyone in the village had the same last name as my father. It amazed me that the mailman could remember who was who.[4]

Male Dominance   Absolute authority lay vested in the eldest male, the patriarch, at least in theory. His role could be compared to that of a benevolent ruler: he represented the family to the outside, oversaw the family operations and took legal responsibility for all the family members. All family members were required to obey him and accord him preferential treatment. He sat at the head of the table, was served first the choicest part of the meal, and went first to bathe.[5]

The successor, most often the eldest son, came next in line for preferential treatment, for when he came of age, he would receive a wife from another household and form the generation to provide heirs to the succeeding one. The other sons rarely shared the inheritance with the eldest son despite the practice of male dominance in the household. They usually split off to form separate, economically independent households when they married. And although they sometimes held close family ties, the ties were more emotional than economic.[6]

---

[3]Harumi Befu, "Patterns of Descent," *Japanese Culture*, (Aldine Publishing Co., Chicago 1962), p. 34.

[4]Personal interview.

[5]Glenn, pp. 202-203. Going first to bathe was a symbolic indicator of privilege in the Japanese home. Wives usually bathed last, after the mother-in-law and daughters.

[6]The fact that "other sons" had limited prospects in Japan lends credence to the speculation that they constituted the majority of Japanese emigrants of that period.

Daughters/Daughters-in-law　　Daughters held low status in the household because they did not figure in the continuity of the family. A daughter usually left to marry and fall into the dreaded fate of the daughter-in-law in the new family. Glenn sums it up:

> The trials of the new daughter-in-law were legion. She was assigned the most menial and onerous tasks. She was expected to rise before anyone else and stay up until everyone retired. . . . As a stranger in the community, she had few or no friends or kin to turn to for support or comfort. Her main reason for being was to work and bear children, especially a male heir. Any children she bore belonged to the household; if she left or was divorced, she had to leave them behind. Yet she herself could not initiate a divorce. If she ran away and returned to her parents, they were obligated to send her back.[7]

The new bride was in addition often dominated by the mother-in-law, whose legendary meanness ranks with that of Cinderella's stepmother. One Issei woman, who had returned to her husband's rural home in Japan, reported being treated so harshly that she regularly retreated to the wilds of the mountains for weeks, at times contemplating suicide. When she came back to the U.S. after the war, freed at last from the tyranny of her mother-in-law, it was, in her words, "*gokuraku*" (paradise).

While women were certainly oppressed, their position in the family was also mobile. By the time the daughter-in-law became the mistress of the household, she had accrued to herself some informal power. Glenn found that women could "attain considerable leverage if they contributed substantially to family income, were skilled, worked hard, had forceful personalities or were clever in manipulating others."[8] Also, she notes, many mothers forged very strong mother-son bonds during the child's formative years, so when the son became the head of the house, she could often exert a great deal of influence.

THE ISSEI-NISEI FAMILY

While the Issei held on to many values of the traditional family system, requisites of the new environment brought about gradual transformation in their own families. Two features, however, remained strong in the entrepreneurial years of the immigrant family: the practice of collective effort and male dominance and privilege.

---

[7]Glenn, p. 204.
[8]P. 203.

When they began to establish themselves in America, the immigrant family took on the character of a typical nuclear family. Issei were starting anew in a new land, more or less untethered to the economics of their kin in Japan. While many Issei couples cherished hopes of returning to Japan, sending part of their hard-earned wages to their households, even recording the names of their children in family registries, the economic arrangement of the immigrant family was, by dint of circumstance, independent of any other household. Other than their own offspring, few Issei heads of households had kin in the U.S., horizontal or vertical, with whom *ie*-like arrangements could be perpetuated.

Being barred from owning land discouraged the development of enterprises that could be handed down. When Issei settled in clustered communities in urban areas, they established small businesses to serve the community. In Seattle, Washington, for example, Issei businesses "were restricted to a narrow range of service-oriented enterprises, including hotels, groceries, produce, houses, restaurants, greenhouses, gardening services, barber shops, laundries, and peddling routes."[9] The Issei frequently viewed their ventures as means of advancing their children's career aspirations more than as a family occupation to be perpetuated.

Although circumstances and aims of the Japanese family in the U.S. had changed measurably from those of Japan, the pillar of the *ie* concept, the primacy of males, would not crumble easily. Women still worked in the fields or businesses, simultaneously taking responsibility for the house and childcare. Men still had ultimate authority and made major decisions without consulting their wives.

To characterize the immigrant family, Harry H.L. Kitano, professor of sociology at UCLA, paints a vivid picture of one at the dinner table:

> All family members are present. The Issei mother announces that she has made a very simple dinner . . . but the children understand that she would say this even if she had been cooking for days beforehand. Her disclaimer is especially loud if there are visitors present, but there are seldom visitors, and almost never non-Japanese guests. The food is a mixture of Japanese and American dishes . . .
>
> Father is served first, then sons in descending order of ages, sisters and finally mother. Conversation is carried on quietly among the children, but

---

[9]Sylvia Junko Yanagisako, "Two Processes of Change in Japanese-American Kinship," *Journal of Anthropological Research*, V. 31, (1975), pp. 201-202.

rarely between the parents, or between parents and children except when direct questions are asked.[10]

Along with illustrating male privilege in the immigrant family, this scene strikingly focuses on other Issei-Nisei behavioral tendencies. One sees the public modesty of the female, the mix of cultural elements (the children have probably prompted the serving of American dishes and are apt to be speaking to each other in English, while the parents speak in Japanese), the insular nature of the family, and the general lack of verbal communication between family members.

THE MARRIAGE

Circumstances in the Issei marriage did not augur well for a lasting union. The disappointments of the arranged marriages, the poverty, the unremitting work, not to mention the age gap of ten to fifteen years that existed between the wife and her spouse and the fact that she often had more education than her husband all pointed to a situation ripe for conflict and disillusionment. In spite of that, the overwhelming number of Issei marriages did prevail.[11] "The disillusionment was there, but not the divorce," asserts Harry Kitano, ascribing this to Japanese values and expectations which militated against a break-up. Too, "expectations of marriage lay not in the traditional American reverence for love and romance, but in the conception of duty and obligation, which, as has frequently been observed, may constitute a more realistic social attitude after all."[12]

Cultural Values   The cultural values to which Kitano refers include *gaman* (perseverance in the face of adversity), *giri* (sense of duty and obligation), and a kind of fatalism that decreed the acceptance of conditions that "couldn't be helped." Also the ideal of *giri ninjo*, which encompasses a range of meaning having to do with carrying out reciprocal obligations and responsibilities accompanied by "heart," strongly impelled Issei behavior. In practice, *giri* ordered a balance between give and take, thus encouraging continuous interaction between human beings and simultaneously strengthening bonds. Certainly, it helped carry marriages through stormy stretches.

Most importantly, the Issei were motivated by a profound commitment to the family: "*Kodomo no tame ni*" (for the sake of the

---

10*Japanese Americans, The Evolution of a Subculture,* (Prentice-Hall, Englewood Cliffs, N.J., 1969), pp 70-71.

11*Ibid.,* p. 156. Kitano found that Issei divorces were estimated to be a mere 1.6 percent in 1960.

12*Ibid.,* p. 64.

children) or "*kazoku no tame ni*" (for the sake of the family) became almost a moral imperative for most immigrants. This commitment all but cemented the marriage.

Michiko Tanaka, who gave birth to thirteen children told her daughter, "The most important thing [for a woman] to remember is her role to marry and raise children."[13] An outspoken, energetic Issei wife, Mrs. Tanaka was nevertheless submissive to her husband. She describes him as having been "severe," one who demanded that she take care of household chores after coming home from work, that she come into the kitchen in the morning fully dressed with her hair neatly combed. After marrying, she says, she never rose after the sun, was never treated well by her husband and rarely had fun. "But once I got married, I never entertained the thought of divorce. As long as he brought home enough to feed the children, I didn't care."[14]

Mrs. Tanaka's husband gambled and drank, as did many Issei men. There is good reason to believe that those habits were acquired in their earlier bachelor days when few recreational outlets were available to them, other than frequenting bars and poolhalls or patronizing Chinese gambling houses.[15] In any case, the drinking and gambling stressed the family's meager budget and caused considerable friction between couples. Glenn remarks that, among those women she interviewed, "the extent of drinking among Issei men can be gauged by the fact that women whose husbands did not drink heavily thought it worthy of comment.[16]

Issei wives had few alternatives to staying married. Unable to speak the language and unable to secure sustaining wages in an alien society, they would have required extraordinary good luck to make a life for themselves and their children. Also, many wives, including Mrs. Tanaka, felt that they could not return to their families in Japan because they either could not afford it, their families would refuse to receive them, or they could not face the "shame" of returning home.

On the other hand, some things had changed for the better for Issei wives. They had, for one thing, been liberated from the control of the mother-in-law of the traditional household. And for another, many women gained considerable authority within the family, particularly if they made substantial contributions to its income and had strong personalities. Mrs. S., for instance, ran a boarding house for bachelors

---

[13]Akemi Kikumura, *Through Harsh Winters, The Life of a Japanese Immigrant Woman*, (Chandler & Sharp Publishers, Inc., Novato, California 1981), p. 76.

[14]*Ibid.*, p. 33.

[15]Ichioka, pp. 84-89.

[16]Pp. 213-214.

in Los Angeles during the late twenties and thirties. She did all of shopping, handled the family budget and made most of the decisions concerning the home and the four children. An active, vigorous woman and a meticulous housekeeper, she would not allow her husband, a gardener, to enter the house through the front door.

Some women whose husbands failed in their occupations or gambled excessively, showed extraordinary spirit. Masako Yamashita's husband had gone back to Japan to start all over again, since his lumber-exporting business had failed.

> I wanted to earn our living expenses . . . and so I made baby clothes and took them to Bon Marche Department Store in Seattle. Since I could not speak English at all, I showed them without a word. Though they couldn't understand my language, they could certainly understand my intentions, and they told me that in spite of the fact that they had never stocked in this manner, they would consider it, and that I should come back again. Taking my children along, I called on them seven times all together [sic] and finally got an order for ten dozen at once, and another ten dozen later. I was to bring them in nine days!. . . For seven nights I didn't go to bed but I managed to finish. When I got sleepy I drank strong coffee and pushed myself on.[17]

Despite the hardships visited upon immigrant women, the overwhelming number of marriages survived. And as Issei women neared the end of their lives, few looked back upon it with bitterness. On the contrary, most expressed feelings of satisfaction. Hagino Matsuoka's statement exemplifies:

> My life in America . . . was not calm nor easy. But all has passed. I, who am 84 years old, consider myself to be fortunate. I cherish each and every peaceful day that passes.
>
> Both my sons have their own families now and live comfortably. I have been blessed with five grandchildren. I have no worries. I enjoy going to church and to the senior center.[18]

CHILDREN

The children for whom these Issei were to undergo all manner of travail began to arrive soon after the couple had established a

---

[17]Quoted in Kazuo Ito, *Issei, A History of Japanese Immigrants in North America*, (Executive Committee for Publication, Seattle 1973), pp. 259-260.

[18]*East Bay Japanese for Action Presents "Our Recollections,"* (hereafter cited as EBJA), (East Bay Japanese for Action, Inc. 1986), p. 95.

household. And the birth of these citizen children marked a turn of mind for the immigrants. Now, in spite of the hostility they were encountering, they considered the prospect of setting roots in the soil of America. In his autobiographical text, Daisuke Kitagawa declared that "the only sense in which Japan was his [the Issei's] frame of reference was as the place to which in the remote future, he would like to retire. He added that it was amazing "how little hostility was to be found among the Japanese toward the American society . . . . No amount of discrimination discouraged them from trying to win acceptance."[19]

Births The period between 1900 and 1920 saw a dramatic increase in the number of these second generation children, or Nisei. In 1900, only 269 children had been born, while by 1910, the number had grown to 4500 and by 1920 to nearly 30,000.[20]

Most children were delivered by midwives (*osamba*), with or without formal training.

Tome Yasutake practiced midwifery full-time beginning in 1909 in Seattle, Washington. She had been trained as a nurse in Japan and had taken the exam for midwives there. In her work, she not only performed the delivery and signed the birth certificates, but gave pre-natal and post-natal care as well. In addition, she often found herself involved in the intimate details of the families' lives and rendering services beyond the call of duty. Listening to the woeful tales of the wives became routine. More than once, the baby she delivered was sired by someone other than the man of the household, calling upon her to act as counselor/mediator. In one instance, she washed diapers for six solid weeks for a woman whose baby she had delivered. Another time, she removed a sixth finger from a baby. Daughter Mollie Fujioka remembers that when her mother returned home reeking of Lysol, she knew that a baby had been delivered.[21]

Not all deliveries were assisted by midwives. Women sometimes gave births unassisted, or husbands performed the duty. That was because, as Gin Okazaki put it, "If we had a midwife we would have to pay $20 to $50, and the doctors were even more expensive." Moreover, Mrs. Okazaki lived in a remote rural area, as many Issei families did, and reaching either a midwife or a doctor was difficult. Thus her husband and she brought four boys and four girls into the world. "It was

---

[19]*Issei and Nisei*, (Seabury Press, N.Y. 1967), pp. 12-13.

[20]Dorothy Swaine Thomas, *The Salvage*, (University of California Press, Berkeley and Los Angeles 1952), p. 577.

[21]Personal interview.

the custom for the mother to take a 21-day rest after delivery," she added. "But as for me, I could only rest three days."[22]

Not much has been written about birth control methods of the Issei, but Mrs. Okazaki gives us some insight: "At that time we knew about family planning. As a matter of fact, peddlers driving a Ford came to Vashon [Washington] too, and sold contraceptives. But since we had been taught that women naturally should give birth to many babies, we didn't think of using artificial birth control."[23]

Unpaid Workers   Mrs. Takaya's poem presented at the beginning of the chapter alludes to the fact that Issei men often looked upon children as assets, as potential workers, to put it crudely, and in their minds, male children added up to a better gain than females on the farm. But, in fact, girls worked right alongside boys as unpaid workers in both rural and urban areas.

As in the case with adults, children living on farms faced longer and more arduous work hours. "Our three children also went into the fields and worked pulling weeds," Yoshiko Ueda stated, "Kikusaburo, at the age of 4, Hirosaburo at 7, and Shige, our 10-year-old daughter, helped us to weed, crawling through the fields."[24]   However, older daughters were sometimes enlisted to care for younger children, while their mothers went off to work in the fields.

In the cities, boys helped their gardener fathers, and sisters joined their brothers to work in the small community businesses like fruit stands and drug stores. Here again a daughter, if an older child, often acted as a surrogate mother to the younger children while her mother went out to work as a domestic or a midwife.

If women suffered hardship and deprivation for the benefit of their children, there is ample evidence that they derived their greatest satisfaction, their very reason for being, from them. In a collection of writings of fifteen Issei women whose average age is 80 years, most expressed gratitude and a sense of reward. Shiki Ito's statement is typical:

> My sixty-four years in America have passed like this in a humdrum way. I am happy that all my children are blessed with fine spouses and living in prosperous circumstances. I have fifteen grandchildren and one great-grandchild. I have no worries. This is something to be thankful for. [25]

---

[22]Ito, p. 250.
[23]*Ibid.*
[24]*Ibid.*, p. 252.
[25]*EBJA*, P. 143.

ABOVE: Immigrant Japanese women participating in a war bond sale drive during World War I, Chicago, 1917. *Photo courtesy Daisy Satoda.*

BELOW: Sewing factories offered one of the few available jobs in cities to early immigrant women, ca. 1920, Honolulu. *Bishop Museum.*

CHAPTER 3

Work and Leisure

The pigs got fat: I got thin.
                    ---Yo Yamashita

"Any Issei woman arriving in the United States could expect to pull her weight economically," asserts Evelyn Nakano Glenn.[1] This meant that in addition to taking the major responsibility for housework and child care, the woman usually assumed a third role as worker. She provided much-needed labor in the form of services in the home as well as in work which produced income. It was a role vital to the survival of the family unit.

But she had limited choices for work outside the home. Glenn outlines four prescriptive features for the Issei woman's choices. She had to find work

1) that enabled her to carry out her family responsibilities, for example, work at home, at places where children could be taken or where hours were flexible; or,

2) with which she was familiar, such as food preparation, laundry, and sewing; or,

3) in "low-technology, labor-intensive field[s] where low wages and long hours reduced competition from white women"; or, finally,

4) in family-owned or ethnic enterprises "where language difficulties and racial discrimination did not constitute barriers to employment."[2]

While the women moved easily between these occupations, they were never employed outside it.[3]

Most women's work closely paralleled that of their husbands'. Whether in the fields, canneries, sawmills, or in laundries, plant

---

[1]*Issei, Nisei, War Bride*, p. 68.
[2]*Ibid*, p. 75.
[3]*Ibid*.

nurseries and restaurants, they worked in "double harness," as Issei were wont to put it.

In the early years, the majority of young brides were initiated into the rigors of immigrant working life in rural areas. Conditions in the home were primitive. Water had to be carted in from wells outside the home and heated atop a wood stove for laundering, bathing and other chores. Wives of farmers labored in the fields from dawn to dusk. Many of these women worked until the day their children were born, rested for a few days and resumed their work, their babies strapped to their backs. Some, like Mrs. Tanaka, would leave the child in a car, or in a shaded area at the side of the field, while they worked.

Shika Takaya's life as a tenant farmer's wife (her husband had been in turn a railroad worker, an ice-cream vender and a restaurant owner) began with relative ease in 1921. She and her family occupied a comfortable farm house on the land, their financial circumstances were on the upswing, and the future looked bright. But year by year, life became harsher with the addition of a child every year and a half, five moves, and the approach of the Depression years. By 1930, she had borne eight children and the family's fortunes had declined to below poverty level. Food came from whatever the fields yielded and whatever else could be canned, brined or dried. Whether new shoes could be ordered from the catalogue so that the children could attend school in the fall became a problem of considerable moment.

A typical day in the summer months for Mrs. Takaya meant rising at five, preparing breakfast and sending her husband and the four older children off to the fields. Often, in addition, there would be a bachelor who had come "to help out." After an hour or so of household chores, such as readying bread dough to be baked and setting out materials for lunch and supper, she herself would leave for the fields, the younger children trailing behind or left at home with strict instructions. She would return to prepare lunch, then work in the fields again until sunset. After cooking supper, and long after her children and husband had gone to bed, she usually sat at the sewing machine, stitching bloomers out of flour sacks or sunbonnets out of inexpensive calico. Often after supper, she would put cauldrons of water on the stove to do the family wash. "It was so unusual to see her rest," said one of her daughters, "that once when I saw her lying prone on the long wooden bench alongside the dining table in broad daylight, I thought she had died. It turned out that she was pregnant."[4]

Many of these pioneering Issei women worked in labor camps operated by their labor-contractor husbands, cooking, cleaning and

---

[4]Personal interview.

laundering for their husbands' work crews, which numbered anywhere between 15-100 men. "Not just anyone could have done the work I did," says Mrs. Tanaka, whose husband was a labor contractor and foreman at Kettleman's. "I sometimes cooked for as many as 50 men (all Japanese) with three big pots. . . rice, *okazu* [meat sauteed with vegetables], *tsukemono* [pickled vegetables], and other dishes. Before I went out to the fields to work in the morning, I would have the food set out so that when I came home, it was all ready to cook."[5]

THE URBAN EXPERIENCE

In urban areas, women worked alongside their husbands in family-owned enterprises such as laundries, cleaners, small hotels, plant nurseries, and eateries.

Boardinghouses   Unlike the hotel, which were usually managed by couples, enterprises like boardinghouses were run nearly single-handedly by women. Except, in some instances, for shopping and collecting money, they performed all the work, cleaning the rooms weekly, laundering linen and preparing two meals daily as well as packing lunches.

Nearly 20,000 single Issei men were left in need of living accommodations, when the U.S. locked the gates of immigration.[6] The boardinghouse provided living conditions for bachelors as near to "home" as they could have wished. It was a place where Japanese was spoken, Japanese food served, where behavioral requisites were more or less understood and where an easy, friendly atmosphere prevailed.

Shika Nakano, a mother of four school-age children, operated a boardinghouse in the 1930s in the western district of Los Angeles where a community of Issei families had clustered. Two other boardinghouses existed on the same block. Between five and seven bachelors, the majority, gardeners, boarded in her two-story rented house. Since her husband was also a gardener, the daily routine for Mrs. Nakano was made simple, if arduous: up at dawn to pack lunches, prepare breakfast and see the children off to school; then cleaning and shopping, followed by preparing supper and cleaning up afterwards.

Like many other boardinghouse operators, Mrs. Nakano regarded her boarders as part of the family. They often sought advice from her, borrowed money, and even accounted to her for their whereabouts.

---

[5]Kikumura, p. 41.

[6]Yamato Ichihashi, *Japanese in the United States* (Stanford University Press 1932), p. 72.

Years after having stayed at her house, one of her former boarders said to his son: "You know, without Nakano-san, I would have been a bum."[7]

Domestic Work   Because it fit nearly all the criteria earlier cited, domestic work comprised over one-fourth of Issei women's work outside the home in 1920, second only to the rate for agricultural work.[8] The work required little training, and only the rudiments of spoken English. Glenn suggests that the language barrier may even have "contributed to the smoothness of relations between the Issei and their employers," in that the "Issei could not 'hear' insulting or denigrating comments."[9]

Although domestic work was considered demeaning by many Issei women, it offered some unexpected benefits. For example, often the employer would leave instructions for the employee and go out, leaving the woman the sense of being her own boss. Also, many workers developed close personal relationships with their women employers, and they learned Western housekeeping practices, like arranging furniture, setting tables and the like. Said Machi Ota of Seattle:

> I learned from her [Mrs.Gow, her employer] how to make coffee, how to fry eggs, how to fry bacon, and many other things I had never known before. Since I was one who had not known even how to set a table or iron, everything was baffling at first. I still remember that on the morning of the second day at Gow's I tried to start a stove. But the fire wouldn't burn in spite of everything. . .so I started to cry.[10]

Because of their diligence, domestic workers were also often given gifts of clothing and bonuses by their grateful employers. Thus domestic work remained one of the mainstays of employment for Issei women even after W.W. II, when many of the women were in their late 60s. Tatsuko Urano worked for one employer for 20 years until she was 80 years old. "I was so lucky," she said. "My employer only wanted me to do the laundry and iron and things like that. I never had to vacuum. Too hard." Mrs. Urano's employer paid for her airfare to Japan twice.[11]

Discrimination   Life was never easy for immigrant women in earlier days, no matter what their country of origin. One thinks immediately of Rolvaag's stirring epic of a Norwegian immigrant family's bitter struggle

---

[7]Interview with daughter Mitsuyo Amano.

[8]Glenn, p. 72.

[9]*Ibid*, p. 159.

[10]Ito, p. 258.

[11]Personal interview.

against the forces of nature in the desolate Dakota territory. The wife, unable to cope with her harsh life, withdraws into a world of religious bliss.   In different ways, but just as punishing, other European immigrants struggled to carve out a place for themselves in the New World.

Yet there was a difference, a significant one, between the experiences of European and non-European immigrants, particularly in the vital area of the family's economic survival. Here, in an excerpt from an account of pioneering women in Arkansas, one gets a glimpse:

> During the period of settlement, the family was of necessity a self-sufficient economic unit, and women were a vital part of that economy. The pioneer wife helped clear the land and build the first shelter. Once the farm was functioning, a division of labor occurred: the husband had primary responsibility for producing the food, the wife for preserving and preparing it.[12]

At first blush, the circumstances seem similar to those of the Japanese immigrant woman, but note that a division of labor has occurred here in the early stages of pioneer life. One imagines the husband outside, tilling the soil or harvesting the wheat, while the woman inside, churns butter, makes jam and tends to the children. Except in times of crises, like the Civil War, this appears to have been the usual pattern for European immigrant women.

The condition for women of color differed in an important way. The period in which they were required to do triple duty (the dual roles of child caretaker and household worker as well as working outside the home) was necessarily protracted. In a racist society, where people of color were systematically barred from favored jobs, unions, and in the case of the Issei, from owning real property, the family's economic well-being was severely thwarted. Thus, almost without exception, Issei women were required to provide labor for an extended period to sustain the family.

Glenn makes a similar point in her discussion of domestic workers. "Daughters of European immigrants," she states, "moved up and were absorbed into the more advanced sectors of the labor force," while the experience of the racially migrant groups was different:

> Recruited to fill temporary labor needs, they were denied basic political and legal rights and were hemmed in by almost impermeable "color" barriers to mobility. People of color were routinely barred from skilled crafts, sales,

---

[12]*"Behold Our Works Were Good": A Handbook of Arkansas Women's History,* p. 12.

clerical work, and even "light" manufacturing jobs that were the steps up for sons and daughters of European immigrants. Domestic service and its close relative, laundry work, were often the only options outside of agriculture for black women in the North, Chicanas in the Southwest, and Japanese American women in Northern California, regardless of education or generation. . . .Women in these groups had to work outside the home even after marriage and motherhood, and they continued to be restricted to the same menial occupations as the immigrant generation.[13]

LEISURE

Most Issei women had little leisure time before the war. And what leisure activities they engaged in were rarely shared with their spouses. While their husbands took part in athletic events and community organizations, played cards or *goh* or went to the neighborhood pool hall, women remained at home. They did participate in church functions and other community organizations and often became members of poetry groups. But for the most part, their leisure time was spent in sewing, handicrafts and shopping. Here again, even in their leisure activities, they showed a tendency toward service.

Transmitters of Culture   It should be noted here that women were often the carriers of Japanese culture, including literature and art. The more accomplished engaged in flower arranging, calligraphy, the tea ceremony, poetry writing, and playing Japanese musical instruments. In addition, notes Glenn, "all women irrespective of education, preserved and passed on everyday aspects of Japanese culture, such as food, folk medicine, peasant lore, and customs, in their families and in the larger community."[14]

13Glenn, pp. 4-5.
[14]p. 38.

ABOVE: FBI agent going through personal belongings of a Japanese American family, December 1941. Many searches were conducted without warrant. *San Francisco Public Library.*

BELOW: Mother on strawberry farm visited by her soldier son just before her internment in a camp at Jerome (Arkansas). Florin CA, May 11, 1942. *Photo by Dorothea Lange. National Archives.*

ABOVE: Nisei and Sansei volunteers at Kimochi's Senior Nutrition Program, San Francisco, 1989. © *Rick Rocamora.*

BELOW: Three generations of women at Kimochi Home Art class, San Francisco, 1989. © *Rick Rocamora.*

CHAPTER 4

Women and the Community

However cut off they were from the larger society, Issei women found sustenance within their own community. The various institutions which sprang up in areas where a sizable number of Japanese had congregated, provided vital aid and comfort and fostered social cohesion as well.

Women's roles in these institutions were roughly analogous to their roles in the family. But occasional opportunities outside these limits presented themselves, and Issei women readily accepted them.

THE CHURCH

Churches, both Buddhist and Christian, became an integral part of the community at the very outset of immigration. They served the particular needs of their segregated flocks not only by delivering spiritual nourishment but by providing practical help.

The Christian Church In the early days of settlement, the Christian church in the Japanese community took on the character of a mission. Under the guidance of former missionaries like the Reverends Merriman C. Harris and Herbert B. Johnson and Dr. E. A. Sturge of the Methodist, Baptist and Presbyterian Churches respectively, the church set up small groups that would meet and take religious instruction. At the same time, it offered lessons in English as well as inexpensive lodging to these newly arrived Japanese. Soon the church became a place where immigrants could gather socially, gain access to employment references and a host of other social services. When enough worshipers began to meet together regularly, they established a church for themselves, sanctioned by the mother church.

Two venerable churches in San Francisco, the Pine Methodist and the Christ United Presbyterian churches, followed this pattern. Both organized as *Fukuinkai*, or Gospel Societies, in the years 1885-1886, These churches thus set a example for establishing segregated Japanese churches, which were to proliferate up and down the West Coast.

As part of their mission work, the Methodist Church established the Ellen Stark Ford Home for Women in 1904. At least one other home for Japanese women had been established by the Presbyterian mission. Havens for prostitutes seeking freedom from bondage, for newly-widowed, abandoned or destitute women, and for orphans, these homes continued their important service for many years. The Ellen Stark Ford Home operated for 30 years.

The significance of the social welfare programs offered by the various churches, a social scientist observes, "lies in the fact that by this work they were playing directly upon the most deeply laid collectivistic sentiments of the Japanese people. . . . Nothing in Japan is more sacred than the helpfulness of one member of society towards another, and the Christian missionaries with their practice of benevolent aid to the young immigrants arriving on these shores must have endeared themselves to these people."[1]

Buddhist Church   Despite the fact that most Issei had come to the United States as Buddhists, the Buddhist church did not become organized in the U.S. until 1898, more than ten years after the Christian Church had begun its mission among the Japanese. The delay was at least partially due to reluctance of the Japanese to establish an institution so intrinsically associated with Japan. Given the anti-Japanese climate in the U.S., some Issei leaders and Consul officials voiced fears that introducing a "foreign" religion in the U.S. could not only arouse further antagonism, but could exacerbate tensions between the U.S. and Japan. At the same time, the Hongwanji (Buddhist denomination which was to become the Buddhist Churches of America, or BCA) leaders in Japan hesitated to commit missionaries and financial resources to the United States, uncertain of what the results would be.[2]

Meanwhile, young males who had been meeting informally, organized themselves into The Young Men's Buddhist Association in San Francisco in 1898, the first Buddhist organization to be formed in the mainland United States. Missionaries were sent from Japan,[3] and the Buddhist Church of America was launched. As evidence of the degree to which the Issei had anxiously awaited the establishment of the church, within a ten-year period, a succession of churches soon sprang up in fifteen locales in California, and one each in Portland, Oregon, Seattle and White River, Washington.

It is a point of irony that the "foreignness" of the religion that had stalled the establishment of the Buddhist Church in the beginning is the

---

[1]Frank Miyamoto, quoted in Hosokawa, p. 129.

[2]*Buddhist Churches of America: 75 Year History*, 1899-1974, pp. 45-48.

[3]*Ibid.*, p. 47. The first missionaries were the Reverends Shuye Sonoda and Kakuryo Nishijima, who arrived in San Francisco on September 1, 1899.

very feature that now attracts a number of non-Asians. Not only are they attracted by the religion itself, but by the celebrations and arts the religion had given rise to. Thousands flock to the Cherry Blossom Festivals (associated with the birthday of the Buddha) and Obon Festivals (a kind of Buddhist memorial day) each year, celebrating the spirit of the day, partaking of Japanese delicacies and participating in the street dances. A host of others take part in *ikebana* (flower arranging) and the more esoteric tea ceremony, both firmly rooted in Buddhistic principles.

Woman's Roles   In both the Christian and Buddhist churches, women were rarely accorded leadership roles in the church's organizational structure. And only later, and then rarely, did they function in ministerial capacities.[4] A few women sat on Boards in the churches before the war, but apart from that, their roles were largely that of support.

Church women commonly organized themselves into *fujinkai* (women's clubs) whose main function was to facilitate church activities. The example of the Fujinkai activities of the Enmanji Temple in Sebastopol, California serves to typify Issei women's work in both the Buddhist and Christian churches:

> All social activities--including refreshments--visitations to patients in hospitals (*omimai*), congratulatory (*oiwai*) obligations, janitorial services for the hall, Temple and the Sunday School classrooms are the responsibilities of the designated . . . group [of the Fujinkai] for that month.[5]

Donating to charities and to various church-related groups, providing equipment for the kitchen and furniture for the minister's residence were also within the traditional purview of the Fujinkai. To accomplish these, the Fujinkai raised funds by contributing handicrafts, needlework and art work for sale at bazaars and by organizing other fund-raising activities. Women were thus able to utilize considerable creativity and judgment in their church work.

---

[4]*Ibid.*, pp. 118-139. This history lists five women among the total of 311 ministers appointed during the 75-year period involved. The first minister was Yurii Kyogoku, appointed in 1955. In the Christian denominations, three Japanese American women have reportedly been ordained, the first being Taeko Okimoto in 1960.

[5]*Ibid.*, p. 360.

THE KENJINKAI

Also contributing to the social cohesion of the Japanese community was the Kenjinkai (association comprised of immigrants from the same prefecture in Japan). Originally an all-male bastion, these Kenjinkai evolved almost automatically.

As was true in the pioneer days in America, the population of the various regions in Japan had developed distinctive dialects and habits, even appearance. People from Tokyo, for instance, were fond of remarking, half-jokingly, that they could not understand a word of Kagoshima *ben* (dialect peculiar to a given region).[6] Thus persons who emigrated from the same prefecture in Japan tended to congregate in certain common areas in the U.S. Seattle, Washington, for example, became home to a sizable number of immigrants from Okayama prefecture. These *kenjin* (persons from the same prefecture) found mutual comfort in familiar accents and shared experiences.

Among the more memorable events sponsored by the Kenjinkai were the elaborate annual picnics. Women would spend the entire day and night before, preparing sushi and other delectables to be shared at the picnic with any family which had spread its blankets nearby. Children would practice for days the various races that would deliver a prize and endow them with one day of glory. At the picnic they gorged themselves on soda pop and ice cream. Women busily served food to everyone around and waited to be coaxed to enter the women's race. Men drank and sang songs. Altogether the picnic afforded a rare occasion for women, who tended to be more isolated than other members of the family, to socialize, renew acquaintances and indulge in plain fun.

The Kenjinkai also offered material and moral support. For example, they often made all the funeral arrangements for a deceased member. The resulting rite usually produced enough *koden* (obituary offerings) to pay for the funeral, with something left over for the bereaved.

Many of these Kenjinkai still exist, though their function is now mainly social. Women now take active part as members.

THE LANGUAGE PRESS

Like the churches, Japanese language newspapers sprouted up in locations where more than a few immigrants had congregated. While

---

[6]Kagoshima ken is located at the southernmost tip of the southernmost island (Kyushu) of Japan, a fair distance from Tokyo, situated in the middle of the main island, Honshu. The language used in Tokyo is considered standard Japanese.

established chiefly in cities, their reach extended to remote farmhouses where few immigrants lived, such as in the states of Idaho and Nebraska.

The first published newspaper, the *Soko Shimbun* (San Francisco News) appeared as a four-page lithographed daily in 1892. Two other dailies soon appeared in the same city.[7] By 1920, newspapers, which published daily or bi-weekly editions became firmly established in San Francisco, Seattle, Los Angeles, Salt Lake City, and Denver. Seldom the flourishing business that marked newspaper publishing in the larger society, the immigrant press, with its limited audience and meager advertising revenue, usually operated on a shoe-string budget.

But here, apart from reading national and international news, immigrants could lay bare their feelings as well as share practical information. They could gossip, debate and let fly their creative imaginations. Farmers shared their expertise--"How to Plant Onions," for example--and traded information about where to get materials and where to sell. Armchair politicos debated Japan's foreign policy. Literary contests were held regularly, and critics voiced their opinions about them. Ads extolled the virtues of various community businesses. Personals advertised for missing wives. In short, the language press not only provided a forum for exchanging information and resources, but entertainment as well. For some, it was the only such source. Thus it occupied a place of extraordinary importance in their households. Most families subscribed to one or the other of the various language newspapers, no matter how great the strain of six dollars or so for the annual subscription or how remote the location of the household.

Women wrote in these newspapers, again in a limited way. They wrote short pieces--stories, essays and poetry, for the most part--rife with feeling and emotion. Mrs. Takaya, who wrote periodically for the *Colorado Times*, decried the lack of "serious" women's writings in one article, attributing this state to the male publishers' prejudice of publishing only those women's manuscripts that were written in "flowery language." Women writers, she contended, were not only discouraged from writing more substantive pieces by this stricture but by the fact that they had to do "double duty as wives and mothers and as workers in the field."[8]

JAPANESE LANGUAGE SCHOOLS

Japanese language schools formed another integral component of Japanese community life. In nearly every site where a dozen or so families had congregated, a language school sprang up. In rural areas,

---

[7]Ichioka, p. 20.

[8]*Colorado Times*, January 1, 1932.

the sessions were often conducted on weekends in the winter, when farm chores were less demanding. But in the cities, boys and girls took instruction in the language school every day after attending public school.

The Curriculum Problem The curriculum usually called for reading, writing, composition, story-telling, singing and *shushin* (instruction in ethical behavior). Although the *shushin* that the Japanese school teacher taught dealt mainly with filial piety and respect for teachers and elders, it became a point of conflict for many parents and intellectuals in the community. In the same way that Buddhist leaders had worried about introducing a "foreign" religion in a Christian country, those involved in language schools worried over the wisdom of teaching *shushin* to their citizen children. Should the language schools be inculcating their children with ethical teachings of the Japanese? Couldn't this be interpreted as seditious? And was this not the reason that regulations against Japanese language instruction had been enacted in Hawaii and California? They had to ask themselves also if inflicting Japanese behavioral dictates might not retard their children's progress in the society-at-large.[9]

At the root of the parents' dilemma was whether they would return to Japan or not. Most wanted to, but they also recognized the possibility that they might not be able to do so. If they did return, language as well as *shushin* instruction would unquestionably benefit the child. But if the child were to remain in the U.S., he or she should become thoroughly "Americanized" in order to succeed. Most parents waffled between those two positions, wanting their children to be inculcated in the Japanese ways of behaving, which most believed superior, and yet wanting them to be "good Americans."

The problem was one which perpetually plagued the Issei, not only in the matter of language instruction, but in decisions they were required to make in their day-to-day dealings with their children. How much "Japaneseness" and how much "Americanization" would best serve their children? Their ambivalence was reflected in the Nisei who, on the one hand, sought desperately to be "American," while, on the other, almost unconsciously, followed many dictates of Japanese behavioral norms.

---

[9]As it turned out, parents and teachers had good reason to be anxious about this matter, for directly after the Pearl Harbor bombing, Japanese school teachers were among those summarily whisked off by the FBI. Since few teachers possessed material wealth or exerted power in the community, the inference to be drawn is that they were likely suspected of teaching seditious doctrine.

the one hand, sought desperately to be "American," while, on the other, almost unconsciously, followed many dictates of Japanese behavioral norms.

Women's Participation   While Issei women did not, as a rule, participate in parent-teacher's organizations at the public school due to language barriers, they took great interest in the Japanese language school. This comes as no surprise, given their extraordinary concern over the welfare of her children. Here, those who were qualified, taught classes. Others organized, and took part in, parent-teacher's meetings and the *undo kai*, the popular sports competitions for the children. More than in any other institution in the community, women exercised decision-making powers in the language school.

Mother and children en route to internment camp. Tags bear family number. Bainbridge Island WA, March 30, 1942. *Photo courtesy Museum of History and Industry, Seattle.*

CHAPTER 5

The War Years and Beyond

The center was a place where Caucasian people governed and Japanese people were governed. Everything they saw, day in and day out, indicated that racial difference was identical with caste distinction.

---Daisuke Kitagawa

World War II brought dramatic changes to the lives of the Japanese in the United States. The bombing of Pearl Harbor by Japan, followed by the incarceration of all persons of Japanese ancestry on the West Coast, unsettled family relationships and caused untold material losses and psychological scars.

A more thorough discussion of this period appears in the Nisei section of this book. Here it will serve to discuss the Issei's experience of the events in light of their status as alien Japanese associated with the enemy.

PEARL HARBOR

As our earlier discussion indicated, the work load of the Issei woman had eased by World War II. The majority of Nisei, now in their late teens or early twenties, lightened household chores and even contributed to the family coffers. With the New Deal policies of President Franklin D. Roosevelt in gear, the country was experiencing a recovery from the ravages of the Depression. In tandem with the rest of the underclass in the U.S., the Issei-Nisei family generally found their economic conditions improving steadily.

In what seemed a period of relative stability, then, Japan struck the blow. Shock and apprehension gripped the entire Japanese community. "*Masaka*!" (It cannot be!) was the nearly universal reaction of Issei. They knew about tensions between Japan and the United States, but few expected this drastic turn of events. Many reproached Japan for its act. Others, whose loyalties wavered, prudently kept their opinions to themselves. But the majority doubtless held strong emotional ties to the country of their birth.

That notwithstanding, the Issei had long considered the U.S. their home. Now the conflict called for a clear decision about where their loyalties lay. In the end, the decision at which they appeared to arrive, was not a political one. Instead, not unexpectedly, it was one based on what they considered to be in the best interest of their children. There was no question as to the Nisei's allegiance to the country of their birth, and the Issei felt bound to support that position. Daisuke Kitagawa suggests that an Issei would have characteristically said, "If I were alone, I might choose to return to Japan, but now I have these children, for whose sake I will stick it out to the bitter end."[1]

But the Issei had scant reason to expect anything but the worst from the U.S. government over this calamity. They had known from the beginning they were not welcome in this country, and nothing had changed. Thus many now feared deportation or a nameless fate even worse.

The FBI Sweep   News that the FBI was sweeping through the community soon reached every household. Families made every attempt to destroy belongings that would impart the slightest suggestion of subversion:

> What could I do if I were arrested? So I started burying things which might cause trouble. Since I was practicing kendo [an art of the sword akin to fencing], I had a lot of materials on it. I put those things together, dug a hole and buried them. Then my wife suggested that burying was not safe enough . . . so we started burning things. Books were especially difficult to burn, so we had to tear pages piece by piece.[2]

Similarly, nearly every family burned or buried articles, some absurdly immaterial to the question of loyalty. Personal letters and photographs from their families in Japan were heaped onto the pyre, as were valuables such as diaries, kimonos, religious paraphernalia and art objects.[3]

Contributing further to the anguish and confusion of the Issei, the FBI began rounding them up for detention on the day after the bombing. No one felt safe. Masao Itano's experience is perhaps typical:

---

[1]*Issei and Nisei*, (Seabury Press, New York 1967), p.32.

[2]Masao Hirata interviewed in Eileen Sunada Sarasohn, ed., *The Issei, Portrait of a Pioneer*, (Pacific Publishers, Palo Alto CA), p. 156.

[3]Recently when the Women's Exhibit Committee of the National Japanese American Historical Society of San Francisco called for photos and artifacts to display in an exhibit dealing with the history of Japanese American women, they reported gaps in their collection because many people had destroyed those items during this chaotic time.

We weren't prepared when they came to pick me up. My wife kept saying we should be packed and ready, but I believed that there was no reason why I should be picked up, since I had committed no crime. We were totally unprepared when they came to take me in.[4]

For women, the situation was no less grievous. Those whose husbands had been taken away were left to manage the household if a grown Nisei was not present to take over. Chieko Sano tells of her despair:

My husband, too, was taken away because of his affiliation with the Japanese Club, but soon released. The hardship and confusion brought on by irresponsible rumors we endured during the six months between the attack on Pearl Harbor and internment were incomparable to anything we ever experienced before. It was like being smashed against a huge wall, unable to breathe or move. . . .

We had just been freed from 20 years of what one might call a nomadic way of life, just finished building a house of our own (although the land belonged to another), and just started to collect some furniture. The more I thought about it, the more miserable I became . . . . In the eyes of the country where we lived, Japanese were regarded as less than maggots, and now, as enemy aliens. I resigned myself to this fate, knowing we were not alone.[5]

Upwards of 2,000 Japanese aliens were seized from Hawaii and the mainland before the FBI closed its net. Included in the round-up were owners of businesses, language school instructors, heads of community organizations, fishermen and gardeners.

Executive Order 9066   Two months later, when the orders came for the removal of all Japanese families on the West Coast to be driven into concentration camps, the Issei responded with relative calm. Like Mrs. Sano, they "resigned themselves to this fate," counseling obedience and order to their children.

Although every Issei suffered humiliation and anxiety as enemy aliens, many remember specific kindnesses extended to them during this period of crisis. "Most of my white neighbors in West Sacramento were kind and good to us," states Kane Kozono. Such was her trust in a white woman who lived across the street that Mrs. Kozono left her with a strongbox for safekeeping before she left for camp. "If the time should

---

[4]Sarasohn, p. 156.
[5]*Ibid.*, p. 187.

come when you have to go to camp," the woman had said, "don't hesitate to let me know whatever you need. I'll be glad to send it to you." She kept her promise. After the war, Mrs. Kozono got her box back with all the valuables and papers intact.[6]

Camps   Some Issei women found being uprooted from familiar surroundings exceedingly difficult. The rugged camp life, with its periodic sand storms, oppressive summer heat and primitive living conditions brought general misery. In addition, a sizable number of women were undergoing menopausal stress, and coupled with the physical conditions of camp, including the lack of privacy, they lapsed into periods of depression. Those whose husbands had been whisked off to separate internment camps early on, experienced desperate loneliness and uncertainty. And many of their husbands, older than they by at least ten years, were beginning to develop serious ailments that required constant care. Kamechiyo Takahashi's husband was among those who died in camp. "My life in camp was miserable," she told an interviewer. "I made a desperate effort to endure the hardship, but I wished I had been sent for by the Lord with my husband."[7]

Issei's Wartime Position   Later, in one of the more ironic twists of the war, many mothers would see their sons drafted into the armed services from behind the barbed wires of camp. A profoundly moving photograph of a mother, Risaku Kanaya, being presented the Silver Star medal, posthumously awarded her son, not only reveals the silent grief of a mother, it is strikingly emblematic of the wartime position of the Issei vis-a-vis the U.S. government.

The photograph shows Mrs. Kanaya, clad in black, standing with her husband before Chaplain (Colonel) Corwin H. Olds, who towers above them. Her downcast eyes are fixed on the medal, while her husband stares straight ahead grimly, his arms ramrod stiff at his side. In the background, a photograph of their son hangs above a simple Buddhist altar. Fruit is offered to his departed soul.

Made prostrate by the hapless circumstance of being identified with the enemy, the Issei stoically faced whatever sacrifice or retribution that might have been exacted from them.

Freedom in Confinement   In yet another irony, some women found in the camps a certain freedom that they had never before experienced. Although they were confined to a one-room living space, they were

---

[6]*Ibid.*, p. 254-255.
[7]*Ibid.*, p. 182.

liberated from the demanding work of the former household. Their obligations as mothers, too, were considerably alleviated by the fact that their children, now mainly in their teens, were making their own choices about where they would eat, what they would wear and who they would spend time with. Their husbands, in like manner, if they were not ill, demanded less attention. Now Issei women could actually choose for the first time, how they would use their time.

Not surprisingly, many able-bodied women chose to work. "I am probably the only person who lived out the four years in camp without working a single day," said Michie Norikane, an Issei who had been constantly in an out of the hospital in camp.[8] Issei women generally worked in the mess halls, where they could find a touch of home, where they could function in a familiar nurturing, serving role. Others found work teaching the arts or serving in the hospital's support force. But their work afforded more leisure time than they had ever had. They used it joyously and creatively.

Riyo Orite remembers that she and a good friend Mrs. Mizobe "had fun together climbing mountains and collecting shells. We didn't have to worry about cooking or buying food in camp." She recalls the English classes, sewing classes and other instruction that "you were free to choose according to your own interests." Mrs. Orite decided to learn English, and the more she began to understand, the more things she became interested in.[9]

In noting the comments voiced about camp "not being so bad," as one Issei put it, one should consider them in the context of the low expectations the Issei had held for their treatment. That they were not, as a rule, physically abused (in the sense of beatings or the like), nor deprived of food or health care, must have come as a relief. Mrs. Kozono, for instance, who said she "thought we had had fun there," had earlier believed that there would be no food for the Japanese in camp.[10] The anxiety about food, in fact, had been widespread. With this state of mind, they might even have been grateful for their present condition.

RESETTLEMENT

During the war, many Issei left camp and migrated eastward, following the lead of their children who had found housing and work in

---

[8]*EBJA*, p. 91.

[9]Sarasohn, pp. 175-176.

[10]*Ibid.*, pp. 193, 194.

places like Boulder, Colorado, Chicago and New York.   By the end of 1944, these resettled Issei numbered about 6000.[11]

In spite of the relatively hospitable climate with which the former internees were greeted in the Midwest and East, settling in yet another strange environment posed difficulties. Issei men, many who were now too old to enter the job market offered by cities, found themselves with little to do. Issei women sometimes worked in sewing factories or did domestic work. But most Issei relied on their Nisei offspring for their subsistence. In the main they viewed this as an interim period. Those who had resettled "felt unsettled," as one report put it, waiting for the day they could return to the West Coast.

THE RETURN

Early in 1945, the Supreme Court ruled it a violation of the constitutional rights of the Japanese Americans to bar them and their parents from returning to the West Coast. After three years of exile, former residents began to return to the West Coast in considerable numbers.

The vanguard of returnees were met with both organized and unorganized hostility. "No Japs" signs flaunted their clear message here and there.   Homes were shot into, and a number of arson cases occurred. In Los Angeles, the Nichiren (Buddhist) Temple, where 600 families had stored their worldly goods, had been ransacked.[12] Many returnees found their nursery greenhouses and farms and homes in ruins.

Housing loomed as a major problem. Returnees faced the wartime housing crunch as well as hostility from renters and were forced to accept anything that provided a roof over their heads. Families stayed in churches, hostels, barns and housing projects.   "It was a pitiful period," says Takae Washizu. I knew one couple with children who rented somebody's basement and slept there like dogs."[13]   Shoichi Fukuda remembers:

> I came back to California in May [1945]. Everybody was afraid of being attacked by the white people. The war was still going on at that time, and prejudice and oppression were very severe. The first problem was that I could not find a home to live in. . . . When houses were found, they were shared by four or five families. When I found a house it was small and dirty.

---

[11]U.S. Department of the Interior, *People in Motion: The Postwar Adjustment of Evacuated People*, (U.S. Gov't. Printing Office 1949), p. 9.

[12]Hosokawa, p. 437.

[13]Sarasohn, p. 251

The owner did not honor his agreement, so we had no light. We lived by candlelight for a month.[14]

But countering the hostility evinced by racists, many white Americans extended welcome arms to the returnees and helped them in a number of ways to reconstruct their lives. Members of Christian churches provided references for work and housing. Neighbors offered food and other symbolic tokens of reconciliation and harmony. Tokushige Kizuka remembers the gratitude he felt toward his white friend in Watsonville:

> He wrote me saying that they had the house ready for us; so we came back and went straight to their summer house without having to stay in the hostel like some other people did. [He] was so nice. He even had food in the freezer. My own family and my wife's relatives all moved in.[15]

The incarceration and subsequent resettlement had resulted in a dispersal of the Issei and Nisei throughout the country. But the majority of Issei looked to the West Coast, which had been their home for over a quarter of a century, as the place where they "wanted to go and die." One Issei, who had returned to Seattle, expressed it:

> In a way it is just like going back to Japan. . . . It may be a fine thing for the Nisei to pioneer to other sections of the country, but when you are 60 years old you want to return home, and Seattle is home to most of us older people.[16]

POST WAR

War with Japan ended in August, 1945. If the Issei did not receive the news with jubilation, they at least felt relief.

Most also felt profound sorrow. The human cost had been staggering on both sides. Many Issei had lost relatives and friends in the bombings, particularly in the atomic holocausts of Hiroshima and Nagasaki. Chieko Sano's hometown of Hiroshima had been completely demolished. Still in camp when Japan surrendered, Mrs. Sano remembers the day:

> The expected had come to pass, and yet we could not keep from weeping. Going to the mess hall, we saw a sign, "Permit us to be closed

---

[14]*Ibid.*, 237-238.

[15]*Ibid.*, p. 250.

[16]*People in Motion*, p. 13.

today," and inside the members of the crew were holding each other, crying out in loud voices. From the beginning, I never thought Japan would win this war, but when I realized it really lost, not even I could understand why I found myself crying so much. I could only think they were the tears of my Japanese blood.[17]

Economy in the Japanese Community   The three-year sojourn of the Issei and Nisei ended with the majority returning to the West Coast. Five years after they had been interned, six out of ten had already returned.[18] As might be expected, the character of the former Japanese communities had changed measurably. The most obvious change took place in the economic structure of the community. While the Japanese population formerly depended for its livelihood on a community-based economy, that is, one basically controlled by the Japanese community, it now became dependent upon employment to be found in the general community. The internment had scattered the people, and the majority who returned to their former communities had to start from the beginning. Even five years later in 1950, "the complex and far reaching structure built around growing, processing and marketing of farm crops had not been revived.[19]

What were pre-war "Little Tokyo" business districts became smaller spheres, dispersed throughout the cities in areas where a number of Japanese families had settled. In cities like Los Angeles, San Francisco and Seattle, Japantowns would not firmly reestablish themselves for a decade. Then, new immigrants from Japan would settle themselves in many of the businesses. By then, Issei leadership had given way to that of the Nisei, and the Japanese community could provide neither the variety nor the volume of employment to sustain the Japanese American population.

Many former farmers "gave up on returning to the farm and decided to work in the city," as Mrs. Sano testified.[20] Men had few job options, since most were now in their lat 60's, but Issei women found themselves in demand. A government study reported that "the most noteworthy departure from the prewar economic pattern in the Los Angeles Japanese American community . . .is the vastly increased number of Japanese American women, both Issei and Nisei, who are now employed. . ." This was no doubt due to the shift of the Issei to

---

[17]*EBJA*, p. 191.

[18]*People in Motion*, p. 47.

[19]*Ibid*.

[20]*EBJA*, p. 191.

urban areas, the removal of some racial barriers and the post-war demand for the kind of work Issei women were willing to do.

According to the 1950 census, of the total of some 5,000 Issei women in the work force, the largest number still worked on the farms, but this was closely followed by workers in factories. Domestic workers and service workers made up the bulk of the remaining work force. By 1970, the Issei women work force had sharply diminished, and of the remaining 3,000, most were in domestic service.[21]

You Can't Go Home Again　Upon returning to the West Coast and resettling, Issei sent clothing and food to destitute relatives in Japan.　Beginning in about 1952, after the Immigration and Naturalization Act was passed (see below), Issei returned for a visit to Japan for the first time since they had set foot in America nearly three decades before.　A deeply-felt obligation to place flowers at the gravesites of their parents or other relatives and to pray for their peaceful repose, urged these visits.[22]

The reunions were emotional ones, rife with the consciousness of one another's suffering, carrying at the same time a sense of apology, the Issei for the ravage which had been heaped upon the people of Japan, and the Japanese for having dropped the first bombs. But the visitors returned to America, with a renewed sense of affirmation, both for pride in their venerable heritage and for the choice they had made to emigrate years before.　Chieko Sako expressed it simply and eloquently: "I paid my respects at my parents' graves, inhaled the pure clean air of my old home to my heart's content, and came back to America."[23]

Naturalization　In 1952, the Walter-McCarran Immigration and Nationality Act was passed, repealing the Oriental Exclusion Act of 1924. It granted token immigration from Japan and allowed Japanese immigrants, at long last to become naturalized citizens.

The Issei rejoiced in the news and flooded classes to study English and American history.　The majority of them, now in their sixties and seventies, passed the citizenship test, took the oath and became citizens. If they no longer had a critical need to be American citizens, to buy land or to run for political office, for example,　they had invested the better

---

[21]Glenn, p. 82.

[22]Most Japanese religions ordain commemorative services for the dead on certain days after death. "It is considered disgraceful for Japanese to disregard or neglect graves" according to an authoritative text on Japanese customs (*We Japanese*, Fujiya Hotel, Hakone Japan, n.d.,).

[23]*EBJA*, p. 195.

part of their lives in America and now sought identification as Americans, side-by-side with their Nisei offspring and Sansei grandchildren. "Issei" had been a term especially coined to designate the first generation of Japanese in America. Now they could lay claim to being first generation Japanese *Americans*, citizen forebears of the generations to follow.

The Late Years   Today, nearly a century after the Issei began their migration to America, their numbers have thinned dramatically. Widows make up the majority of the group, most now in their 80's and 90's.

In their declining years, their children, the Nisei, along with the grandchildren, the Sansei, have seen to their care and comfort. The Nisei have taken primary responsibility for supplying the needs of parents who are ailing or who have lost their mates, caring for them in their homes; only reluctantly have they arranged institutional care for them.

The Sansei, with their talent and resourcefulness, provided the impetus for setting up structures for the care of the Issei in the various communities. In the California cities of Berkeley, San Francisco and San Jose, for instance, they initiated the establishment of Senior Centers geared specifically toward the needs of the aging Japanese population. The services these centers provide include nutritious lunches, food distribution to shut-ins, recreation and excursions to places both near and far. A few living units and nursing care homes have also been established.

For their part, the Issei have almost universally expressed gratitude for the state of their present lives. One sense that they feel amply rewarded for the hardships they endured "for the sake of the children." Chieko Sano sums it up:

> It has been a long and difficult journey for me. Now I am a grandmother of ten and a great-grandmother of four, living as happily as any ordinary grandmother. Sometimes I look at my ugly wrinkled hands and thank them for having worked so hard and so long for me. I also feel deep gratitude for the Nisei and Sansei who give us the credit as being the building blocks, and in our lonely old age, comfort us and make us happy in so many ways. I thank them very much from the bottom of my heart.[24]

---

[24]*Ibid.*, 197.

LEGACY

Since Issei women had given over their lives for the sake of their children, it seems required of this account to sum up the legacy they left. For, as we have seen, the contributions that Issei women made toward the survival and success of their progeny, and ultimately to the country itself, are not ones easily measured. Nor do they lend themselves to public acclaim. Even as Issei women took part in the institutions of the Japanese community, shored them up and helped sustain them, they took no part in formal decision-making. And because of language barriers, prejudices of both gender and race and cultural imperatives, their efforts were noticeable mainly within the narrow confines of their families and communities.

Up close, however, we have had a glimmer. We have seen a portrait of a woman standing beside her spouse and a large brood of children. The garment she wears is most likely the only "dress up" garment she owns. She has subordinated her own wants and needs for those of her children so that they could present themselves in the best possible light to the world outside her own. Apart from running her household, she has toiled as an unpaid worker outside. Or, she has earned a few dollars by doing piece work at home, by working in the fields or fisheries or by cleaning other people's houses.

The family has been her central concern: it is largely she who has forged the bonds of family which carried it through its travails.

She has tried to instill in her children a sense of duty and responsibility and has transmitted a sense of the value of education. She has also passed on the inclination to work hard and to persevere in the face of adversity.

In short with little visible notice or fanfare, she managed the critical task of preparing the ground on which her children could survive, and survive well. It would be an enduring legacy, the significance of which she could never know.

"Threads of Remembrance" quilt, depicting a 100-year history of Japanese in America. NJAHS Women's Exhibit at The Oakland Museum, 1990. © *Rick Rocamora.*

ABOVE: Pole pea farm at Los Osos near San Luis Obispo CA, 1926.
Photo courtesy Grace Shibata.

BELOW: Mother, son, daughter and family friend in candy store.
Hanford, CA, 1932. *Photo courtesy Hatsumi Wada Iishi.*

PART II

Okaasan
(Portrait of an Issei Mother)

by Grace Shibata

For my mother Take Eto
whose boundless patience, strength and understanding
sustained me.

Publisher's Note: Grace Shibata had not laid eyes on the manuscript of this book when she wrote this moving portrait of her mother. But as if to flesh out the text of the foregoing segment, "Okaasan" (mother) gives us a real life story of an Issei woman, which, in its broad outlines, parallels exactly the historical account that author Mei Nakano has set down. When Nakano read "Okaasan," she wondered aloud if it could somehow be included in her work, knowing full well that such an inclusion would defy conventional publishing practices. We found a way. With Shibata's permission, we placed her writing here, an appropriate transition, we thought, between the "Issei" and "Nisei" segments. Grace Shibata's deeply felt portrayal of her Issei mother adds richness and texture to our understanding of the Issei woman.

Okaasan

"*Tadaima, kaeri mashita,*" (I'm home) I would call as loudly as I could, as I rushed into the house. Laying my books on the dining table, I would listen for Mother's soft and reassuring voice, which soon came: "*Okaeri na sai.*" (Welcome home.) Mother always spoke to me in Japanese. Satisfied, I would bound up the stairs to my bedroom to change my starched school clothes to jeans, shirt and scruffy shoes.

Through the open window came the sound of splashing water, and I knew Mother must be in the garden watering plants. Outside, I walked quickly over the gravel path, which was bordered with quarter-inch board and lined with chicken and hen cactus, to find her. She heard my footsteps, looked up and smiled, still holding the long, black hose. "*Kyo wa do deshita ka?*" (How was your day?) She was always interested in what I did.

At age forty-three, Mother is slightly under one hundred pounds, energetic and fit. The soft-spoken Issei woman stands five feet tall, looking relaxed in her print cotton dress, which falls loosely to her ankles. Under her wide-brimmed straw hat, her straight, black hair is pulled softly back to a bun. Her eyebrows are just two light puffs. Her skin, void of any makeup, is smooth and soft as a young girl's. Her small eyes dance as she smiles easily. She is enjoying one of her favorite pastimes, gardening. Early mornings and late afternoons, she tends her snapdragons, sweet peas, dahlias and myriad other flowers which bloom in their season.   At the far end of the garden are several golden sunflowers, full of dark seeds, towering perhaps eight feet tall.   A chubby yellow and black bumblebee searches for nectar on a dahlia, and two small white butterflies flutter silently, dipping left and then right. The serenity of the garden befits Mother's character.

This scene of Mother in the early 1930s seems placid enough, but it veils the hardships endured by a woman who had pioneered the frontier days in San Luis Obispo County with her husband Tameji Eto. Resourceful and patient in time of need, she stoically endured unbelievable odds to make a home and living for her family as a pioneer woman in the new world.

Born in 1889 in Okunaga village, Chida City, Kumamoto-ken, Japan, the third child in a family of six, Mother had a relatively easygoing, happy childhood.   Her parents, prosperous farmers, gave their children a warm and cheerful environment and encouraged them to play as well as study.

After *Jo-gakko* (high school), attending nursing school was Mother's dream, but as nursing was considered demeaning in those days, she could not get her parents' consent.   Instead, she went to a weaving school and became an adept seamstress.   Little did she know how useful this training would be when she raised eight children in America.

I often wondered why Mother came to America.   All four of her brothers in Japan were university graduates and professionals: the eldest, a city councilman; the second, a dentist; the third, captain of a freighter; and the fourth, a mining engineer.   Did she feel she had to accomplish more to keep up with them?

For his part, Father had landed in San Francisco in 1904 and after doing odd jobs, growing fava beans, sugar beets, potatoes and onions, had become foreman for the Pacific Coast Railroad Company.   He then started a modest farm and soon after asked for Mother's hand by letter to his family in Japan.   Father had been a classmate of Mother's eldest brother and used to see her playing at school, an image that had apparently stayed with him.   The brother encouraged the parents to accept the proposal and after much thought, they agreed.

In those days in Japan, a young girl married without question whomever her parents chose for her, but Mother must have considered this marriage something of an adventure as well as a challenge. Although shy, she could be spirited and plucky.   She was an avid *karuta* (card game played on New Year's Day) player, for example, and could easily trounce her brothers.   She was also a strong swimmer and a fast and lithesome runner.   She enjoyed competition and liked to win.

Clutching a photo of this man she did not know, Mother and her father boarded the train to Yokohama where a ship waited to take her to the United States. She was nineteen, leaving her family for the first time to wed a man who was a stranger. Too, she was destined for an alien country to be confronted with a completely foreign culture and language. For her future, she had relied solely on the judgment of her parents and eldest brother in whom she had absolute trust.

On the train, passing rice fields reminded her of home in Okunaga. It made her suddenly sad.

The *Minnesota* took about thirteen days to reach Seattle. Aboard she met a dozen or so other picture brides, and the kimono-clad young women compared photos of their future husbands, discussing their anxieties, sometimes joking uneasily about their future. The journey was pleasant enough, but Mother was soon struck by the cultural differences she faced. For example, in the dining room she was bewildered by the array of silverware before her and waited, shy and uncomfortable, until a kind waiter inconspicuously pointed out the correct one to use. One evening she lost her appetite at the sight of the main entree, meat with bones attached to it. In Japan, only thinly sliced meat was served. Another time a beautifully rolled yellow globular object had been placed on a small dish. Thinking it an egg yolk, she put the whole thing into her mouth, only to experience a horrid taste in her mouth. Too shy to spit it out, she swallowed it, an egg-yolk sized blob of butter. Many more cultural shocks would follow.

Upon reaching their destination, all her new acquaintances joined their spouses or spouses-to-be. But Mother's excited hopes of seeing the United States and meeting her future husband were dashed when immigration officers detained her because of a possible eye infection. The young couple had to be content to communicate by letter for ten days of quarantine. When Father at last saw Mother, he was surprised to see a plump young woman instead of the slight and sprightly girl he had remembered. *"Sumo tori ga kita to omotta,"* (I thought a sumo wrestler had arrived) he would tease her later. But she was not to keep her extra pounds very long.

Mother, on the other hand, was pleased to see Father standing straight and tall with lots of hair. The picture that she brought with her had not deceived her. In fact he was quite handsome. And he seemed kind.

The couple was married at the U.S. Immigration Office by the assistant minister from the Seattle Buddhist Church, Rev. E. Fujiyeda, on May 21, 1908.

When Father took Mother to a Seattle department store to purchase western clothes for the trip to California, she bought a dress with puff shoulders, long sleeves and a tight-wasted, long skirt, a wide-brimmed hat with a feather, and high laced shoes. She looked lovely but felt constrained by such apparel.

After another a boat trip from Seattle to San Francisco, the newlyweds boarded a train to San Luis Obispo. By horse and buggy they traveled to Arroyo Grande where Father's brother, friends and neighbors gave them a wedding reception at the Parrish ranch. Wash tubs were used as drums to hail the new couple, and the event was published in the *Arroyo Grande Recorder*. Mother was touched by the kindness of these rural people.

Arroyo Grande was a frontier town set in a valley of sloping hills, scrub oaks and green grass. Deer, coyotes, raccoons, jack rabbits and opossums roamed the area, and neighbors lived miles away.

From the very first day, Mother plunged into a mental and physical endurance test of frontier life, meeting the challenge head-on. Her husband's brother taught her cooking and house chores, which included starting a fire by gathering dry kindling, chopping wood, drawing well water by bucket and pulley and carrying the filled container to the house.

She learned how to stoke the fire in the wood stove, and to "read" the oven temperature by placing her hand for an instant inside the big black oven. She learned how to make yeast and bake bread, biscuits and pancakes, to kill, dress and cook a chicken. She learned to wash, rubbing the yellowish-brown soap into the clothes over a washboard. She learned to heat the heavy black iron on the hot stove, making sure the fire did not go out. Water had to be kept hot for washing and rinsing dishes. These were all back-breaking chores, but she labored, uncomplaining, patient. For a woman who had lived a relatively tranquil, easy life back in Japan, pioneering was a jolting change. Fortunately she was healthy and strong.

Mother kept the rustic house clean and tidy, and she soon learned the necessity of keeping a watchful eye on the pantry inventory. Once, she forgot to put "rice" on the grocery list. That resulted in one of the few times Father gave her a stern lecture: it required a full day's walk with a horse to Oceano from Arroyo Grande to purchase the rice, which meant the loss of a day's work. A year later Father made enough profit on his farm to buy a buggy. This made shopping much easier.

The hired men enjoyed Mother's cooking and even on Sundays hung close during meal times. To this day, some of them recall nostalgically the sweet delicious taste of her *dango-jiru*, a red bean soupy dessert with sweet flour dumplings. But even Sunday was not a day off for Mother. This was the day for laundering and ironing in addition to cooking three full meals. Her chores usually ended at midnight. She would be up again at four in the morning to start the fire for breakfast.

"It was not easy," she used to say later, "but it was my future as well as his, and I wanted to be a part of it. Father never demanded I work so hard. I did it because it was necessary and I wanted to." This attitude and support freed Father from daily problems to concentrate on his farm full time.

I should add that with his loud voice Father seemed gruff, but he was in fact a kind and humane man who treated mother with respect and kindness.

In 1909, a year after arriving at Arroyo Grande, Mother gave birth to my oldest sister, Kofuji, when she was twenty years old.

The following year, the family moved to Oso Flaco where Father worked for the Waller Seed Company and later contracted growing seeds for them. Mother, now with baby Kofuji on her back and another on the way, helped pick nasturtium seeds. To harvest these flower seeds, the nasturtium bushes were pulled by hand, stacked in piles, then pitched on to a horse-drawn wagon. The bushes were then dumped on a large canvas and beaten with pitchforks to separate the seeds from the plants. However, many of the seeds, the size of green peas, fell to the ground while harvesting, and Mother and the other women gathered them up. "It was like picking up money," she said. "Nothing went to waste."

In 1910, a second child Toshiko was born during a particularly cold and rainy season in December. Not only was the cold weather difficult, Mother had a terrible time trying to dry the diapers. Four years later, in the summer of 1914, Alice, another daughter, came into the world. Mother was now caring for three children, at the same time doing the house chores and helping on the farm. Her workload had become ever more demanding.

But in spite of her arduous schedule, Mother always made time to plant vegetables. She loved to see the plants grow. She was also a practical, resourceful woman, and knew the garden would supply her with instant groceries when she needed them: eggplants, carrots, cucumbers, and a host of other common vegetables, not to mention the more esoteric Japanese vegetables, like Japanese pumpkins.

During the winter months when farm production was low, Father would go surf fishing in Pismo for perch and bullheads. There he observed that it was not bitter cold during mid-winter when Oso Flaco was frigid and white with frost. Why not grow English bush peas which would command high winter prices in the market when the item was scarce? he thought. Soon after, he leased some land in Pismo and moved his family near the Pacific Ocean. Having made this fortuitous decision on a hunch, he succeeded handsomely as a pioneer in bush peas. This earned him the name "Pea King."

Since there were no wells for irrigation, Father had to dry farm. This required planting a crop after the first rain, usually in December. To preserve moisture and to draw it from the bottom, he would repeatedly cultivate the soil to create a mulch. Father and Mother referred to this work as *kana beta* (cultivating). For years, we children used to say "kana beta-ing", as if it were a regular English word. Japanese English became a part of our daily conversation.

At the height of the pea season, Mother would go out to the fields. Squatting between two rows of bush peas, her hands moved rapidly as she picked the peas, careful not to ruin the vines for future crops. She was undoubtedly the fastest pea picker, for the men would grudgingly but good naturedly say, *"Eto no obasan ni wa kanawanai na!"* (We're no match for Mrs. Eto!)

With three children under five years of age and another on the way, our parents became concerned about the youngsters' education. Afraid the children might lose their heritage of the Japanese culture and language, they anguished about what to do, but finally decided to send the two older daughters to their grandparents in Japan. Many years later, when one sister asked why they had been sent away, Mother replied that their parting had been like a knife piercing her own flesh and that the pain in her bosom remained for months. But at the time, she explained, Father and she both thought they were doing what was best for the children. Although the pain of separation had been severe for both children and parents, the sacrifice enabled the two daughters to learn the Japanese language and be exposed to its culture. Father and Mother felt that was important.

In 1916, Father's two brothers sent for their pictures brides in Japan. Though nine months pregnant, Mother prepared a huge wedding party when they arrived. The very next day, she gave birth to her only son, Masaji. After three daughters, this ten-pound baby caused quite a stir. Now Father had a son to continue his farm.

In the midst of all these demands on her, Mother managed to find diversions. To expand his production, Father and his brothers purchased 125 acres of Morro Bay farm land to grow flower seeds and later, artichokes. Consequently, he had less and less time at home. He taught Mother how to hitch a horse and buggy so she could go to town for shopping. She would dress up the two younger children and go to Guadalupe for Japanese groceries or to San Luis Obispo for mail and other farm necessities. (At this time, Pismo consisted of only a few tent houses and one hotel.) As Mother gained confidence in her new-found independence, she began to visit her friend Mrs. Oishi, the wife of a labor contractor, on the way home from shopping. Her "shopping day" became longer each time, and Father teased what a mistake it had been to teach her to drive the horse and buggy.

Mother always took advantage of what nature had to offer. Pismo clams were plentiful back then, and waves scattered them over the long stretch of sand. There were so many that Mother used them as chicken feed as well as for food for us. She often drove the horse and buggy on the wet beach sand while her two sisters-in-law stooped to pick up the clams. In later years, one of them lamented laughingly, "Take-san would just sit there holding the reins while we had to do the hard work!" Mother would break into a smile and claim, "But I was the only one who could handle the horses."

Daughter Mary's arrival in 1918 was an especially joyous occasion, as she was born on March 3, Girl's Day. Since Mother cherished tradition and festivities, this event could not have pleased her more.

Although petite, Mother was courageous and stout-hearted in many ways. Many evenings she was left alone in the house with her three young children when Father went to San Luis Obispo to bank and to take his products to the train station for shipping. Other times he would go as far as Morro Bay. The house was located close to Highway 101, and many hobos used to come knocking at her door. One late evening, there was a banging that would not stop. Mother lay quietly in bed, hoping the children would not waken. She could hear footsteps circling the house and ultimately stopping under her window. When she asked what he wanted, the stranger replied that he needed a place to sleep. She asked if he smoked, and when he said no, she gave him permission to use the barn. Next morning, while preparing breakfast, she was startled to see a huge, burly, disheveled hobo standing silently by the door peering down at her. Heart pounding but outwardly calm, Mother offered him coffee and then added some toast. She found the hoboes generally honest and harmless, and they often offered to do chores in exchange for this kind of favor. But she always declined, happy to see them go.

Strong though she was, there were times when sadness and nostalgia overwhelmed Mother, like the time she discovered a large red abalone on a rocky promontory on the beaches of Pismo. Anticipating that she would return to Japan in the not-too-distant future, she polished the beautiful rainbow-colored shell until it shone, carefully wrapped it and stored it in her steamer trunk. There were no shells so lovely in Japan, and she wanted to share it with her family. Many years later, after having borne more children, and having moved once again, Mother's hope of seeing her homeland had dissolved into a dream. Reluctantly, she gave away the treasured shell. Then there were those quiet evenings, her chores done, the children asleep, when she would stand outdoors and face East toward her homeland, and tears would well in her eyes.

Mother was a skillful doctor and nurse at home. She adeptly bandaged our cuts and bruises and performed whatever other remedies necessary to keep us in good health. We never went to the doctor except when we had tonsillitis. In addition, all of us were born at home.

As a child I used to wonder why other Issei commented on how amazing it was that all eight of us grew up healthy. Much later, I realized it was because fatalities among young children was not uncommon in those days for at least one member in the family, as grave markers in Japanese cemeteries attest. No doubt we were spared the same fate because of the infinite care Mother had given us.

After five years in Pismo, Father wanted his own farm to grow products that brought year round income. He left the Pismo farm to his elder brother and the Morro Bay Farm to his younger brother and then struck out on his own, purchasing 150 acres in Los Osos Valley. Here the Eto family settled permanently. It was the place I would call home.

The Alien Land Law, which prohibited Asian non-citizens from owning land, forced Father to buy his farm under the name of a Caucasian friend. He formed a corporation of three officers: Brown-san, a Japanese accountant, and himself. Then he brought his family of five to this new farm in the bulky horse-drawn seed wagon loaded with household goods.

This was in December in the year 1919. Mother was again heavy with child, her sixth. The next weeks would severely test her fortitude and patience, for the former owner refused to vacate the house, and the family had to live in a tent and endure the bitter cold with their three children, aged six, four and two. This was the coldest part of the valley in winter; it was not unusual for the temperature to plummet to 26 degrees F. But the family was finally able to move into the three-bedroom, 1200 square foot, wooden farm house. Shortly thereafter, on January 14, 1920, number six child, Susie, was born.

Mother was always supportive of Father, however bad things seemed, and worked right by his side. She was a vital moral and spiritual strength to him. Father started his newly acquired farm by growing sweet peas and English bush peas. Production was high, but no matter how well the farm did, Brown-san constantly drained the profits. Father could not seem to get ahead: one way or another, Brown-san continued to deplete his assets until Father was slowly becoming immersed in debt.

Mother had never seen Father, an optimistic man by nature, so depressed. This must have been one of their darkest moments. Out in the dusk, as Father worked late, Mother quietly reassured him: "Even if we have to eat as little as one grain of rice a day, we'll somehow survive. Let's free ourselves of 'Osca-san' and try it alone."

Father eventually dissolved the corporation, established a new one in his children's names, and started all over again. Gradually, Father's and Mother's diligence and determination began to pay off, and the family farm began to take hold and grow.

Another daughter Nancy arrived on Girl's Day, March 3, 1923. In spite of her growing family, Mother's amazing stamina and fortitude enabled her to care for them as well as cook for a crew, now forty to fifty men, working on the farm.

The kitchen and the dining area where the employees ate were in a separate building. There were huge black woks, or "kama" in a row. She would start the fires inside the three tunnel-like openings below the cement structure that held the woks. The first wok contained rice, the second hot water for tea, and the third a concoction of meat and vegetables, or sometimes chicken or seafood. For breakfast, she always served "Mother's Oats." In addition to the regular crew, during the height of a season, neighbors came to help as was the custom in those days, and Mother would set extra places at the table.

Finally, the farm became established to a point where Father and Mother, along with their youngest daughter, were able to take the long-awaited trip to Japan for a whole month. It had been fifteen long years that Mother had been away from family and friends. What a joyful reunion that must have been!

By this time, Father and Mother had long considered the United States their home, feeling their roots grow deeper in American soil. The children were citizens by birth, spoke English, attended American schools, and had many friends. They too were becoming more integrated into the Caucasian community as well as the Japanese community.

My father helped establish the Guadalupe Children's Home, a very important event for my mother, for then she was able to recall her two older daughters from Japan. This home was a dormitory school where children were taught the Buddhist religion and the Japanese language, after attending American school. Now Mother had all her children nearby.

Father, with Mother's help, was constantly expanding and improving Los Osos Farm, and its operations became extensive. He introduced the first truck farming in San Luis Obispo County by growing lettuce, celery and later, tomatoes and asparagus. He started shipping produce to San Francisco and Los Angeles through the Post

Office and later built a packing house in San Luis Obispo to ship produce to the East by refrigerated freight trains.

Father finally hired a cook for the working crew, which gave Mother more time for herself. She used these extra hours to design clothes for her children, stitching them up on her treadle sewing machine. Mother had an artistic bent as well as being adept with her hands. She often did exquisite embroidery work in the evenings. The piece I remember best is a black silk cushion with a peacock's brilliantly colored tail spread out like a fan.

She also made butter from the cow she milked. She even had an ice box, but as it was a twelve-mile trip to town to purchase ice, she usually had an ice-box with no ice.

Mother sometimes showed her spunk in unexpected ways. Father had bought a black Dodge, which she had not learned to drive. One evening, when Father had had one too many at a Guadalupe party and had fallen asleep, Mother put the car in low gear and slowly drove thirty miles to Los Osos Valley. In those days, the road was windy, narrow and sometimes hilly. It was a very long drive in low gear, but Mother negotiated all the curves and made it home safely.

In 1925, I was born in mid-December, the last of the Eto children.

Father negotiated for the first electricity and telephone service to be brought to Los Osos Valley. He also led the Japanese Association drive to import 200 cherry trees from Japan to donate to the local Senior High School. The lovely trees lined both sides of a wide avenue, beautifying the entrance to the school. This was a source of great pride to mother, not only because of the beauty the trees provided, but because she felt a part of Japan was here.

During prohibition days, Mother made *sake* for Father who liked to have a drink with dinner. She mixed *koji* (fermented rice) with cooked rice and water in a ten-gallon crock and stirred it periodically for several weeks while it fermented. It was tightly covered and, as the days passed, it started to bubble and foam. She poured this concoction into a clean linen sack which had been placed in a square wooden box, v-shaped at the bottom. With a weight on the sack, there came the drip, drip, drip of *sake* into the jug below. Father happily drank his sake with dinner.

The 1930 depression years were difficult. Peas sold for three to five cents a pound, from which the freight cost to the market had to be subtracted. A three-layer box of tomatoes sold for thirty cents. Wages were about ten cents an hour, but at times Father could not even pay that. Piano lessons were often paid for with eggs, fruits or vegetables. Mrs. Riley from Baywood came to barter for fresh vegetables with her clams.

These were harsh times, but Mother never complained. Instead, she taught us not to waste anything and to take good care of our possessions. She carefully rolled up string from packaged goods and used it to tie pole beans or sweet peas. She saved newspapers for starting fires, and even cut the blank column on the side to use for scratch paper. Vegetables and fruit peelings were buried to fertilize the soil. No matter how tired and late it was, she would tidy up the washing machine and cover it carefully when the laundry was done, never overloading it when in use. "A machine is like your body," she would say. "If you want it to last, do not abuse it." I learned the value of not being wasteful from her.

Mother was also creative in her frugality. She originated a simple but delicious dish she named "hamburger peas." It was inexpensive and easy to prepare, consisting of hamburger, sliced onions and fresh green peas, flavored only with salt. To this day, I have not seen or heard of anyone else making it, but it remains a favorite dish in our family.

Father was away a lot, organizing the Southern Central Japanese Agricultural Assn. to help support the price of produce. He created the San Luis Obispo Packing House Exchange and helped strawberry growers and many others who needed advice. Therefore, Mother's responsibility overseeing the farm while Father was away became extensive. She helped by supervising the planting and harvesting and by generally keeping the men busy. In addition, she had enough energy and patience to raise five hundred egg-laying chickens. Ever resourceful, she bought newborn chicks and kept them warm with a kerosene heater under a brooder. When they became stronger, they were let out to the larger chicken compound. With the help of my brother, Mother built a large chicken coop facing southeast to catch the morning sun.

Mother was a gracious and able hostess. The Los Osos Farm was midway between Los Angeles and San Francisco, and many friends made their stop at the ranch home. Mother and Father shared their food, drinks and sometimes lodging. When unexpected guests arrived, Mother never seemed harassed. Quietly, she would go out to the backyard, catch one of her chickens and proceed to prepare dinner. With the vegetable garden providing the greens, she somehow always managed to prepare a respectable meal. Because she was extremely well-organized, she performed her work inconspicuously and efficiently. I never realized, until much later, the enormity of her task.

Mother also showed unlimited patience with us children. None of us can recall her ever being angry or raising her voice, unbelievable though this may be.

In 1932, she received the honor of being named Mother of the Year from *Shin Nichi Bei* of Los Angeles. It must have come as a great surprise to her, for she sought no honor and believed what she did was nothing unusual.

In spite of her huge responsibilities, she encouraged us to have fun. She said she had wonderful memories of her childhood and wanted us to have the same. "There is enough work and commitment after you grow up and get married," she used to say. Work for my sisters and me extended to helping with the housework, doing the washing and ironing and occasionally assisting in the packing shed. At the same time, we planned picnics, played tennis, climbed mountains, or went walking to the beach with our red wagon packed with *onigiri* (rice balls), linked wieners, marshmallows and cold water. We stripped willow branches to roast our hot dogs and marshmallows. We always remember those fun activities linked with warm memories of Mother who encouraged them.

When sister Mary was studying Shakespeare, we improvised plays and dragged all the empty lettuce crates, which had been stacked neatly by the barn, to make castles, moats and drawbridges. We performed *Hamlet* and *Romeo and Juliet* and asked our neighbors to attend our production. Once, we asked Mother if we could charge a penny for our performance, but she said no.

Mother loved the outdoors and the sea and made the most of it whenever she could spare time from the farm. She watched the tide by the position of the moon. Whenever it was close to full moon, the tide low, she would urge Father to drive us out to Pismo Beach for clams, or more often, to Pecho for abalone hunting. Mother took four or five sacks and tire wrenches to pry the mollusks from the rocks. With our trousers rolled up, we scrambled down the craggy hillside to the rocky beach below. Carefully stepping from one slippery, seaweed-covered rock to another, we'd peer under a large boulder to find abalone, always with one eye to the oncoming wave. Mother was always quickest to find her limit of five abalone. Then she would come to help us find ours, we meanwhile having been more interested in playing than looking for abalone. We also found among the tide pools, crabs, mussels, small black sea snails and sea urchins. Mother would boil these in a huge pot as soon as we returned home. Eating these delicious morsels capped our day.

Masaji, our brother, used to hunt for rabbit, duck and quail at the farm, which contained a five-acre lake, surrounded by lush pampas grass. Some of the best lunches Mother packed for us included roast quail with *onigiri* (rice balls). When Masaji had luck hunting, he brought down mallard ducks or sea brant geese and occasionally, a Canadian goose. Mother saved the soft down to make pillows and cushions. While dressing the wild game or fish, she would explain the anatomy of the carcass to us.

Mother loved to go mushroom hunting.   She found small mushrooms, firm and white, in the willow forest, or *kashi naba* (oak tree mushroom) under large oak trees, surrounded by peat moss about a foot deep. She also picked mushrooms from pastures, miraculously never poisonous ones. How she knew the difference remains a mystery to me. I used to watch her put a dime into whatever pot the mushroom was cooking to see if it would turn black, but in later years, I learned that this was not an accurate test of toxicity.

Once a week, we went shopping, usually on Saturdays when Father was available to drive. This was a big day, going into "town," and we all had something on the list. Grocery shopping came last so the food would not spoil in the car. The best part was in the end, when Father would say: "Orai, (all right) everybody finish?" And Mother would say, "Hai, Papa. Ice cream wa doh?" That was music to my ears, for I knew Father would say with a grin, "Orai, orai." Our heads poking out the window, we eagerly watched Father come out of the ice cream parlor with six vanilla cones stuck firmly in a cardboard container. They dripped a little on the side, softening the white paper napkins wrapped around them. Mother beamed as she looked at our happy faces.

Mother was philosophical, and the Buddhist religion meant a great deal to her. Our parents worked on Sundays (crops had to be readied for the Monday market), but they sent the children to the San Luis Obispo Buddhist Sunday School. Father was one of the founders of this church and was largely responsible for acquiring the original ten acres on which the church sat. Mother always wanted to know what we learned in class and the songs we sang. She impressed on us the importance of remembering what we had learned.

When Alice was attending Mills College and Masaji going to California Polytechnic School, the four younger sisters, Mary, Susie, Nancy and I spent a lot of time together. During Hana Matsuri (April 8, the birthday of Lord Buddha), we would go out to our neighbor's pasture early in the morning (with their permission), duck under the barbed wire fence and pick baskets and baskets of buttercups and lavender lupine. We would return to the car, the lower parts of our skirts dripping wet from the dew, our shoes muddy. Shivering, but invigorated by the early morning adventure, we would drive to church where we joined other members to decorate the *Hana Mido* (altar for the Lord Buddha), using the yellow and lavender blooms. Usually it was the girls who performed this service, since the boys were helping on the farm.

On December 7, 1941, I was setting the table for lunch, as music flowed from the radio in the living room. Suddenly, the program was interrupted again and again by the newscaster announcing that Pearl Harbor was being bombed by Japan. Was it really true? Mother could not really understand the broadcast, but was concerned. When Father came home and heard the news, there was total disbelief and bewilderment on his face. *"Sonna koto wa nai hazu da!"* (That cannot be!) But as the news continued, reality sunk in, and we became somber. Mother turned pale.

Early the next morning when I came downstairs, I found Mother sitting silently by the unlit wood stove (the stove was now used as a heater), one light still on. She looked up, but did not give her usual smile. She appeared not to have slept. Her clothes were the same as the ones she had worn the day before, and her hair had not been combed. And she wasn't bustling. Mother was always bustling in the morning.

"What happened Mama?" I asked, puzzled.

"Around eleven last night, after we all went to bed, the police came and took Father away," she explained, her voice grave. "They were very apologetic and polite, saying it was FBI orders and that they were instructed to take him in for questioning. He complied without hesitation, for he knows these men, and there was no reason to be afraid. But it's 4:30, and he still has not returned. I'm afraid something serious has happened."

"Why didn't you wake us?" I pressed.

In typical fashion, she said, "You had school, and there was no reason you should lose sleep over this. I thought he might be home by this time."

Unknown to us, the FBI had picked up numerous community leaders, Buddhist priests, Japanese school teachers and other "dangerous aliens."

Immediately, my brother went to the police station, but was unable to see Father or get any information about his whereabouts. In the meantime, there was a call for sister Mary from the police station. Father told her he was well and would be sent south. He was allowed to speak only in English, and that was the end of the conversation.

The very next day, the *S.L.O. Telegram Tribune* ran an article about Father's arrest. Rumors in the Japanese community were rampant as to where the Issei were being detained. Several weeks passed before Mother received a letter from Mrs. Matsuura of the Guadalupe Buddhist Church, informing her that Father was in the Santa Barbara jail and was anxiously waiting to see his family.

Masaji, Toshiko and Mother hurriedly drove to see him. Nancy and I stayed at home because Mother did not want us to see Father in custody.

At the jail, the visitors were allowed three minutes each. The usually robust Father appeared drawn. My sister asked how he was. "I'm fine," he said, "but I miss the outside, the fresh air." Masaji wanted to know what he could get for him, and Father asked for some clothes and cigarettes. Mother told Father, "Don't worry, Papa. Everything is being taken care of. Just take good care of yourself."

My sister and brother were informed the detainees would be transferred again, so gathering articles Father had asked for, they rushed back to Santa Barbara. By this time, aliens were restricted from traveling, and Mother could not go to see Father. When Toshiko and Masaji got there, Father was already gone. If the wardens knew where he was, they feigned not to. My sister and brother were sent to the Los Angeles FBI office for information and, after a lot of running about, they were finally able to locate his whereabouts: the CCC Camp in Tujunga.

Toshiko and Masaji stayed overnight in Los Angeles and left early the next morning for Tujunga. It was a long, lonely ride, but they were overjoyed when they were permitted to visit Father.

With guards hovering nearby, Father came out to the open-fenced compound. He looked much better than when they had last seen him. They were allowed five minutes. Father asked about Mother and the family and then discussed with my brother what should be done about the farm. "Drive carefully," were his parting words, as he stood and waved until the car turned the corner and they could see him no more.

At home, my brother conferred with Mother daily on how to take care of the farm. Amidst rumors of an evacuation, the farm still had to be operated. Mother's judgment was vital, now that Father was gone. In the event of evacuation, the ranch had to be leased, or goods packed, the equipment and trucks sold. Then there was the furniture, the chickens, the cars. The Buddhist Church property had to be tended to, besides. We depended on kind and helpful friends like Mr. Ernest Vollmer, Mr. Pete Bachino and Dr. George Dunklee during these uneasy times.

We received word one day that Father was to be transferred to someplace very cold and would need warm clothes, also that his train would be passing the San Luis Obispo station that evening. It was Christmas Eve, and all the stores had already closed. My sister Kofuji called Mr. Sinsheimer, the owner of a department store and the city mayor for twenty years, to explain our problem. Mr. Sinsheimer knew Father well, for he had entertained many of his guests from Japan. He kindly opened his store, and my sister came out with a bundle of warm clothes.

We waited at the train station for several hours, to no avail. Masaji found out when the next train was due, and we waited for that one too, but Father was not on it. We waited past midnight, and when told there would be no other trains that night, we went home despondent and worried. We were to learn much later that Father's train had been rerouted through Barstow, the southern route. Mother had had such high hopes of seeing Father and had been so eager and bright at the station. Now she looked sad, but did not let down for an instant.

Meanwhile, our phone lines had been tapped, and the road to our farm was under surveillance. We knew this because the FBI came often to the house and questioned us about those who had called or visited us. Sometimes while Mother spoke on the phone, a voice would say, "Speak English." She was cut off from all other Issei and must have felt very much alone, though she never complained. However, Rev. Todoroki, a fearless Buddhist priest from the S.L.O. Buddhist church, visited her often to offer encouragement and strength. He himself was eventually picked up by the FBI.

About thirty miles north of our farm, a mini-Japanese submarine attacked an American oil tanker near the coast. A local paper accused Father of plowing his farm so that the furrows pointed to the ports where the ships had been anchored. The newspaper also charged that it was known to the authorities that Father had secret meetings with Japanese spies. Mother gasped at the accusations and grimly shook her head. My older sisters, however, incensed, wrote a letter to the newspaper, repudiating the false allegations. It was more than a welcome comment, then, that came from my English teacher, Miss Katherine Sharpsteen, the next morning: "Good, for the Eto sisters!" she announced to the class. "These are trying times, and we must remain calm."

The evacuation orders which first came, divided California in three zones vertically. Zone one covered west of Highway 1 near the coast where we lived, and we were required to move by March. Zone two was west of Highway 99, and we were told we would probably be able to stay there permanently. Not wanting to be too far away from home, we joined our sister Kofuji and her husband, who had rented a farm in Ducor, near Delano. We left Los Osos in March 1942 and slept under the stars in the open field at Ducor.

Even as we unpacked and began constructing makeshift living quarters, Mother put vegetable seeds in the ground so we would have fresh vegetables and *tsukemono* (pickles). She remained calm throughout these hectic times, trying to maintain some sort of normalcy. My brother-in-law planted tomatoes as soon as possible, but about four months later, Ducor was declared a restricted zone, and he was forced to leave his plants. We would have to move again.

Discouraged by this latest government order, we lost the will to fight and decided to enter a government relocation camp instead of trying to relocate ourselves elsewhere. So, we boarded a train in the hot July heat for Manzanar, a camp in the California desert. My sister Toshiko, a nurse, had volunteered to work at the Manzanar hospital on the condition that our family could stay together.

Having grown up in the open spaces, we found Manzanar life oppressive and stifling. Not only were the living conditions inadequate, being thrown in with ten thousand other strangers in one square mile of desert was utterly depressing. We felt like cattle in a corral. People from our home town had gone to Arizona, and we were virtually strangers here. Mother tried to keep our spirits up by telling us how great it was that we didn't have to cook three times a day. She reminded us we should be grateful we were together as one family.

As usual, Mother adapted to the new situation gracefully and kept herself busy knitting dresses for us or creating garments, like the lovely cape, lined in red, which she made from a black pea coat. Not surprisingly, she was thinking of others despite worries of her own: Father had been interned in a high-security concentration camp, and she was having trouble with her dentures. Just before we left for Manzanar, the dentist had to pull out all her teeth. The swelling of her gums had not subsided when the dentures were fitted, so they were painful to wear. She was grateful for the kind cooks at Block 34 mess hall, who were aware of her problem and tried to give her soft pieces of food.

Mother received letters from Father periodically, but a large portion of the letters were cut out or blanked out in ink, censored. She was, however, grateful that Father appeared to be in good health.

We were anxious to leave Manzanar. It was an abnormal way to live without a family life, as we had known it. Also, I was still in high school and wanted a legitimate diploma to continue my education.

Seven months after our internment, we left for Payette, Idaho, where sister Alice and her husband had leased a farm. They gave us housing and work for the duration of the war. Mother cared for her son's first daughter, Lois, and also helped on the farm. She was grateful to her daughter and son-in-law for taking care of her family and wanted to do her part. Only fifty-four-years old, she had already experienced more than a lifetime of events.

In the meantime, Father was being shifted with other internees to concentration camps in Montana, Oklahoma, Louisiana, Texas and New Mexico. We were never sure why all this movement was taking place, except that people were continually being taken into these camps, as for example, persons of Japanese ancestry from South American countries. We wondered if the camps were getting overcrowded.

When Father was in Louisiana, Mother learned that sister Susie from an Arkansas camp was able to visit Father with her husband, who had already been inducted in the 442nd Combat Team. My sister recalls how impressed she was at Father's understanding and compassion. "This is your country," he had said, "and I am proud my son-in-law is serving. You do your best to fight for your country. My internment should make no difference." The son-in-law was to give up his life on an Italian battlefield.

One day, Mother received a odd letter from Father, asking her opinion about the family repatriating to Japan. We thought his morale must have been very low to even ask such a question. Mother's answer was a resolute no. "The United States is our home," she said. "Our family is here, and I do not wish to leave this country."

Mother was overjoyed when Father was finally released from the New Mexico internment camp in the fall of 1944 to join his family in Payette, Idaho. The FBI was not able to charge Father with any wrongdoing. Since he was passing Boise, Idaho, where Nancy and I were going to school, we went to meet him at the train station. With a guard beside him, Father got off the train briefly to see us. I was appalled at his ashen face. Although he stood straight and tall, his clothes hung loosely on his thin body. I admired my sister, so strong and controlled, greeting father and talking with him. I could only hold onto his sleeve and cry, happiness and sadness filling me at once.

In October of 1945, Mother returned with the family to Los Osos to find their yard and home in total disarray. Weeds were so high, they could hardly see their home. The door was partly off the hinge and would not close. To make the deteriorated house somewhat livable, required at least two weeks of repair and cleaning. What had been locked upstairs in a room, had been stolen or thrown out of the window. Mother found the remnants of the beautiful *O Hina Sama* dolls she used to display each year on Girl's Day broken and strewn on the ground.

Nothing could be planted in the fields because the tomato crops were being harvested by the tenants, and they did not want to give this up. Mother, Father and my brother and his family had to make a new beginning.

At age fifty-six, Mother was again helping on the farm as it slowly became reestablished, bunching broccoli, asparagus, or packing tomatoes. It was not easy, but she was determined to get the family back on its feet. "We have been through worse times," she said. "This is nothing."

The city of San Luis Obispo had honored Father before the war by naming one of its streets Eto Street. During the war, it was renamed Brook Street. The message was loud and clear. The Eto's were dishonored simply because they were Japanese. This greatly pained my parents, for they had always tried to live uprightly and had contributed to the community as though they were bona fide citizens.

In the summer of 1953, I had to give Mother the bad news that Father must undergo a cancer operation. The doctor later claimed the surgery a success and told us if the cancer did not return in five years, he should be all right. Mother stayed by his side throughout his ordeal and nursed him back to health.

In December of that same year, my parents' lifelong wish was realized, when they proudly became citizens of the U.S. Mother did not speak English fluently, but understood it enough to receive her citizenship. Now America had become their country, and their roots had become firm in the country of their choice.

Father's commitment to public service became even stronger during the post-war period. He wanted the relationship between Japan and the U.S. to improve and thus became involved in an agricultural exchange student program. The students from Japan learned about America as well as agriculture, an important feature of the program to Father and Mother. Even before the war, he used to tell me how crucial people-to-people relationships were between countries. He felt wars were created by heads of governments and that private citizens should get more involved to influence the leaders.

When the Oyama case was brought to court, challenging the Alien Land Law, Father had joined in with many others to support the case.

My parents' public efforts did not go unnoticed. In 1954, they were honored as "Mr. & Mrs. Issei of the Year" at the annual Los Angeles Nisei Festival. Other events followed, but one that I can remember well was when Lord and Lady Abbot Otani from the Nishi Hongwanji of Kyoto visited their home for lunch. Mother prepared her meal, using many ingredients from her garden. The guests were especially thrilled with the abalone and the clam *sashimi* served in their own shells. "Everything in America is so large," they commented, "even the abalone and the clams."

In 1956, Father received the Fourth Order of the Rising Sun from the Emperor of Japan for his service in bettering relationships between

Japan and the U.S. He was privileged to receive it at the Emperor's Palace in Tokyo. Mother was very proud and could not help but reminisce about her many years with him since coming to America.

Perhaps the proudest moment in Mother's life came in January of 1959. A statue of Father was built in his honor at Chida City, Kyushu, Japan for his continuing aid to the Kumamoto citizens who had sought help in the United States as well as his support to the orphanage and schools there. Mother accompanied him for this cherished moment inasmuch as this was also her home town. Little did she dream when she left for America some fifty years earlier that fate would bring them to this happy end.

That very summer, Mother and Father celebrated their 50th wedding anniversary. Father, however, was starting to lose weight. The cancer that had invaded his body five years ago, had reappeared, this time in his liver. He had won many battles in the past, but this was one he could not win.

Mother cared for him and was constantly by his side. When the end was near, Father said goodbye to his family. Then Mother cradled his hand in hers and said, "Please go peacefully. You must not worry about anything, the family or the business. I wish you rest in peace."

Father had always called her his best nurse, his "number one nurse." When he died at 75, Mother was 69 years old. They had lived a full life together. Mother grieved silently and sorely missed him, but she said she had no regrets. "I did everything in my power for him while he lived, and he knew that. That is all that matters."

Life had not been easy many times, but Mother and Father had managed to send seven children to college. Now she had time for her own pursuits. At age seventy, Mother began to study *ikebana*, the art of flower arranging. She continued to grow her own flowers and took pride in taking them to her class and sharing them with her friends. She actively participated in arranging flowers at her local Buddhist Church at *Obon* Festivals (memorial festivals of the dead) or during special occasions such as weddings and community functions. My eldest sister Kofuji took her to lessons in Arroyo Grande regularly twice a month. She was happy to see Mother so interested in her classes.

At home, until the age of ninety, Mother made *sushi,* prepared *sashimi,* and even took active part in the *mochi tsuki* by rolling the mass of hot *mochi* with her bare hands while it was being pounded. She also had her vegetable garden, and she took pleasure in the visits from family members.

She asked for so little and gave so much, it was a great pleasure for my sisters, brother, and me to give her a ticket to the Hawaiian Islands to celebrate her 88th birthday. My husband and I accompanied her.

She was still very lively and curious, thrilled to see the proteas, anthuriums, the pineapples and the sugar plantations, and eagerly climbed a volcanic mountain. Her eyes shone like a young girl's. Before leaving the Islands, she carefully hand-carried the beautiful flowers given her and wrapped the stems in wet, paper towels to bring them all the way home to Los Osos Valley. Next to her family, plants and nature had been her life.

Mother had many friends. Many came from neighboring towns to see her in her later days. They kindly brought her flowers and vegetables from their own gardens, or fresh fish from the sea. Since she went out very little during these days, she appreciated their company. She was walking more slowly now but took daily walks and enjoyed feeding Buster, Masaji's dog. Her favorite pastime was watering her plants and gazing at them as she rested.

Mother lived to be ninety-six years old. In the end, this diminutive woman struggled against all odds, but could not overcome the stroke that befell her. She died three months later.

One of her favorite Buddhist songs was "*Kokoro Hare Bare*," sung at her funeral in October, 1985. Part of the translation reads: "There will certainly be rainy and stormy days. But whether sunny or cloudy, my days are embraced by an emancipating path, the *nembutsu* (Buddhist invocation) of a bright, clear *kokoro* (heart; spirit)."

In every sense, Mother was the embodiment of the words, "*en no shita no chika mochi*," a pillar to her family. She loved us all with boundless patience. Her strength and understanding sustained us, embraced us with comfort and security. Her name, Take, or bamboo, befitted her: she knew how to bend with the wind; she grew straight and strong and had put firm roots in the ground.

Mother's memory evokes happiness, sadness and warmth all at the same time. Her life is an inspiration to me. I cannot adequately express the gratitude I feel for what she has given me, what she was, and what she accomplished in her lifetime. This story, then, is but a token tribute to that end.

ABOVE: Temporary camp at Salinas, April 1942.   *Photo by Clem Albers. National Archives.*

BELOW: Bringing only what they could carry.   Temporary camp at Salinas, April 1942.   *Photo by Clem Albers. National Archives.*

ABOVE: Vegetable garden outside barracks. Temporary camp at Tanforan CA race track, 1942. *Photo by Dorothea Lange.* *National Archives.*
BELOW: Doing the family wash. Temporary camp at Santa Anita CA race track, 1942. *Library of Congress.*

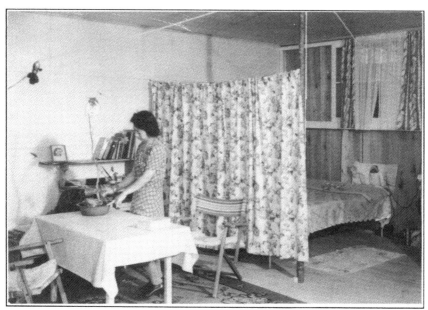

ABOVE: Typical barracks unit, furniture of scrap lumber. Woman brightens room with *ikebana*. Jerome AR concentration camp, November 17, 1942. *Photo by Tom Parker. National Archives.*

BELOW: Line to mess hall snakes past latrine. Temporary camp at Tanforan race track, June 1942. *Photo by Dorothea Lange. National Archives.*

ABOVE: Girls from Minidoka camp topping sugar beets near Hunt, ID. *National Archives.*

BELOW: Blue Star Issei mothers (mothers with sons in the U.S. Army) and Nisei women with their visiting soldier husbands at Granada CO camp. June 23, 1953. *Photo by Joe McClelland. National Archives.*

ABOVE: Nisei Women's Army Corps (WAC). Nisei WAC Detachment at Fort Snelling, Minnesota, 1945. *Photo courtesy Miwako Yanamoto.*

BELOW: Gold Star Mother. Issei parents accepting the Silver Star Medal awarded their son killed in action near Bruyeres, France, October 1944. *Signal Corps photo.*

PART III

The Nisei

CHAPTER 6

Before the War

life's so strange
before the war
I had a name.
     ---Janice Mirikitani

Since the Issei could not gain citizenship and the rights and privileges attendant to it, they worked unstintingly toward the welfare of their citizen children, the Nisei, as we have seen. What had at first been a misty vision of their future in America, forged itself into a fierce dream.

But being citizens did not automatically confer on the Nisei their birthright of liberty and equality under the law, nor did it present a horizon bright with hope of personal fulfillment. Moreover, the Nisei female found her life constrained by the same dual evils of racism and sexism that had beleaguered her mother.

While striking similarities existed between the Nisei female and her mother, there were significant differences. The foremost of these was that the Nisei was native born: she could speak the language, read the paper, drive a car. These few circumstances alone offered opportunities quite beyond the bounds that held her mother.

On the other hand, precisely because she operated "out there" in the outer community, she was more vulnerable than her mother to damaging experiences because of her race. Verbal assaults in the public arena, as well as limits put on her choice of careers, housing and where she could go for entertainment could not help but exact stiff costs from her feelings of self-worth.

But the Nisei woman experienced measurable transformation in tandem with the changing times. Indeed, one might make the case that she experienced her life in at least four distinct phases: in the period before World War II, during the war, the post-war period, then the period after the sixties.

Beginning with her youth and naivete before the war, passing through the climate of hostility and cruelty during the war years, then struggling with marriage and motherhood, she would finally come of age in her maturity, nurtured by a more favorable socio-political climate.

Thus while the Nisei female's life paralleled her mother's in significant ways, it nevertheless differed from hers markedly. Both were shaped by the inexorable circumstances of American history.

BIRTHS

Nisei females came into the world in a relatively short time frame, the majority arriving between 1915 and 1940. Statistics further reveal that their births occurred with the greatest frequency between the years 1918 and 1922.[1] Owing to the immigration patterns earlier discussed, i.e., the flow of picture bride immigration beginning around 1908 and ending abruptly in 1920, followed by the total exclusion of Japanese immigrants in 1924--the births of Nisei came to a virtual standstill by 1940.

This phenomenon of their births concentrated in a discrete, relatively short, period of time, resulted in a remarkable number of shared generational experiences and character markings in the Nisei woman. And, because discussions of these phenomena, inevitably invite stereotyping, it seems worth repeating that the generalities presented here illustrate *typical* cases, and that no one Nisei woman experienced every event in the same way, nor would she fit every characteristic described.

IDENTITY

Shaping their identities presented at least two interrelated dilemmas for the Nisei: while they struggled to incorporate American values into their attitudes and behavior, they could not cast off the values they had learned from their parents; and while they wanted desperately to be Americans, white Americans did not want them. Neither comfortable in the larger society nor in the Japanese society, they developed their own particular subculture.

For the most part, the Nisei woman grew up in humble, but not severely impoverished, circumstances,[2] largely due to her hard-working parents and the solidarity of the family. Having absorbed the lessons of her mother well, and having lived through the Depression, she was apt to be frugal and hard-working as well as resourceful, attributes that

---

[1] Evelyn Nakano Glenn, *Issei, Nisei, War Bride*, (Temple University Press, Philadelphia 1986) p.51.

[2] Roger Daniels, *The Politics of Prejudice* (University of California Press, Berkeley 1962), p.14.

contributed immeasurably toward her and her family's material well-being in later years.

"Good Japanese"/"Good Americans"   The Nisei female was typically bilingual and bi-cultural. At the same time that a teenage girl spoke Japanese to her mother, while helping prepare a supper of *miso* (bean paste) soup, rice and *okazu* (mixed vegetable and meat dish), she might be thinking of her date that evening with a zoot-suiter who would take her to a jitterbug palace. Afterwards, they would likely stop at a drive-in eatery to order hamburgers and a milk shake. Thus buffeted between her identity as both a Japanese and as an American, she nevertheless learned to move in both worlds with a certain facility.

"It's a wonder we aren't all schizo's," one Nisei woman said jokingly. "Our parents were always telling us to be 'good Japanese'. Then they'd turn right around and tell us to be 'good Americans'."

But the speaker well knew, as did most Nisei, that this double message was not all that baffling. For, being a "good Japanese" or a "good American" referred exclusively to behavior and had little to do with divided loyalties. The Issei never challenged the obligation of the Nisei to hold allegiance to their native country, America. What is more, the two injunctions were not necessarily antithetical.

To be a "good Japanese" meant bringing pride and honor to the Japanese race. One did that, not surprisingly, by complying with the earlier discussed catalog of Japanese behavioral norms like *gaman* (perseverance) and *enryo* (self-restraint, reserve) and *giri* (sense of duty and obligation). One should also strive to be *majime* (serious, honest) and *sunao* (gentle, obedient), and, by all means, hold *oya koh koh* (filial piety) among the highest of ideals.

Most Nisei find these terms familiar, for parents invoked them pitilessly. In addition, parents called forth the specter of *haji* (shame, disgrace) to drive home their injunctions. Errant behavior not only brought *haji* to themselves, Nisei were told, but to their parents, the family, the community, and finally, by extension, to the entire race. Emphasis on misbehavior reflecting badly on one or the other of the social groups to which the offspring belonged, operated as a potent means of control. Said one Nisei woman:

> I do recollect generally throughout my childhood, my parents' concern that we be well-mannered and well-behaved, that we wouldn't bring shame upon the family. But I think a lot of their restrictions might have been

precipitated by prejudice, not to look and sound in ways that would be shameful or [make us] stand out as a Japanese group.[3]

The Issei well knew that anti-social behavior on the part of any Japanese would make them "stand out" because of their race, further jeopardizing their already tenuous position in the society.   This heightened consciousness of their actions bears on what they meant by being a "good American."   It was, in effect, a prescription for Nisei behavior outside the parents' domain, one predictably weighted by the parents' own Japanese values.

Embracing the values of both cultures, however, did pose some difficulties for the Nisei female. Not the least of these was the conflict between the deeply ingrained group or consensus orientation of Japanese society and the one of the larger society that championed the primacy of the individual. In glancing over the ideal behavioral modes of the Japanese cited above, one sees a marked tendency toward group orientation, an acute consciousness of how an individual's actions impinge on the group.   *Enryo* and *gaman*, for instance, require superseding one's private needs for the good of the larger group. And *haji*, or shame, calls into play the motive to act out of obligation to the group.[4]

Thus inculcated, the Nisei female tended to feel more comfortable with consensus than with independent decision-making and she worked especially well cooperatively. Her "Japaneseness," moreover, made it difficult for her to express strong personal opinions or act in a manner that might call attention to herself.

White Americans no doubt wondered at the lack of verbal contributions the Nisei made to a group, while Nisei often complained that *hakujin* (white Americans) were "long on talk and short on follow-through." The two modes were strikingly exemplified at school where teachers often observed that the quiet, well-behaved Nisei contributed little to oral discussions, but usually came to class with their homework completed, while the opposite was likely true of many other students.

Group orientation with its de-emphasis on ego-centeredness tends to produce few heroines. Its primary aim, after all, is to promote the greater good of the whole. For Japanese Americans, this mode of

---

[3]Anonymous. Interview conducted by Marion Natsue Wake.

[4]It might be noted that the U.S. manufacturing industry, striving for greater productivity and a superior product, became intensely interested in the dynamics involved in what they called "the Japanese method," one using group-centered management practices. But one could reasonably expect that, without the cultural drives that produce the dynamics, the results would likely be only marginally successful.

operating worked felicitously, for the solidarity it fostered in the early years in their families and in their communities proved to be critical to their survival, as has been shown.

Going Along To Get Along   But as any student of psychology knows, one of the consequences of this group orientation is a tendency toward conformity. While conformity helps one "to get along," it has its inherent drawbacks. Going along to get along results in actions that are not always moral or just, nor even in the best interest of the whole, since it lacks the benefit of keen critical judgment. Professor Kitano remarks that "for many of the same reasons that the Japanese show little negative deviant behavior . . . they also show little positive behavior (noncomforming) such as creative forms of rebellion, disagreement, and individualism." And, in a population that is highly educated and skilled, he adds, where one could expect to find [Japanese American] individuals making notable contributions in the so-called rebellious and "creative" areas of artistic, scientific and academic endeavors, that has not been the case.[5]

For many Nisei women, cultivating characteristics like assertiveness and independence, would be a lifelong struggle.   An impressive number would succeed in attaining a fine balance between independent effort and collective endeavor, between satisfying their own needs and serving the interests of the group.

Generation Gap?   Much has been hypothesized about a generation gap that might have existed between the Issei and the Nisei. Granted, their experiences had been markedly different, and the age differential between them was greater than the norm.[6] With these differences in age and experience as well as in nativity and citizenship, conflicts did arise. The Issei communicated in Japanese, worked and socialized within their own communities and observed the behavioral norms of their own culture. They often expressed alarm at what they saw as the too-rapid acculturation of their children. The Nisei, on the other hand, spoke English almost exclusively to their peers and operated at school

---

[5]Harry Kitano, *Japanese Americans, The Evolution of a Subculture,* (Prentice-Hall, Englewood Cliffs, N.J. 1969) p. 129. One should note that this work was published about the time Nisei women were "coming of age," as it were (see next section), and before the Sansei had reached maturity at which time they would make considerable progress in the very areas of which the writer speaks.

[6]Dorothy Swaine Thomas, *The Salvage,* (University of California Press, Berkeley and Los Angeles 1952), pp. 18-19. In 1941 the median age of Nisei was 17 years, Issei males 55, Issei females 47, and Kibei 26.

and in their social lives in a world of which their parents were mainly ignorant. And, as they struggled to shape their own identities, they often rebelled against parents' strictures.

But the Issei had sacrificed abundantly for their children and had instilled in them values that tended to bind the family, values like filial piety, the importance of family and working together, so that the conflicts in their day-to-day lives tended to be short-lived and superficial. Too, as Glenn astutely points out, "In a racist society where members were exploited as individual units of labor, the family was a necessary counterforce. It was the one institution that Japanese Americans could turn to for comfort, affection, and an affirmation of their individuality and self-worth."[7] While the relationship between the Issei and Nisei might not have been "close", as defined by Western cultural standards, it was generally one of mutual affection, respect and support.

Political Identity   But even as Nisei had been imbued with many Japanese cultural values, there is little doubt that they identified with America rather than Japan. America was where they were born and where they would live out the rest of their lives. It was the country to which they owed their whole-hearted allegiance. Kitagawa makes these pertinent observations:

> When . . . the Issei emphatically supported the "glorious" war effort of Japan in the 1930s, and when he sent packages to relatives in Japan to help Japanese soldiers in Manchuria, he was like a football fan rooting for his favorite team. His act indicated emotional self-identification with the team, but not actual participation in the game itself. All this was distasteful to the Nisei, and he would have tolerated it as an idiosyncrasy of the oldster had it not been for the danger it might bring upon the Nisei's position in American society. The Nisei was just as emotional in this as the Issei, and he could not see anything good in anything Japan was doing at home or abroad. Neither Issei nor Nisei, of course, knew much about contemporary Japan, nor had either of them any real stake in Japan.[8]

In the matter of political activity, Nisei involvement was negligible. For one thing, they were young. For another, a general mood of acceptance of the status quo prevailed around the country. "Racial consciousness," as we have come to know it, had not yet surfaced noticeably. That Paul Robeson could perform before millions and not

---

[7]P. 199.

[8]Daisuke Kitagawa, *Issei and Nisei*, pp. 35-36.

be welcome at the front door of a nightclub, that members of colored minorities could not join the major labor unions or live in a place of their choosing, appeared not to strike most Americans, including the Nisei, as intolerable.

But the Nisei were not inclined to confront issues of race or inequality head-on, in any case. Instead, they generally followed the lead of their parents: they worked hard, kept out of trouble and tried otherwise to prove themselves worthy of American citizenship.

The Japanese American Citizens League (JACL)   To promote this latter aim, a few Nisei men, mostly professionals, formed the Japanese American Citizens League (JACL) in 1930. Evolved from a group known as the American Loyalty League, the JACL sought throughout its formative years and World War II to cultivate a more favorable image of Nisei as loyal and productive Americans. At the same time, it sought to generate political savvy among the Nisei, and to encourage them to become more involved in the political process. But to arouse interest in politics in the Nisei, who were young and who had always operated on the fringes of the mainstream, was difficult:

> The JACL tried valiantly to get the Nisei interested in political matters. It was easy enough to get Nisei registered to vote, but rounding them up for a meeting with candidates was a more difficult problem. On many an occasion candidates for local, county and state offices showed up to address JACL-sponsored political meetings only to find a mere handful of Nisei present.[9]

In these pre-war years, JACL could be seen, in many ways, as a microcosm of the Nisei community: apolitical, its leadership all male, its purposes clearly announced in its slogan, "For Better Americans in a Greater America." And although it had defined itself as a national organization and stated its lofty aims, it had no clear agenda.[10]

During the war, JACL leaders would come under heavy criticism by Japanese Americans themselves for their near-fanatic determination to demonstrate the super patriotism of Japanese Americans. (See following chapter.) After the war, however, the JACL spearheaded successful drives to eliminate discriminatory statutes such as California alien land laws and immigration and naturalization laws.

---

[9] Bill Hosokawa, *Nisei, The Quiet Americans* (William Morrow and Co., New York 1969) p. 200.
[10] *Ibid.*, pp. 201-202.

Through the years, the JACL has been charged with holding too closely to a middle-class conservative agenda, tending toward re-active rather than pro-active approaches to issues. But it had attained national stature during the 1950s, and since it remained the only Japanese American national organization, its membership continued to increase. Indeed, JACL came to be regarded as the organ through which the collective voice of Japanese Americans could be heard and consequently gained increasing influence in tandem with the economic growth and political influence of Japanese Americans themselves.

EDUCATION

Education had always taken a high place in the order of priorities in the Japanese family. This fact derived from interrelated motives: cultural predilection, means of elevating status and means of securing the Nisei's long-term occupational goals.

The degree to which the Japanese emphasized the importance of education is revealed in the disparity between school attendance figures in the Japanese population and those in the general population in 1940. At ages 18-19, when high school graduation normally takes place, 60 per cent of Nisei males, compared with 44 percent of the general population and 54 percent of Nisei females compared with 38 percent of the general female population were attending school. The percentage of Nisei completing high school exceeded that of the population norm by a significant margin.[11]

The majority of Nisei were in school on the eve of World War II. Available data suggests that the majority did not expect to go to college. In 1940 the proportion of Nisei females who finished high school exceeded that of the population norm, but the proportion completing from 1-4 years of college dropped significantly below it.[12] In high school, they typically took general education or commercial courses (basic secretarial skills) or courses based in homemaking.

On the whole, Nisei women appear to have had pleasant experiences in school, especially in the elementary grades. Because of the emphasis placed on education in the home, many Nisei excelled in school and, at least in the lower grades, enjoyed popularity among the students. "We were well liked, and in a number of classes--3rd grade, 4th grade--I had to tutor some of the other children who were slow in spelling or arithmetic . . . and being teacher's pet. . . I made a lot of friends," said one woman. Other Nisei women tell of similar experiences.

---

[11]Thomas, p. 72.

[12]Ibid., p. 611.

Bradford Smith reports that a study found that Nisei students made more high marks at every level except in the last term of high school. Other investigators, he writes, concluded that Nisei suffered from a language handicap because English was not spoken at home and that "in intelligence they were equal to other children but in effort superior."[13]

High School   In high school, where social interaction and school politics gained importance, racial division increased in proportion. Nisei made non-Japanese friends but danced amongst themselves at the high school hops, went to football games together and dated other Nisei. Social segregation outside of school remained in force for even the most popular and active girls. Although the recollections of Nisei women are often couched in terms like "I didn't feel comfortable (dancing with, dating . . ., etc.) them," putting the onus on themselves, they were quite conscious that an invisible line barred them from interacting with white students in those social matters.

Thus, if there were a dozen or more Nisei students attending a high school, they often formed a Japanese Club, not for political purposes, but mainly to carry out a social agenda.

Generally, Nisei did not participate in student politics. One woman told an interviewer, "We realized that all the girls who were student body officers were very rich and attractive, and although we thought it would be nice to be part of the student body [government], we didn't even try. We knew there was no chance." However subjective the statement, it clearly reveals the lower economic and social status which underscored most Nisei's experience in high school.

But in some high schools where a large mix of ethnic minorities comprised the student body, many Nisei took leadership roles. A striking example existed at Roosevelt High School in Los Angeles where students from Jewish, Japanese, Mexican and African backgrounds made up the majority. There, Nisei were routinely elected to the highest offices, including the office of Student Body President.

Masaye (Nagao) Nakamura, a student at Roosevelt from 1938-1941, recalls that her closest friends at school were of Jewish, Mexican and Greek descent. "I felt very comfortable there," she reports, "not *different* because of my race." Nakamura, who had won a number of oratorical contests at the school, was elected to the office of President

---

[13]*Americans from Japan*, (J.P. Lippincott Co., 1948), p. 252.

of the Girl's League in 1941, the year that Pearl Harbor was bombed.[14] Interned in a concentration camp during the war, Nakamura left it to attend college in Missouri, then went on to Columbia University to earn a Master's degree. A year of teaching in Hawaii followed, after which she became the first Japanese American teacher in the Oakland school system in 1949. "It was difficult finding a teaching position then," she says. "I was a bit amused when they published a photo of the new teachers for that year, and referred to me as 'Hawaiian'." Nakamura was honored as Oakland Unified School District's "Teacher of the Year" in the 1978-79 school year and went on to distinguish herself as an administrator in the district before she retired.[15]

The impressive achievements scored by Nisei was, in many cases, due to their good fortune in being able to attend schools like Roosevelt High School which nurtured their talent and intelligence.

College   In spite of the great emphasis that the Japanese family placed on education, Nisei women did not aspire to a college education in great numbers for a variety of reasons. First, many families could not afford to send them, particularly if there were males in the family, who usually got priority.[16]   In many cases, the female sibling worked to support the family while her brother attended college.

Secondly, Japanese American women had a limited choice of professional careers open to them, usually in the health care or scientific fields. Accountants, teachers and social workers found it next to impossible to find jobs. "On the other hand some technicians, for example, biochemists and dieticians, were working in fields for which they had been trained, and there was little discrimination against nurses."[17]

Third, most females at the time viewed marriage and motherhood as their ordained destiny. "I never thought about it much," said one Nisei woman. "Being a wife and mother, it's just something you did."

Anne Saito Howden was an exception.   She attended the University of California at Berkeley in the 1930s.   The elder of two daughters from Hanford, California, she was encouraged by a high

---

[14]In the same year, Susie (Hattori) Narahara had been elected Student Body Secretary at RHS. Also, a number of other Nisei girls in the school had taken active roles in scholarship, service and athletic organizations through the years.

[15]Personal interview.

[16]Thomas, p. 611. Thomas reports that 10.3 percent of Nisei males had completed 1-3 years of college in Washington and California in 1940, compared to 6.6 females in the same year.

[17]*Ibid.*, p. 42.

school teacher and her parents, especially her mother, to continue her education. A minister friend, the Reverend Hata, arranged a "school girl" domestic job for her in which she would help with meals in exchange for room, board and carfare.[18] Howden recalls:

> I vaguely thought of becoming a teacher, even though I didn't know of a single Nisei woman teacher. But I wasn't one of those career-bound people, you know. A whole new world had opened up to me, and I was determined to make the most of it. I found myself taking English literature courses and some business courses on the side.[19]

Only a handful of Japanese Americans were enrolled, as Howden remembers it, and they established their own social program. "It was so exciting," she says, "to meet Nisei men who were actually going to college!" Almost in the same breath, she said she realized that she might never have gone to college had she been blessed with a brother. After graduating, Howden went to work at the International House in Berkeley, where she was eventually appointed a staff member.

Medical Training   Against formidable odds, a few Nisei women graduated from medical schools, among them, Yoshiye Togasaki. Dr. Togasaki estimated that there might have been about ten Nisei women in medicine:

> I didn't know them all. For instance, my two sisters and myself--that was three. There was the Yamaguchi family in Los Angeles, and there were two or three of [them]. And there was this gal, [Masako] Kusayanagi . . . . That was seven. I am sure there were at least three more somewhere in the United States.[20]

---

[18]Encouragement from parents and a teacher, coupled with help from other community network sources became a pattern which enabled many Nisei to enter college. It should also be noted that one of the first community service activities that Japanese American organizations engaged in was offering student scholarships. These scholarships have greatly increased in scope and amount through the years.

[19]Personal interview.

[20]Interview conducted by Eric Saul, National Japanese American Historical Society Oral History Project, February 1986. Not mentioned in Dr. Togasaki's interview were Drs. Bertha Akimoto and Sakaye Shigekawa. The author was unable to obtain information about the former, but the May 26, 1989 issue of *Pacific Citizen* reveals that Dr. Shigekawa had graduated from Loyola Medical School in Chicago, one of four women in her class. After practicing in Santa Anita detention center, Shigekawa left camp to practice in

Having graduated from U.C. Berkeley in Public Health in 1929, Togasaki was admitted to the John Hopkins Medical School. Later, when she sought employment in public health work, she often faced the response: "Sorry, we would like to employ you, but the other members of the staff and the community will not accept you."

Togasaki would later become the chief of the Division of Preventive Services in Contra Costa County, California.

Nurses' Training   A considerable number of Nisei women aspired to nursing, not only because it was in the tradition of women to be care-givers, but because opportunities for employment in the field were fairly decent.   Also, nursing drew respect and prestige in the Japanese community akin to that of teaching.

Yet the effort was not easy. Setsuko Shimizu took her pre-nursing education at Los Angeles City College along with five other Nisei women.   "But very few private hospitals would accept Japanese American women for training," Shimizu recalls, "so we took it at Los Angeles County General." But while they received vigorous training in the spectrum of medical problems there, the hospital did not provide training in the refinements of nursing care such as private hospitals afforded. "So I had to look around for a private hospital to finish my training, and, as far as I know, the Seventh Day Adventist hospitals, White Memorial and Glendale Sanitarium, were the only ones that accepted Nisei women." Shimizu had only four months of training left at White Memorial when she was recruited as part of the vanguard health care group to go to the Manzanar concentration camp. During her stay there, she had to be escorted to Los Angeles by MP's to take her State Board examination.

Shimizu eventually became a surgical nurse. She recalls that, while Nisei women did find nursing jobs during the war, they were sometimes shunted off to places like the supply room, as she was, in one Chicago hospital. Such a witless waste of human resources did not prevail for long, however, due to the wartime shortage of nurses.[21]

Japanese School   On weekdays, young Nisei attended public school, after which they would likely attend Japanese school. The conflict provided by these institutions was palpable: not only were the languages to be learned derived from different streams, having no cognates, the

---

Chicago and later in Los Angeles, specializing in obstetrics. She delivered over 20,000 babies and at this writing practices general medicine at the age of 75.

[21]Personal interview.

shushin, or rules of conduct, taught in the Japanese schools were often at odds with what the student knew to be operative rules of conduct in the dominant society. Writer Monica Sone describes her experience:

> Nihon Gakko was so different from grammar school I found myself switching my personality back and forth daily like a chameleon. At Bailey Gatzert School I was a jumping, screaming, roustabout Yankee, but at the stroke of three when the school bell rang and doors burst open everywhere, spewing out pupils like jelly beans from a broken bag, I suddenly became a modest, faltering, earnest little Japanese girl with a small timid voice.[22]

"It was a farce!" insists one Nisei. "We went because our parents made us go. I didn't mind much because all my friends went. . . . I don't think I learned a darned thing, though, except maybe *kana* [the Japanese syllabary alphabet] and a few *kanji* [Chinese ideographs].

Later, during the war with Japan, the U.S. Army discovered a need for interpreters, and after a thorough check of all Nisei in the concentration camps, they came upon the astonishing fact that only 15 percent could speak passable Japanese while only 5 percent could pass a reading and writing test.[23] Said Smith, "There was irony in the fact that after intensively educating themselves for American life, getting farther up the educational ladder than any other group of any ancestry, what the nation wanted of them after all was simply to know the language of their fathers--the very thing they had, in their desire to be American in all things, done their best to forget."[24]

RELIGION

"Christians and Buddhists had little to do with each other," wrote Father Daisuke Kitagawa. "Each religion had several denominations, and one's denominational affiliation went far in determining one's social circle."[25] In fact, the opposite may be more to the point: one's social circle and circumstance frequently determined one's religious affiliation. Significant differences existed between the religious preferences of the Issei and Nisei and between rural and urban residents before the war. Rural Issei remained overwhelmingly Buddhist (over 80 percent), while only 32-36 percent of Nisei in urban areas professed that religion. Correspondingly only 11-12 percent of Issei rural residents

---

[22]*Nisei Daughter*, (University of Washington Press, Seattle and London 1953), p.22.

[23]Smith, p. 253.

[24]*Ibid.*

[25]*Issei and Nisei*, (The Seabury Press, New York 1967) p. 16.

claimed Christianity as their religion, while the proportion of Nisei urbanites reached well over 53 percent.[26]

But as a rule, the differences in religious preferences between the Issei and Nisei did not provoke conflict between them. Traditionally, Buddhism took a more eclectic and tolerant approach to religion than did Christianity, and most Issei Buddhist parents reflected that approach. Margarette Murakami of Sebastopol, California recalls that her parents, who were Nichiren Buddhists, often attended Christian services held in the home of a friend before a Buddhist church was established in that small town. "It doesn't matter what church you go to," they told her. "The main thing is that you believe in God." As a child, Murakami began going to a Christian church with a friend and became a lifelong adherent of that religion. Her friend, Pat Shimizu, on the other hand, attended Sunday school in whatever Christian church her *hakujin* friends happened to attend. "My father told us to go to church, so we went," she said. But when the Buddhist Temple was established in 1934, Shimizu, along with many other Nisei teenagers, became members of that church.[27]

The Buddhist church in rural locales like Sebastopol counted an appreciable number of Nisei among its adherents at least partly because Japanese Christian churches had not been established in most rural areas before the war. And while the Buddhist church was to later adopt many of the formal practices of the Christian church to accommodate the needs of the English-speaking Nisei, it remained for the most part Japanese in character.

Nearly all the various Buddhist sects on the West Coast had their home base in Japan. Priests came from the home country to serve in the churches. Efforts to develop a Nisei ministerial program did not get underway until 1932, and then, the students were sent to Japan for training. Sunday School was conducted in Japanese.

In urban areas, such as Los Angeles, San Francisco and Seattle, Nisei attended Christian churches in greater numbers than they did Buddhist churches. Theological considerations aside, Nisei attended Christian churches partly due to their eagerness to be identified with anything American, partly because services for them were held in English, and because they provided social and educational activities that were more in line with contemporary American life. "I remember feeling superior to Buddhists," said one Nisei woman. "They seemed so

---

[26]Thomas, pp. 66-69. Survey was taken in 1930, and included only those 14 years of age and older. But another survey taken in concentration camps in 1942 more or less confirmed these findings.

[27]Personal interview.

Japanesey. It's funny now. . . that's the very thing about the Buddhist church that we find attractive."

In the early years, when very few Nisei had become ordained ministers, Caucasian lay people or ministers sent from the parent church presided over the segregated Nisei congregations. Nearly every Nisei who regularly attended the church in those years remembers a spinster missionary or a minister and his wife who served their church. Kindly and solicitous, they were regarded with the same deference as were teachers, and with the same distance.

But many of the Nisei congregations had already developed an organizational structure by 1941. The Reverend Paul Nagano, a retired Baptist minister, cites the Southern California Japanese American Christian Church Federation as an example. An umbrella organization, it coordinated the activities of different denominations, frequently matching ministers with congregations and arranging interdenominational services on special occasions. Financial independence had not yet been achieved by the larger denominations, such as the Baptists, before the war, but smaller, more fundamentalist churches like the Holiness Church functioned independently.

For Nisei girls and women, the church offered spiritual nourishment and education as well as an important social base.

WORK

A Nisei woman, about to join the work force, knew that her choices would be slim. She knew that she would not be hired in situations in which she would be visible to the public, even in as commonplace a position as a clerk in a department store. She knew that if she joined the legion of clerical workers, she would likely not rise above the middle rung of that group, no matter her ability or the effort she put forth.

"Back then [ca. 1938], Japanese could not find jobs except in Japan Town and China Town," says Yuri Kochiyama. "It seemed impossible to get an ordinary job in town. Even when I finished junior college, I was one of the only Japanese Americans who was working in San Pedro proper and I heard it was the first time that a five-and-dime store hired Japanese. Woolworth hired me where three other five-and-dime stores wouldn't even let me make out an application." Kochiyama was hired only as a fill-in for summer vacations and holidays. "Par for the course," she remarks, "for all Japanese were either working in a vegetable stand or doing domestic work."[28]

---

[28]In "Fishermerchants Daughter: Yuri Kochiyama, an Oral History," v. 1, (Community Documentation Workshop 1981), pp. 5-6.

Indeed, out of a total of 6,884 employed Nisei women in 1940, the greatest number were employed in domestic service (1,771) followed by farm workers, both paid and unpaid (1,675), then, clerical workers (1574). Others found work as seamstresses or in ethnic enterprises as clerks, salespersons or bookkeepers. A mere 300 were employed in the combined category of professional and technical workers.[29]

Urban Nisei, according to Evelyn Nakano Glenn, had life a bit easier than those who lived in rural areas. In their early teens, girls who lived in cities helped at home or contributed toward their own support by baby sitting, working at the family business or doing light domestic work. Many did not work at all until they finished school. Most finished high school and a few managed to attend business college.[30]

Domestic Work   Nisei women took domestic work for some of the same reasons that the Issei did: the work was available and familiar and the hours flexible. But, unlike the Issei, indications are that many, if not most, Nisei viewed domestic work as an interim occupation, while, for instance, they attended school or looked for other work. Some did "day work", working one day a week in the homes of different employers. Others worked for a short length of time for one employer, then moved on to some other activity. During the war, many Nisei wives left concentration camps to take domestic work near the camps where their servicemen husbands were stationed. Today, few Nisei women can be found who have *not*, at one time or another, worked as domestics.

Farm Work   The work experiences of rural Nisei women differed significantly from those who lived in cities. Women who had worked on farms remember their lives as only slightly less grueling than their mothers'. "It was a *hard* life," said one woman. "We were always working. No vacation, no nothing. And the worst of it was, we always seemed to be poorer than everybody else." She recalls having moved at least four times during her school years, and was forced to quit school in her senior year to work as a domestic in the city in order to help support the family. Her experience was not uncommon among Nisei women on the farm.[31]

Adding to the drudgery of their lives, young Nisei females on farms often lacked social contact with their peers, unless they had access to a Japanese American church or other Japanese American organizations.

---

[29]Glenn, p. 86.

[30]*Ibid.*, 56-57.

[31]Personal interview.

Thus, when they came of marriageable age, many of their marriages were arranged through intermediaries.

Mrs. K., a widow in her seventies, whose family had moved from the farm to the city when she was 21-years old, reports that her parents had presented her with three marriage prospects, one after another. But, she believes, because of her lack of experience ("I didn't know anything about men because I had never dated,"), the man she selected turned out to be a "wrong choice" and the marriage an unhappy one. "If I were a Sansei, I would probably have gotten a divorce," she states.[32] "But then I guess I'm glad I didn't," she adds hastily, "because of the kids."

Plant Nursery Workers   Women who worked in plant nurseries, usually family-owned or -managed, trod the line between urban and rural living. They worked hard and lived a relatively secluded life, but not as secluded as women on the farm.

Eiko Sugihara, the only daughter born into a family that owned a nursery in Redwood City, California, recalls that by the time she was eight years old, she was cooking for the whole family because her mother was ill much of the time. About fifteen Japanese families lived in and around the area, and she remembers a generally happy and satisfactory social life, attending Japanese School and Japanese Student Club functions at the high school. Unlike girls on the farm, Sugihara did not work in the family business, the nursery, except for light chores on weekends and summer vacations. She remembers with pleasure the occasions when "nursery people" would come together to help one another, filling labor shortages or putting up the cheese-cloth frame houses in which the seedlings were nurtured. On the latter occasions, a spirit of good fellowship reigned as the families gathered to work together and to share the great mounds of food which always appeared on the table.

For all the pleasant experiences Sugihara derived from her life before the war, she never ventured farther than Monterey, California, about a two-hour drive from her home.[33]

---

[32]Personal interview. The speaker refers to the fact that Sansei enjoy more independence in decision-making, are more assertive and less inclined than Nisei to carry on an unsatisfactory marriage. Sansei also have greater social and job mobility than their elders, which makes them better able to sustain themselves as independent householders or single parents.

[33]Interview for OHP.

THE MILIEU

In many ways, the years just preceding World War II was a heady time for urban Nisei females, filled with the scent of gardenias, and the excitement of romance and dating. Dual exhaust pipes cracked loudly on the streets, proclaiming the presence of young males in the neighborhood. The most pressing business involved going to school, activities with a social club and being "popular."

With President Franklin Roosevelt's New Deal programs in gear, Japanese Americans found reason to look optimistically to the future. Most families had recovered from the ravages of the Depression. Some owned homes; most owned a car. Many Nisei had gone to work, fresh out of high school, to plunk part of their wages into the family cash pool. Now they could go to a movie, take a ride to the beach or the mountains, or go out for a hamburger or a plate of chow mein without too much strain.

Outside of school, social engagement between Nisei and other races rarely occurred before World War II. A date with a *hakujin* would no doubt provoke strong censure from her parents as well as his. Asked how she felt about not being included in the social circle of her white friends, one Nisei woman responded: "Oh, I don't think I minded. If you don't expect it, you don't care."

But it was precisely because they were barred from participating in the social activities of the majority culture that the Nisei had, by the late thirties, established a broad network of organizations for social activities within their own ethnic communities. Youth organizations in the churches, literally hundreds of clubs organized solely for social purposes, and YWCA and athletic groups offered diversion as well as a means of establishing friendships and maintaining communication and support. One researcher found that over 400 such clubs could be counted in 1938 in Los Angeles alone. Young adult Nisei maintained control over their own groups with little or no interference from their parents.

Dancing was a favorite pastime for teenage Nisei in the thirties and forties. In Los Angeles, various athletic and social clubs sponsored dances, inviting one or two other clubs to the event. Donning short skirts, Sloppy Joe sweaters and saddle shoes, the bobby soxers (the term was invented for them) jitterbugged, Lindy-hopped, fox-trotted and waltzed to the music of the big bands like Tommy Dorsey, Duke Ellington and Glenn Miller that blared from radios and phonograph machines. Occasionally, they would slip into high-heeled shoes and fancy dresses, their hair done in a high pompadour, to dance at the Palladium in Hollywood, or Lick Pier at Ocean Park (which cost their escorts 10 cents to go through the turnstile for each dance number).

The Issei, observing this, what they somewhat deprecatingly called "jitabata", were genuinely bewildered by the phenomenon.   As Hosokawa noted, they often grumbled, "Too much-i dan-su, dan-su."

The pre-war years was also a time of "innocence," guided by the understanding that proper male-female relations meant dating, going steady, necking, but not "going all the way." Marriage was held sacred, a union somehow ordered in heaven.   Trust in authority and the instruments of government held sway.

Nisei girls held to these norms perhaps more constantly than did their counterparts in the majority population because of the insularity of the society.   However, occasionally a girl would disappear from the social scene, and rumors would fly that she had been hustled off to Japan because she was pregnant.

KIBEI

Nisei who had been sent to Japan in their early years, often for economic considerations but also to obtain a Japanese education, eventually returned to the U.S. and came to constitute a sub-category of the Nisei known as Kibei.[34] By World War II, close to 10,000 Kibei were counted in the Japanese American population.[35] The greatest number had returned between 1935 and 1940.

The Question   To send or not to send their children to Japan became a large question among the Issei in the twenties and thirties.   With its moral overtones, the issue was hotly debated around pot-bellied stoves in farmhouses, in the parlors of rooming houses and in the language press.   Junsuke Takaya, an Issei writer presented the argument in an illuminating essay, summarized here:

"I say it's wrong, a big mistake, to send the girls to Japan now," says a man named Yamane.

"You don't understand, you a bachelor," counters Mr. A. "See, time is the important thing now. We want to send the older ones over to learn a little Japanese, get a little refinement, you might say, before they start thinking about boys. Too late then, you know."

Yamane, indignant, calls that thought shallow-brained. "It's just not right," he adds, "to send children away to Japan, no matter what you say. When they're grown up, all right. Same as it's all right to send students from Japan here to study."

---

[34]"Kibei" is translated literally "returning to America."

[35]Thomas, p. 580.

Another man joins the debate: "But, Yamane, you know the old saying *'Kawaii ko niwa tabi wo saseyo'* ["Send a beloved child on a journey."]. To send a child away is a hard thing, of course. But then they gain strength from the experience--far better than getting spoiled as they do in this country, no?"

Yamane is not moved. "Fools!" he shouts. "It may be that children here tend to be *wagamama* (spoiled), but it's downright stupid to think you can't raise them up to be decent here, same as in Japan. To tell the truth, I think parents send their children off to Japan because of money more than anything else. Too much in a hurry to get rich. They want to save money by working in double harness, husband and wife, without the responsibility of the children."[36]

The harsh indictment uttered by the last speaker contained some truth: sending children away to Japan freed the mother to work alongside her husband. It was also less expensive to sustain children in Japan than in America. But contrary to the impression given here, there were usually other children in the household who had to be provided for, so that parents were not entirely "without the responsibility of the children." And, as the main speaker argues, many Issei had genuine concerns about educating their children in the culture of Japan, which they thought superior to that of the western world.

Also, sending children to their grandparents was undoubtedly underlaid with the assumptions of the traditional Japanese family system. In that context, returning the child to the head of the household in Japan was conveyed to the child as a privilege. Be that as it may, Kibei suffered from their sojourn. Some had endured the trauma of feeling rejected and experienced difficulty renewing an affectionate relationship with their parents when they returned to the U.S.

They had spent the better part of their lives in Japan, a greater proportion even than had the Issei, and had been more thoroughly schooled there.[37] Thus they spoke Japanese more fluently than English, and their political views tended to be more staunchly pro-Japanese than those of either the Issei or the Nisei.[38] In addition, socializing with the much older Issei often proved unsatisfactory to the Kibei, while their approximate age cohorts, the Nisei, rejected them as being "too

---

[36]From *"Sei Wo Shiru Musume"* (A Girl Awakened) in *Colorado Times*, January 1928.

[37]Thomas, pp. 64-65.

[38]There were, of course, exceptions as in the case of Karl Yoneda. A Communist worker, he took a strong stand against the military policies of Japan before the war. In W.W. II, as a Military Intelligence serviceman, he demonstrated his loyalty to the U.S. in the Pacific theater.

Japanese."   As a consequence they tended to associate among themselves and became a minority of a minority group.

Because of their lack of English skills, the Kibei were also handicapped in their choices of occupations. In her interview sample, Glenn found that in the families that had sent some children to Japan and kept others in California, the "Kibei siblings were employed in service and blue-collar jobs, while their Nisei brothers and sisters worked in white-collar jobs."[39]   Thomas confirms this finding: "An appreciably greater proportion of them [Kibei] than of Nisei were working for other Japanese, and they were disproportionately in agricultural rather than in urban pursuits, in manual rather than clerical activities."[40]

Kimiko Tamura's poignant story illustrates the dilemma which beset many Kibei. Taken to Japan by her mother when she was five years old upon the divorce of her parents, Tamura remembers little of those early years in the U.S. She returned in 1935, a young adult, speaking no English and with few marketable skills. Nevertheless, she found work as a waitress in the Ten Cents A Meal restaurant in the skid row section of Los Angeles. After serving up meals for three months, she fortunately found work as a typesetter for the *Rafu Shimpo* language newspaper. She spent her leisure time with other Kibei, joining the Kibei Club, a kind of literary group in which members shared short stories and poetry.

During the war, Tamura and her husband, Akira Itami, also a Kibei, were incarcerated at Manzanar. After six months in camp, Itami volunteered for the Armed services, anxious to serve his country. The Army pressed him into enlisting in the Military Intelligence Service at Camp Savage. Kimiko Tamura left camp with her new daughter to be with him in Minnesota, taking a job as a domestic. His training over, Itami was sent to Japan to interrogate prisoners of war and, later, war criminals. In the service, in Japan, Itami began to agonize between loyalty to the United States and his love for Japan. He had, after all, spent his impressionable years in Japan, and could not sever the strong emotional bonds that held him in thrall. Unable, finally, to resolve his dilemma, he committed suicide.[41]   By this time, Kimiko Tamura had joined him in Japan, and suffered the entire ordeal with him.

---

[39]P. 53.

[40]P. 42.

[41]The political and moral thicket into which Itami was snared, became the subject of a 3-volume novel *Futatsu No Sokoku* (Two Fatherlands) by the noted Japanese novelist Toyoko Yamasaki. The work was dramatized into a 50-hour weekly series by NHK TV in Japan. When the prospect arose of showing the film in the U.S. in 1984, many Nisei

Later, however, having returned to the U.S., she remarried and made a good life for herself and her daughter. Now 75 years old, she is a fine potter, and still attends a community college to polish her English.[42]

While the Kibei experienced more than their share of difficulties in the United States, particularly during the war when they came under intense suspicion and scrutiny, most made post-war adjustments well, contributing to the pluralistic landscape of America. One is, however, left with the conviction that a definitive story of this oppressed minority is yet to be written.

WAR CLOUDS

By 1940, the mood of the country was edged with anxiety. Wars that had been raging on the European front and in Asia threatened to disintegrate worldwide balances of power so that they could no longer be ignored by the U.S. Mussolini had earlier seized Ethiopia and Hitler's troops had stormed relentlessly through Austria, Czechoslovakia, Holland, Belgium, Poland and France. In July, they had begun bombing raids on Great Britain.

On the Asian front, Japan had seized Manchuria in the early thirties and had won control over northern and central China by the end of 1938. Some historians even date the beginning of World War II from one or the other of these two events. When France fell to Germany in 1940, Japanese armies invaded French Indochina. The United States cut down its sales of scrap iron and oil to Japan. Soon afterward, Japan signed an alliance with Germany and Italy, which only served to exacerbate the already heightened tensions between Japan and the United States.

Meanwhile, here in the U.S., the attitudes of white Americans toward Japanese Americans, never amiable, turned increasingly ugly with each aggressive step that Japan took.

Then, in 1941, diplomatic relations between the United States and Japan deteriorated with alarming speed. In July, the U.S. stopped the sale of much-needed oil to Japan completely and froze all Japanese assets in the United States. Great Britain followed the action of the United States. Japan retaliated by freezing American and British assets. The stage was set.

---

objected vociferously, charging that the public perception of the Nisei would be distorted by the tragic story of this man. They also objected to what they saw as the depiction of the Nisei as mere caricatures. As a result, the film was never shown in the U.S.

[42]Personal interview.

CHAPTER 7
Crisis

One hundred thousand persons were sent to concentration camps on a record which wouldn't support a conviction for stealing a dog.
                                                    ---Eugene V. Rostow

PEARL HARBOR

On Sunday, December 7, 1941, Japan attacked Pearl Harbor. The following day, the United States declared war on Japan.

This war was to produce the single, most wrenching episode in the lives of Japanese Americans. On February 19, 1942, fully two months after Pearl Harbor, President Roosevelt signed Executive order 9066, giving authorities the power to remove all persons of Japanese ancestry from the West Coast. The Nisei, together with their children and their Issei parents, were driven from their homes and businesses and banished to concentration camps without charges or due process of law.

The question of how such a breach of the Bill of Rights could have occurred has been discussed in great detail in a number of publications. It is not within the purview of this book to cover the same ground except to provide a historical framework of the event sufficient to explore the Nisei woman's experience within it.

It should be understood, at the same time, that the outline of these events rests on the findings of the U. S. Government's own investigative commission, namely that: 1) General John L. DeWitt (Commander of the Western Defense Command) *"relied heavily on civilian politicians rather than informed military judgements in reaching his conclusions* [that exclusion of persons of Japanese ancestry was necessary]," and 2) the decisions leading to the exclusion *"were not driven by analysis of military conditions. The broad historical causes which shaped these decisions were race prejudice, war hysteria and a failure of political leadership."*[1]

---

[1]Report of the Commission on Wartime Relocation and Internment of Civilians, (hereafter CWRIC), *Personal Justice Denied,* (U.S. Government Printing Office, Washington, D.C., 1982), pp. 8, 18. *(Author's emphasis)*

"A Jap is a Jap"   For decades, anti-Japanese forces had been at work on the West Coast, fueled by racist groups and powerful agricultural and labor interests who felt threatened by the inroads being made by the resident Japanese.

Prejudice against the resident Japanese sprang from another source too. The tide of public opinion towards Japanese Americans had always surged for good or ill in direct relation to the current political climate between the United States and Japan. When the U.S. locked its gates against Japanese immigration in 1924, culminating a series of hostile moves against that nation, Japan was outraged. One historian went as far as to assert that this one event had a major influence on every antagonistic event that took place subsequently between the two countries.[2] In succeeding years, Japan had been engaged in a series of successful expansionist wars, provoking hostility, fear and not a little envy in the United States.

Now, with the bombing of Pearl Harbor and with Japan marching relentlessly towards its goal of hegemony over the Philippines, Burma, Malaya and the East Indies, Secretary of War Henry L. Stimson called for threats of reprisals against Japanese nationals in America.[3]

That a certain amount of hostility felt towards Japan might be transferred to the Issei might be expected. But white Americans had always had difficulty making a distinction between the citizen Japanese, the alien Japanese and the Japanese in Japan. To most, the term "Jap" meant anyone with a Japanese face, an abstraction insinuating danger and inscrutability (therefore, treachery) to be guarded against. "A Jap's a Jap," Lt. Gen John DeWitt was to declare as a rationale for the exclusion of citizen Japanese from the West Coast. ". . . There is no way to determine their loyalty . . . . It makes no difference whether he is an American; theoretically he is still Japanese and you can't change him by giving him a piece of paper."[4]

---

[2]Robert Aura Smith quoted by Carey McWilliams, *Prejudice*, Little, Brown and Company, (Boston 1944), p. 68.

[3]Michi Weglyn, *Years of Infamy*, (William Morrow and Company, Inc., New York 1976), p. 55.

[4]DeWitt uttered this infamous statement in testimony before a congressional committee in 1943 as a rationale for removing the Japanese from their homes. He had been designated by the Secretary of War to carry out the removal orders. Parenthetically, many researchers have concluded that once the responsibility to handle "the Japanese problem" had shifted from the Justice Department and the more flexible Attorney General Francis Biddle, to the War Department with its cadre of rigid Army personnel, the die was cast for mass exclusion of the Japanese.

"Remember Pearl Harbor"   Not surprisingly, when Japan attacked Pearl Harbor, a firestorm of intense hostility towards the resident Japanese burst over the West Coast. "Remember Pearl Harbor" swiftly became a rallying cry, resonant with hate and an ugly mood for reprisal. But in mocking irony, the Nisei were to have more reason than any to "remember Pearl Harbor."

Yo Nagata:

> I had gone to a Nisei basketball game in Oakland when the attack was announced. I guess I didn't quite believe it, or I wasn't quite sure of its significance. Anyway, I went to a movie that afternoon with Mort [her future husband]. They kept interrupting it with announcements of the attack and calls for all Navy personnel to report to their ships. Then I began to feel frightened . . . and guilty. As if I personally had something to do with it.[5]

Akin to Nagata's state of mind, feelings of guilt resided in the far reaches of every Nisei's psyche, gnawing and debilitating. Almost unconsciously, they had long carried the weight of "racial guilt," the guilt of being born to a race despised by their fellow citizens. The bombing by Japan served to heighten this curious sense of culpability.

Monica Sone:

> I felt as if a fist had smashed my pleasant little existence, breaking it into jigsaw puzzle pieces. An old wound opened up again, and I found myself shrinking inwardly from my Japanese blood, the blood of an enemy. I knew instinctively that the fact that I was an American by birthright was not going to help me escape the consequences of this unhappy war.[6]

Mary Ann Utsumi, a new bride, had just sent her husband off to work when a Caucasian neighbor came to tell her that Japan had attacked Pearl Harbor.

> The neighbor seemed very angry that the Japanese--and I think that included us--could do such a thing. We had been congenial before that, but after that the relationship became touchy. Anyway, I quickly relayed the news of the bombing to my father-in-law, and he said, 'Never. That could never be.' The next day, the FBI came to the house and boarded up the door

---

[5]Personal interview.
[6]Pp. 145-146.

and windows and ordered us to stay in the house. They put a watch on us around the clock.[7]

The Utsumis never found out why they were forcibly confined to their house, but they suspected at the time that their father, who was one of the few Issei dentists in the San Francisco Bay Area, was under suspicion. After the family was released from their confinement, they could not go out without feeling that they were being watched.[8]

If war with Japan was not exactly a surprise to government officials, it came as a shock to most Americans.[9] Not since the Civil War had major hostilities been fought on American ground. Now, on the West Coast, the air laden with rumors of Japanese submarines lurking near the shore and radio signals being flashed to the enemy (allegedly by the Japanese on the West Coast), fear mounted daily that a bomb attack was imminent. To heighten the public's anxiety, large cities on both coasts were ordered blacked out. Air-raid sirens wailed ominously in the night, accompanied by rumors of enemy planes looming over the horizon.

As the resident Japanese had feared, they became the victims of the public's anxiety. At least nine racially-motivated deaths of Japanese occurred, one of a Nisei who had just been honorably discharged from the U.S. Army.[10]

The Nisei became prime targets since they were perforce in public places. But conditioned as they were to being treated like enemy aliens and not a little daunted by the bombardment of wartime propaganda, they behaved in a manner that would provoke the least animosity. They waited for buses that would not pick them up, and tolerated being turned away at restaurants as well as at public places like the municipal swimming pool.

They were even prevented from making a livelihood. Many were fired from their jobs. Employers told gardeners they had no more need for their services; the civil service fired Nisei without hearing or accusation.

---

[7]Personal interview.

[8]Personal interview.

[9]Weglyn, pp. 33-34, writes that coded messages going in and out of Tokyo had been intercepted and decoded by Washington cryptoanalysts. Moreover, she notes, a report by the Army Pearl Harbor Board investigating the attack found that "Washington was in possession of the essential fact as to the enemy's intentions and proposals."

[10]Jacobus tenBroek, Edward N. Barnhart, Floyd W. Matson, *Prejudice, War and the Constitution*,(University of California Press, Berkeley and Los Angeles 1954), p. 72.

At work in a produce market in Southern California, Miyo Senzaki heard the news of the bombing blared over the radio.

> The manager called us in back and gave us our paychecks and that was it. We were terminated, and then we got scared. . . . On the way home, I noticed they had barricades set up. Certain streets you couldn't get into; you had to sort of detour to go home. Then after that it was just a daze.
> The next day, Dad got scared and started to burn all the books, Japanese books. He was panicking; he said to get everything out--all the records--and we just built a bonfire, busted everything, you know. . . . My mother kept on saying, "No matter what happens they're not going to do anything to you because you're an American citizen."[11]

As it turned out, Senzaki's mother's faith in the inviolability of the rights of citizenship was shattered. Miyo Senzaki was sent to the Santa Anita detention camp and later to Rohwer, Arkansas concentration camp. There, she endured separation from her parents and family and suffered the traumatic episode of her new husband grappling with death because of a blood clot near an ear bone.

Within hours of the bombing, FBI agents swept through the Japanese communities, rounding up civic, business, professional and religious leaders, not to mention those perceived as promoting Japanese culture. More than 1800 were interned for the duration of the war, most never informed of the charges against them, many shifted from camp to camp for whatever purposes the Justice Department deemed fit.

Chiye Tomihiro's recollection of her father's arrest on December 7 typifies a pattern of disbelief, powerlessness and a veiled sense of betrayal experienced by relatives of those caught in the FBI net.

> My mother and I were not home that evening. . ., and when we came home, they had ransacked the apartment, taken a lot of things, and left the door open, unlocked. Then we learned that my father had been taken away . . . .
> At the time we thought it was because he spoke English well and because he was prominent in the community, that they probably needed him for some interpreting or some darn thing like that. Never, you know, realizing that he was going to be interned. They stuck him in the Multnomah county jail. . . then they brought him back to pick up some things, and he said, don't worry, don't worry, but we didn't see him after that until we went to visit him in Santa Fe, New Mexico, where he was interned.[12]

---

[11]John Tateishi, *And Justice for All*, (Random House, New York 1984), p. 101.
[12]*Ibid.*, pp. 239-240.

Undoubtedly, a major reason for the roundup together with freezing the bank credits of the Japanese was to disable the community. The strategy succeeded admirably, forcing the closing of businesses, depriving the community of resources, and leadership and the established community infrastructure.

Through December, voices mounted with increasing intensity for the removal of all Japanese from the West Coast. "Patriotic" organizations like the American Legion, Daughters of the American Revolution and the Native Sons and Native Daughters of the Golden West fanned the fire of hate, as did resurrected racist groups, demanding that the "enemy Jap" be excluded from the West Coast. By January, 1942 they had reached a crescendo.

The press, at first tolerant and fair, turned strident: "Let us have no patience with the enemy or with anyone whose veins carry his blood. . . . Personally, I hate the Japanese. And that goes for all of them," said Henry McLemore, syndicated columnist.[13]

Even the urbane newspaperman, Herb Caen, later to be dubbed "Mr. San Francisco" was not immune from Jap-bashing. In his *San Francisco Chronicle* column of April 19, 1942, Caen reprinted a letter sent to him by Sam Murata. Murata, taking the JACL line, stated that the majority of Japanese Americans were "willing to put up with evacuation as the greatest good for the greatest number." He explained that the Japanese American had been vilified by name-calling, like "yellow worm" and "Jap" but their faith in the government was not broken, and they were in the mood to cooperate fully. He ended his letter by pledging that "when the democratic countries win this war, the Japanese, especially the Japanese-Americans, will build side by side with their white-skinned friends a new home proving themselves 'A Greater American in a Greater America'."

Caen's response: "The only thing we'll build side by side for the trans-Pacific Japzis will be--graves."

On February 13, the West Coast Congressional delegation recommended to the President that all persons of Japanese ancestry be removed from the West Coast. The then Attorney General Earl Warren of California warned against persecuting enemy aliens, but in the next breath urged that they and their children be evacuated.

---

[13]Morton Grodzins (*Americans Betrayed*, Univ. of Chicago, 1949), who made an extensive study of the involvement of the California press during this period, found that among newspaper columnists, only Ernie Pyle (Scripps-Howard newspapers) and Chester Rowell (*San Francisco Chronicle*) wrote columns sympathetic to the Nisei.

EXECUTIVE ORDER 9066

Then what most Nisei had decided could not happen, happened. On February 19, 1942, President Roosevelt signed Executive Order 9066, granting Secretary of War Stimson the authority to designate military areas within the U.S. to which "any persons whose presence was deemed prejudicial to the national defense" should be excluded. Although "Japanese" was nowhere mentioned in the order, upon being implemented, over 112,000 persons of Japanese ancestry, aliens and citizens alike, were   removed from their homes in California, Washington and Oregon and forced into concentration camps.

For the Issei, this cataclysmic event represented a culmination of the heavy-handed treatment they had received from the beginning of their stay in this country. The Nisei, on the other hand, were stunned. Even leaders of the Japanese American Citizens League, who had been in touch with government officials seemed unprepared for the sweeping inclusiveness of the order.

Parenthetically, it might be well to note that the JACL played a controversial role in the matter of incarceration and has come under fire recently by both historians and Japanese Americans themselves.[14]

In the absence of Issei leadership, the JACL had come to be regarded as the de-facto political voice of the young Nisei population, since its leaders were slightly older than the average Nisei. Three of these leaders, Mike Masaoka, Dave Tatsuno and Henry Tani, had testified at the Tolan hearings, which had convened "to inquire further into the interstate migration of citizens" and "the evacuation of enemy aliens and others from prohibited military zones." Masaoka's statement before that hearing has come to be regarded as altogether too accommodating, even obsequious.[15] His claim of speaking "on behalf of the 20,000" members of JACL was inventive, according to James Omura, who asserts that the number was closer to 7500. Moreover, the rank and file of the membership, many who had only lately joined so that they could be apprised of developments, had hardly had time to gather their thoughts into a collective position regarding the impending exclusion.

---

[14]Among the severest critics is Richard Drinnon, (*Keeper of Concentration Camps*, University of California Press, Berkeley and Los Angeles 1987) who excoriates Mike Masaoka "and his JACL brethren." They became "one with the colonizer," he says, exhibiting super-patriotism at the expense of the masses of Japanese in America. Many Nisei and Kibei have made the same charges.

[15]For full text of Masaoka's statement, see Bill Hosokawa, *JACL In Quest of Justice*, (William Morrow and Company, Inc., New York 1982), pp. 361-363.

Others condemn JACL for providing informers to the FBI, an accusation not denied. They also charge that Masaoka made every effort to quash dissidence, for example, successfully urging JACL not to support Minoru Yasui, an attorney who had been imprisoned for deliberately violating the curfew order as a matter of principle.

In defense of Mike Masaoka and the JACL, Bill Hosokawa writes that they had no better choice than to counsel cooperation, given the circumstances. The alternative, he says, would have been disastrous. "Revisionists would have us believe that JACL forced its views on a reluctant community. The opposite is true. The community sought leadership and guidance and JACL chose the only possible course of action."[16]

Second Roundup   "I couldn't believe that American citizens were being uprooted," says Violet De Cristoforo, voicing the sentiments of many Nisei. "I was unable to answer the question myself as to why such a thing was being done to us . . . . Why? What necessity? It just didn't make sense."[17]

The hardships immediately visited upon persons because of the order were brutal. Helen Murao, a fifteen-year-old orphan from Portland, Oregon, had been shunted from home to home along with her two younger brothers before the war. In April, 1942, while living with a caring Caucasian family, she received a phone call informing her that her sister, Mary, who had been confined to a tuberculosis sanitarium, was critical. In order to visit her, Murao was first required to obtain permission from the Western Defense Command to travel to Salem because of the newly decreed curfew order.[18] After an interminable delay at the offices there, she was finally granted permission, but by the time she got to the sanitarium, her sister was dead.

> Her room was empty. Her name was still on the bed, so I knew we were in the right room . . . . In fact I didn't know she was dead, because I couldn't find her. I couldn't find anybody who could tell me anything about her. Somebody, I don't remember who . . . told us, yes, that the patient had died

---

[16]*Ibid.*, p. 160.

[17]Tateishi, p. 124.

[18]The curfew order imposed in March, 1942, prohibited German, Japanese, Italian aliens and "all other persons of Japanese ancestry" (meaning citizen Japanese) from leaving their homes between 8 p.m. and 6 a.m. And in the same month, Japanese were barred from traveling beyond a five-mile radius from their homes. The Army never saw fit to explain why the curfew suddenly became necessary, after more than three months had elapsed since the bombing and no sabotage by the resident Japanese had taken place.

...It was yes, the patient had died, and they didn't know where the body was. No official confirmation, no nothing.[19]

Others experienced the period between the bombing and the impending evacuation in more typical ways:

Yuri Tateishi:

When we were to be evacuated, there were some people that wanted to go east to Colorado or Utah, but of course we knew no one back there, and so my husband went to Colorado to see if he could meet with any Japanese people [who could help us] get something started. But it was quite difficult, and while we were back there the curfew went into effect, so he had to rush back.... [20]

When the evacuation came, we were renting a home and had four kids. It was terrible because you had to sell everything. We were just limited to what we could take with us, and so everything was just sold for whatever we could get.

Tateishi was unhappy about her internment, she says, but not bitter.[21]

Observes Professor Kitano: "With no one to turn to, with their structures and institutions dismantled, with little political or economic power, with cultural norms and values emphasizing conformity and non-conflictual behavior, with a lack of feasible alternatives and facing the awesome power of the United States Government, the Japanese marched into camp. Could they have really done otherwise?"[22]

Thus the Herculean task of forcibly removing over 112,000 persons from their homes and transporting them to assigned camps, like so many heads of sheep, was accomplished with summary dispatch.[23]

---

[19]Tateishi, pp. 41-42.

[20]After E.O. 9066 was issued in February, 1942, persons of Japanese ancestry were encouraged to move out of the excluded areas voluntarily. However, hostility soon developed in those areas where the evacuees had moved, and the movement was stopped by another proclamation which forbade change of address by persons of Japanese ancestry.

[21]Tateishi, pp. 23-26. For losses incurred because of exclusion, see following chapter.

[22]Comments at UCLA symposium, printed in the *Pacific Citizen*, June 9, 1967, p. 2.

[23]Three Nisei men challenged government orders. Min Yasui of Portland, Oregon defied curfew orders and Gordon Hirabayashi of Seattle, Washington refused to obey curfew and exclusion orders, both deliberately, on principle, and were sent to prison. Fred Korematsu defied the order for personal reasons, was caught and dispatched to an Assembly Center. He also spent time in prison.

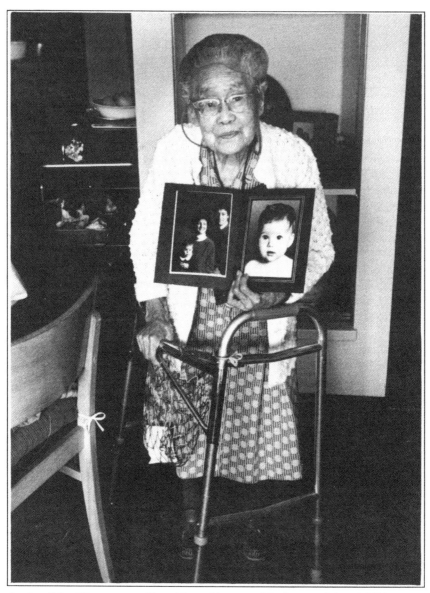

Issei at Eden Terrace, an elder citizens' home, with photos of grandchildren and great-grandchild, Hayward, CA, 1989. © *Rick Rocamora.*

CHAPTER 8

Camps

This is what we did with our days.
We loved and we lived
just like people.
                    ---Mitsuye Yamada

If ask a Nisei woman what she did in the war is to hear a story, unique in the annals of American history. Yes, she did tend the hearth, as women of that era were wont to do. But Nisei women tended the hearth in at least three different places, in one, imprisoned, while their men lay costly sacrifices more on the altar of *loyalty* than freedom.

The Exclusion Order   The bold heading on the exclusion order, posted in various neighborhoods where Japanese lived, read: INSTRUCTIONS TO ALL PERSONS OF JAPANESE ANCESTRY: ALL JAPANESE PERSONS, BOTH ALIEN AND NON-ALIEN[1], WILL BE EVACUATED FROM THE ABOVE DESIGNATED AREA BY 12:00 O'CLOCK ON TUESDAY..."

Although Japanese families had been informed that they would be removed from their homes sometime in the dim future, most were caught unprepared when the Army ordered them to leave in the early months of 1942. They were allowed an average of six days to ready themselves for pickup. The Order included these instructions:

Evacuees must carry with them on departure for the Assembly Center the following property for each member of the family:
  (a) Bedding and linens (no mattress)
  (b) Toilet articles
  (c) Extra clothing
  (d) Sufficient knives, forks, spoons, plates, bowls and cups
  (e) Essential personal effects

---

[1]The government used various buzz words to blunt the harshness of the removal orders. Here, "non-alien" refers to citizens.

All other property had to be sold, stored, or given away. The government agreed to store "more substantial household items," but at the "sole risk of the owner."

Economic Impact   Bargain hunters swooped down into the Japanese ghetto neighborhoods, telling the anxiety-ridden families that the government intended to seize their properties. In the absence of official statements to the contrary, victims tended to believe them.[2] This, together with the uncertainty of future and the pressure of time, caused many Japanese families to sell everything--real property, businesses, personal items and household goods--at whatever price they could get.

> We sold some of our things in the time we had but we didn't get very good prices because it was all too rushed. We owned three automobiles and we left them with friends who promised to sell them for us and send us the money later. We never did get the money for one of the cars. We had a lot of things scattered around the house and the people in the neighborhood went right through like vultures after we left. They took all of the small items like lamps and furniture so that our friend who was supposed to gather up all of these loose ends found nothing there when he arrived. My brother disposed of his produce market at quite a loss. I had two pianos of my own which cost me $1,200. I only got $30 for one of them. We had paid $300 for a phonograph about a year before the war and we had to sell it for $50. . . . If we added up all of our losses, it would run up into a few thousand dollars at least, maybe as much as $5,000.[3]

It is impossible to calculate the economic losses sustained by the evacuees today because of the time lag and because many evacuees failed to keep records. In 1948, attempting to compensate evacuees for "damage to or loss of real or personal property" caused by the exclusion order, the U.S. government distributed among them a total of $37 million through the Japanese-American Evacuation Claims Act. But an impartial study, admittedly conservative, estimated that actual losses totaled $77 million, more than twice the amount paid out by the

---

[2]Although the Federal Reserve Bank of San Francisco, the Farm Security Administration and the Office of Aliens Property Custodian had been charged with handling evacuee properties, few evacuees appeared to have received guidance from any of these agencies. Later the War Relocation Authority (WRA) assumed responsibility for handling evacuee's properties.

[3]Anonymous interview in Thomas, p. 494.

government.[4] Over the years, writers have bandied about the figure of $400 million as the Federal Reserve Bank's estimate of evacuee losses. "We now know that this figure was a postwar invention," writes Roger Daniels, surmising that it came from a figure quoted by JACL official Mike Masaoka at a hearing in 1954. "Until further research is done, we simply will not know its valuation. Clearly, it [property losses] was worth hundreds of millions of dollars."[5]

Evacuees incurred economic losses not only by underselling, vandalism and stolen goods, but by the immeasurable cost of lost wages and earning power. They could never reclaim the time spent in exile which virtually put them three years behind in their economic progress.

FIRST MOVE: TEMPORARY COMPOUNDS

With stunning speed (28 days), the Army established 16 temporary compounds to confine all persons of Japanese ancestry from the West Coast. In facilities like race tracks, fairgrounds and livestock exhibition halls, workers hastily devised living units out of existing structures, like horse stalls. They also built row upon row of tar-paper-covered barracks to accommodate the overflow.[6]

Called "Assembly Centers" by the Army, these temporary compounds would eventually detain upwards of 112,000 persons, two-thirds, or nearly 72,000 of whom were citizens of the United States.[7] Just less than half of these citizens were Nisei females, the majority between 15 and 30 years of age, densely clustered around age 17.

Stepping off the bus onto the grounds where they were to be imprisoned, the arrivals found nothing to allay their anxieties. The bleak compounds had the unmistakable look of a prison camp, ringed with barbed wire and punctuated by guard towers. Guards patrolling the borders with machine guns brought sharply into focus the reality that they were indeed penned in, prisoners.

---

[4]Leonard Broom, Ruth Reimer, *Removal and Return* (University of California Press, Berkeley 1949), pp. 202-204.

[5]*Asian America*, (University Washington Press, Seattle and London 1988)pp. 290-291 and n.8.

[6]Twelve such camps were built in California and one each in Washington, Oregon and Arizona.

[7]One should bear in mind that the total number of those affected by the exclusion order was considerably higher than the figure given here. Counting those who had been interned earlier on, aliens and citizens evacuated from Hawaii, those who had voluntarily moved eastward out of the West Coast states, and those born in camp, as many as 120,000 persons came under WRA custody.

Here, they were to spend from one to six months, although they had no way of knowing that. In fact, the vast majority knew very little about their present circumstances.

The living quarters of this temporary compound would have disheartened even the most optimistic among the arrivals. Artist Mine Okubo, arriving at the Santa Anita racetrack in southern California, described it:

> We walked in and dropped our things inside the entrance. The place was in semidarkness; light barely came though the dirty window on either side of the entrance. A swinging half-door divided the 20 by 9 ft. stall into two rooms .... The rear room had housed the horse and the front room the fodder. Both rooms showed signs of hurried whitewashing. Spider webs, horse hair, and hay had been whitewashed with the walls. Huge spikes and nails stuck out all over the walls. A two-inch layer of dust covered the floor, but on removing it we discovered that linoleum the color of redwood had been place over the rough manure-covered boards.
>
> We opened the folded spring cots lying on the floor of the rear room and sat on them in the semidarkness. We heard someone crying in the next stall.[8]

Recalls another Nisei woman: "The thing that I remember most is lines, lines, lines. You got into lines to get shots, to eat, to get a job, even to get into the toilet and the showers." Or, as Michi Weglyn tersely put it, "Evacuees ate communally, showered communally, defecated communally."

Diarrhea afflicted nearly everyone, and the heat put such heavy demands on the showers that they often overflowed. For females, the lack of privacy in the latrine and showers was especially galling. Stalls had no doors, and having to function in the sight of those waiting in line so assaulted their sense of modesty that they often waited until the late hours of the night to visit the latrine and showers.

In the cramped quarters of the barracks, where as many as seven persons occupied one unit, sheets or blankets were hung to partition off spaces, rendering some units useless for anything but sleeping.

Life never took on a sense of normalcy at these way stations, for inmates soon learned that they would be shifted elsewhere in due time. So they tolerated the insipid food, the cramped living quarters, the odious smells, and waited.

---

[8]*Citizen 13660*, (University of Washington Press, Seattle and London, 1983 edition), pp. 35-36.

Medical facilities, post offices, police and fire protection services, temporary educational services and canteens were soon set up in each camp. Evacuees enlisted in the work force to operate them.[9]

Young Nisei parents were particularly concerned with trying to maintain a life for their children comparable to the one they had been living on the outside. They sought, most of all, to minimize the trauma of the imprisonment. They could not satisfactorily explain the presence of soldiers patrolling the fences with menacing weapons. Nor were they inclined to tell their children that they had been forced into these enclosures because of the color of their skin. They could only try to protect them by attempting to carry on "normal" activities, as did Lillian Omi of Santa Anita:

> After being settled in the barracks . . . I called on the Director of the Assembly Center about the education of my three children. I was told to start a class in the main building of the race track if I was that concerned. After requesting books, some of us managed to have a makeshift school. In the beginning when we assembled the classes in the main lobby, the teachers ended up with laryngitis after a week, the result of trying to make themselves heard. We then scattered to various parts of the building. The classes in the bleachers had to move elsewhere when the huge camouflage nets full of dust were put up. The betting booths of the hall became our stockroom when we received discarded books from public schools.[10]

Instruction for grades 1 through 12 was soon organized at the camps, though loosely, at whatever space available. In a bit of under-statement, Anthony Lehman writes of the arrangements at Santa Anita: "Classes, remarkably, were held in the lobbies of the grandstand in front of the pari-mutuel betting windows, a somewhat questionable environment for the education of the young."[11]

Leisure activities in these temporary camps included movies, concerts, dances, all sorts of athletics and board games. For younger folk, Scout troops were organized in some camps as well as arts and crafts activities.

Anxious to move the evacuees to more permanent camps inland, the Army began to close the smaller temporary compounds as early as

---

[9]Wages per month were $8 for unskilled workers, $12 for skilled and $16 for professionals. Later, the pay scale went up a notch to $12, $16 and $19.

[10]Newsletter "Kokoro no Tomo," December 1988.

[11]*Birthright of Barbed Wire*, (Westernlore Press, Los Angeles 1970), p. 50.

June 1942.[12] By the end of October, the last one, Santa Anita, which held over 18,000 inmates at its peak, was emptied.

THE SECOND MOVE: "PERMANENT" COMPOUNDS

With the exception of those ordered to camps in California, inmates travelled two or more days to their destination in the second phase of their exile, sometimes over circuitous routes, often under grueling conditions. The elderly, the infirm and the babies found the trip particularly difficult. At least two infants died during the journeys.[13] Violet De Cristoforo testified:

> My youngest daughter, born under . . . adversity in a horse stable, and only 18 days old when we were moved to Jerome, Arkansas, had to make the four-day, four-night trip in a dilapidated coach, amid much filth . . . in the stale air of the coach because the windows and shades were always drawn for security reasons. In the extreme heat, and in such adverse conditions, she developed double pneumonia on the train and, upon our arrival at Jerome, she had to be rushed to the still incomplete hospital.[14]

De Cristoforo's child would suffer the trauma of her debut into the world for years to come.

The Army erected ten, what they euphemistically called "Relocation Centers" in sites outside the designated military zones on the West Coast.[15] Meanwhile, they transferred the responsibility of administering the camps to a newly-created civilian agency, the War Relocation Authority (WRA), initially headed by Milton Eisenhower, later by Dillon S. Myer.

"We arrived in the middle of a dust storm when the dust was flying all over," said one woman who had been ordered to a camp in Poston, Arizona. "There were times when the electricity went off and we had no water. It was hot and dusty. And no shelter and no cooling system and over 100 degrees. For the first couple of weeks, if they wanted to kill us,

---

[12]The exception was Manzanar, which served both as a temporary and permanent camp. The little-known compound at Mayer, Arizona (holding 250 inmates) was closed on June 2, just shy of one month's existence.

[13]Report of the Commission on Wartime Relocation and Internment of Civilians (hereafter CWRIC), *Personal Justice Denied*, (Washington D.C., 1982), p. 151.

14Testimony before the CWRIC, August 1981.

[15]Camps and maximum population: Topaz in Utah (8130); Poston and (17,814) Gila, (13,348) in Arizona; Heart Mountain in Wyoming (10,767); Jerome (8,497) and Rohwer (8,475) in Arkansas; Manzanar (10,046)and Tule Lake (18,789) in California; Minidoka in Idaho (9397), and; Amache (7318)in Colorado.

all they had to do was turn the water off."[16]   Indeed, it was as if the Army and the WRA had conspired to locate the camps in uniformly desolate, sand-swept sites, searing in the summer and, some, bitter cold in winter. The two camps not located in the desert lay in the hot and humid swamplands of Arkansas.

Evacuees had been led to believe that these more permanent centers would be "resettlement communities," not prisons. But when they found their new quarters fenced in with barbed wire and guarded by military police, they were not surprised. At the camp in Minidoka, however, residents were to discover that the fence had been electrified and became duly incensed.[17]

Facilities   In its haste to transfer inmates out of the temporary compounds, the Army ignored warnings from the WRA that the new camps had not yet been completed. Eventually each block would have a mess hall, laundry, toilet, shower room and a recreation hall.

But in the beginning months, in many camps, evacuees were forced to walk to other blocks to eat, tote their laundry and to shower. In Amache, as in other camps, outhouses were hastily erected, having to accommodate vast numbers of people.

Even after the initial shortcomings of the facilities had been remedied, the primitive accommodations were particularly trying on mothers of babies, the elderly and the ill. Everything they needed, from food down to hot water for bathing infants and shut-ins required a trip outside the living quarters. The daily routine for a parent or a care-giver included two or three trips to the laundry room to tote back buckets of water.

Mothers planned an hour a day over the washboard in the laundry room to do the baby's diapers. If sheets or heavier items needed to be laundered, reluctant husbands were enlisted to help. In the winter, when clothes could not be hung outdoors, the laundry room became a forest of sheets. Miraculously, few disappeared. When one did vanish, the owner often asked that an announcement be made at the mess hall that someone had "mistakenly" taken the wrong item home.

As in societies where women have found comfort and joy in each other's company while doing the wash at places like the river's edge, many women in camp enjoyed socializing in the laundry room. They indulged in gossip, exchanged information and forged lasting friendships over their washboards.

---

[16]Anonymous. Interview conducted by Marion Wake.

[17]Weglyn, p. 90.

Administration   When completed, each camp was virtually a small city with its   own municipal government, utilities, school, hospital, police and fire departments and businesses.

A Project Director, appointed by the WRA to head each camp, functioned somewhat analogously to a mayor and city manager combined. He directed a staff, all Caucasian, which supervised various departments under Civil Service.   Evacuees worked under these supervisors on the lowest level.

This three-tiered system was often a source of irritation to the evacuees, in that regardless of how much better qualified they were than their supervisors, they could not fill those second-tier slots, nor could they rise above the maximum monthly pay of $19.

"Self-Government"   The camps were governed by what appeared on the surface to be a democratic system. Called "community government" by Project Directors, it included a Community Council comprised of representatives elected from each block, all Nisei, overwhelmingly male. But as the writer Michi Weglyn points out, "the function of Council members amounted to little more than acting in an advisory capacity to the camp director and seeing to it that rules and regulations handed down by Washington were enforced by the block managers." She adds: "In neo-colonial fashion, the Project Director held the reins of power tightly, maintaining the absolute power of the veto over his youthful Council members."[18]   Because of this and because Issei were barred from being elected to the Council, many evacuees considered that body a sham.[19]

The CWRIC found that, instead of the Council, Block Managers functioned as the real channels of communication.[20]   Generally Issei men, they were appointed by the Project Director after being nominated by block members. While drawing respect from most, they sometimes incurred the same irritation that police incur, for they had the unenviable job of enforcing rules and regulations and handling routine complaints about heat, supplies, and the like. Soon, "The Blockhead" became the favorite, good-humored epithet for the Block Manager.

LIFE ON THE INSIDE

The New "Home"   The camp residential section was divided into blocks comprised of a dozen or so identical barracks, 120 x 20 feet. Each barrack consisted of 6 one-room units. A unit 20 x 16 feet, the size

---

[18]P. 121.

[19]CWRIC, p.174.

[20]*Ibid .*

of a small bedroom, accommodated a family of three, while the larger one 20 x 25 feet held up to seven persons.

The evacuees found their living quarters about as hospitable as Army barracks, after which they had been modeled. Cement or bare boards covered the floor, the walls revealed 2 x 4 studs or, in extremely cold areas, they were covered with fiberboard. In some compounds, a niche was provided so that the occupant could install a crossbar on which to hang clothes. A bare bulb hung in the center of the unit. Each occupant was supplied with an Army cot, the only piece of furniture provided. In camps where winter temperatures plummeted below zero, a pot-bellied stove was installed in one corner of the unit. A statement issued by the Project Director at Amache read:

EVERY FAMILY WITH SEVEN PERSONS OR LESS IS ASSIGNED ONE OF THESE ROOMS AND ALLOWED TO MAKE IT AS HOMELIKE AS POSSIBLE.

"Allowed" this great privilege, evacuees hunkered down to the business of making their lives as pleasant as possible in their bleak environment. As soon as they became settled, women ordered muslin or calico from Sears Roebuck (which had been designated the official mail-order house) and put up curtains. Men salvaged lumber from wherever they could to build shelves and crude furniture. "My husband got wood from outhouses they broke down," said one woman. "He made a chest of drawers and frame for a couch out of it, and when he sanded the wood and varnished it, it looked good!" Gardens emerged under the expert hands of the Issei. At some camps, they created aesthetic rock gardens to blend in with the desert scenery.

Feeding the Multitude   As is prevalent among populations which have lost control over their lives, food loomed as a large concern for camp inhabitants. At least part of the unrest that took place in Poston, Manzanar, Tule Lake and Topaz was related to food.

Contrary to public perception that the Japanese in camps were eating "high off the hog," they literally ate much lower off the animal, at least in the beginning. The WRA had established a policy that provided no more than 45 cents per capita daily for food and strict adherence to wartime rationing.[21] Not only because of this spare budget but because of poor judgment in procuring food and poor management policies, evacuees found an excessive amount of products made from the innards

---

[21]In most camps, the allotment for food was closer to 40 cents per day per capita. In Poston I, for example, administrators allotted 38 cents.

of animals on their plates in the first months. Most evacuees, especially urbanites, had never partaken of foods like liver, hearts, tripe and the like before. What the quartermaster corps (which procured camp food) referred to as "edible offal," the evacuees acidly called "awful edibles."

At certain camps, like Poston, considerable acrimony took place over the amount and quality of the food. Alexander Leighton, a psychiatrist sent there as an analyst for the government observed:

> Although the meals varied a good deal from one block to another they were in general very poor, lacking in variety, insufficient in quantity and not at all comparable to Army rations. Men going out to work frequently complained that they could not get enough to sustain them. There was no adequate means of feeding infants and small children if the parents did not have the money to purchase their specialties and the situation was similar for invalids who required diets.[22]

At least part of the overall problem with food had to do with poor menu-planning and cooking. Many of the male head cooks had had no experience at cooking, let alone planning menus. Granted they had little to work with, but with some experience, they might have produced a more balanced diet than the all-starch meals or the repetition of entrees that appeared on the mess hall table. "Often a meal consisted of rice, bread, and macaroni, or beans, bread and spaghetti," writes Mine Okubo, imprisoned at Topaz. "At one time we were served liver for several weeks, until we went on strike."[23]

Clearly, a lack of understanding on the part of the administrators about the history of the Japanese in America is revealed in their failure to enlist as women as head cooks. With their experience of having cooked for work gangs or their extended families, they commanded more knowledge and skill about the myriad needs of cookery. As it was, these women served in the mess hall largely as cook's assistants or waitresses.

But more important than the quality of the food was the quantity. There was simply not enough of it, according to Leighton. "The funds allotted were ample, but there were serious difficulties in securing what was wanted . . ." and there appeared to be a discrepancy between the budget allowed and the food which appeared on the mess hall tables.[24]

Some of the food shortages were undoubtedly caused by the evacuees' pilfering or taking advantage of their access to the food. But

---

[22]*The Governing of Men*, (Princeton University Press, Princeton, 1968), p. 116.
[23]P. 143.
[24]P. 116.

group ethics which directed their behavior, that is, that one should never take more than one's share at the expense of the group, would have been a powerful inhibitor to such action. And the stigma of getting caught would have undoubtedly rendered the culprit a pariah, a thing to be dreaded in a closed community. Too, evacuees had no way of storing perishables, so their pilferage would have had to be niggling, in any case.

On the other hand, "suspicion that staff was stealing and selling food was widespread."[25] Evacuees reportedly observed white stewards and other workers who had access to the food, committing outright thefts. One Nisei truck driver, for example, tells of seeing a man stuffing a quarter hind of beef into the trunk of his car at Amache. He didn't bother to report it, he said, because it seemed to be common practice.[26] At Tule Lake, Violet De Cristoforo's brother, a cook in the mess hall, "was aware of the considerable pilferage of food from the warehouse by Caucasian personnel," and became part of a team to investigate the problem. For that, says De Cristoforo, he was labeled a troublemaker and locked up in a stockade and beaten repeatedly.[27]

To provide a better balanced diet, to economize, and to put inmates to work, the WRA took advantage of their skill and experience and launched an agricultural production program on camp lands. Eventually, all the camps produced vegetables, and most had animal and poultry operations. The results were impressive. For example, by the end of 1943, the first harvest year in most camps, they were producing 85 percent of the vegetables they consumed.[28] According to Director of WRA, Dillon S. Myer, the total yield of vegetables had an estimated gross value of over $3.5 million during the camps' existence. The hog farms produced meat valued at $1.5 million, while poultry products added up to about $470 thousand.[29] If evacuees began to have something resembling a balanced diet in their menus it was in large measure due to their own enterprise.

For women, concern about feeding their families had not been totally alleviated. Although they had been relieved of the ordinary duties of planning and cooking meals, they usually assumed the responsibility of attending to the special nutrition needs of babies, the elderly and the ailing. The task was complicated by the lack of running water or cooking units in the barracks, and whatever food was available

---

[25]CWRIC, p. 176.

[26]Personal interview.

[27]Testimony before the CWRIC, August 1981.

[28]CWRIC, p. 168.

[29]*Uprooted Americans*, (University of Arizona Press, Tucson 1971), p. 34.

for these needy ones, had to be picked up outside the living unit for every meal.

Evacuees bought hotplates to warm the baby's formula and to modify food doled out by the mess hall to make it more suitable to the diet for the ill. One Nisei woman, about seven years old at the time of imprisonment, recounted:

> I remember eating scenes at the mess hall. Because my youngest brother was so sickly, we had to take turns and ration our milk and one of us had to give up our milk for the day for our brother.[30]

Family Life   Few elements in the camp environment inspired a stable, pleasurable family life. Conjugal relations were severely tested by the lack of privacy and conditions that tended to disrupt relationships rather than foster harmony. Young couples occupying the same room with their children, or worse, with persons outside the family, found little opportunity for intimacy. "We put up sheets to partition off our bed from the boys' beds," said one Nisei woman. "But we were always aware that they could hear everything, even a whisper. Sometimes we just went for a long walk in the middle of the night."

Other mothers recall rocking their babies at all hours so that their cries would not disturb the neighbors through the thin walls. "At least my husband took turns with me walking the baby," said one. "Otherwise, I wouldn't have gotten any sleep at all. Our baby had his days and nights mixed up and would be awake a lot at night."

Furthermore, the traditional roles held by members of the family underwent radical transformation in the camps. The Issei father, normally the breadwinner and decision-maker, found himself earning the same low wages as his Nisei daughter or son, even his wife. Because they no longer depended upon him for their daily necessities, family members were more inclined than ever to make independent decisions. All of this was bound to diminish the father's status in the family, not to mention his ego.

As well as the change in family roles, the housing units, barren and cramped, hardly provided an environment conducive to family togetherness. Families were deprived of the kitchen, the literal and symbolic center of family life. Little shards of experience that tend to bind families together, like children doing their homework on the kitchen table while inhaling the familiar and reassuring odors of their mother's cooking, were altogether wanting.

---

[30]Anonymous. Interview conducted by Marion Wake. Milk was rationed out only to children and to those with doctor's permits.

Camp life also dictated that most activities take place outside the home. "Home" here was not a place to which one could invite friends, if only for the lack of furniture and space. Thus Nisei teenagers spent most of their leisure time away from home with friends. It was not unusual for them, especially males, to wake in the morning, have breakfast in the mess hall, and disappear all day somewhere in the maze of barracks, only to come home to roost at night.

The traditional family ritual of eating together often disappeared as well. Children as young as ten sometimes chose the company of friends at the mess hall tables as did some men. In some camps, tables were set aside in the mess halls for families, but attempting to force children, particularly teenagers, to sit at the same table with their families was difficult. Some families tried to overcome this problem by carting their meals to their own living units from the mess hall.

Even celebrations and holidays tended to be public, shared with friends or block members in the mess hall. New Year's, a major celebration in nearly every Japanese household, became a communal one in camp. Teenage birthdays were often celebrated among friends rather than with the family.

And if strains existed in family relationships, they were bound to be exacerbated by the prevailing stressful conditions. At times, stress showed itself in aggressive acts. As Dr. Leighton wrote: "The considerable scientific work that has been done to understand the nature of *aggression*, indicates that it is *not so much an innate quality or instinct as it is a way of reacting to stress*."[31] Reported one former evacuee:

> In our block, there was a woman whose husband began to beat her. Of course, everyone knew about it. How could you hide such a thing in those barracks? She was so ashamed that she wouldn't come out of her unit for days, even to eat. Then one day--and I still don't know how she did it--she left camp, her husband, and her two small children. She must have suffered a lot to leave her children.[32]

Other reports of spousal abuse circulated around the camps. For the most part, neither the camp police nor the officials appeared to have become involved in these affairs. A cursory look through camp newspapers produces no report of spousal abuse.

But in spite of these assaults on family life, evidence strongly suggests that the disintegration the family experienced in camp tended

---

[31]*The Governing of Men* (Princeton University Press, Princeton, N.J. 1968), p. 167.
[32]Personal interview.

to be temporary. Parent-child bonding in the Issei-Nisei family had already taken firm hold, and it thus weathered the buffeting conditions of camp. When, for example, Nisei outmigrated to cities outside the military zone, they called for their parents as soon as they became established. Many, if not most, would provide economic support to their parents through this resettlement period and provide for their care and well-being for the remainder of their lives.

In like manner, Nisei family units held together for the most part. Quality of married life aside, the traditional pattern of family solidarity remained strong.[33] And it was the women who shouldered the bulk of the responsibility.   Following the archetypical model of their foremothers, Nisei women saw to the physical and emotional needs of the children, made and cemented social ties and often acted as intermediaries between their husbands and children.

"It's incredible, as I think of it now," said Helen Murao, to whom had fallen the responsibility of holding the family together in camp. "But we lived as a family unit. I don't know what gave me the strength to do it, but I can't help but feel that those early years with my parents must have given it to me." [34]

Health Care   Health problems in camp were legion. The extremes in the climate of the camps that West Coast inhabitants were not accustomed to, and the ongoing stress under which they carried on from day to day, took their toll.

WRA Director Myer noted that flu epidemics struck two centers in the winter of 1943-44.[35] He also observed that a "rather high incidence of peptic ulcers was found at most of the centers, which was not surprising when we consider the tensions and frustrations that most of the residents experienced during the early months."[36] His succeeding observation, however, are questionable:

Undoubtedly many of the residents received better medical care during this period than ever before. There were reasons! The professional care was excellent; it was free; and the center residents had time to go to the doctor or the clinic when ill.[37]

---

[33]Harry Kitano, *Japanese Americans* (Prentice-Hall Inc. Englewood, N.J 1969), p. 156. Kitano reports a low 1.6 percent divorce rate among Nisei, ages 20-44 in 1960, the same rate as the Issei.

[34]Tateishi, p. 47.

[35]*Uprooted Americans*, p. 53. Myer does not specify which centers were involved.

[36]*Ibid.*, p. 55.

[37]*Ibid.*

The Director's perceptions do not square with testimony from former inmates.

Dr. Yoshiye Togasaki dealt with medical problems both in Manzanar and Tule Lake. "We had five doctors to take care of 10,000 people," she recalled. "There were open sewers; the barracks had no water, no stoves. And we had young families, many with new babies, and no vaccines, or DPT shots, or sanitary conditions for making baby formulas." Trying to persuade the Army bureaucracy of the need for basic health-care items, and for things like lab facilities to diagnose illness was often a futile exercise, and the doctor was forced to write to friends outside for needed supplies.[38]

At Tule Lake, Dr. Togasaki and her sister, also a doctor, disobeyed the Medical Director's edict to cease treating Caucasians (Japanese were ordered not to treat Caucasians because of the presumed danger to the latter) and "doing obstetrics" outside the hospital.[39] When the two doctors continued treating those patients because they thought the hospital staff so poor, they were branded "disruptive" and dismissed from the camp.

One has only to listen to a few women's voices to sense the extent of evacuee's problems related to health.

Mabel Ota (Poston):

There was only one obstetrician in that camp of ten thousand people, at the beginning anyway. And many women there were in the child-bearing years like myself. . . . My husband Fred left to go to New York to become an assistant manager of a cooperative [saying] that he would be back in time for the birth of the baby. But she came one month early, and when I went to the hospital, the nurse said the doctor had collapsed during the course of the previous day or night. He had delivered two babies and he had been on his feet all this time without help, so he collapsed and had gone back to the barracks to sleep.

Ota was in labor for twenty-eight hours, during which time, no doctor came to check on her. When the doctor finally came and examined her,

---

[38]Chizu Iiyama, reported in *Nichi Bei Times*, August 22, 1985.

[39]The Medical Director being referred to here was Dr. Reese M. Pedicord, who was later beaten by inmates at Tule Lake. According to Richard Drinnon, *(Keeper of Concentration Camps)* p 304, Tule Lake Director Raymond Best told the FBI that the beating "was provoked by the fact that Peddicord [sic] was disliked by the Japanese, as he runs the hospital in his own way, takes no dictation from Japanese and refers to the Japanese as 'yellow bellies,' without respect for their feelings."

he told her that they could not perform an operation (presumably, a Caesarean section) because there was no anesthesiologist in camp. "They took me to the delivery room and gave me a local and I could see the knife to cut me. Then he used these huge forceps and I kept watching that clock. He really had a hard time yanking her out, and I was conscious all the time. So it was a horrible experience." Ota is convinced that her baby suffered permanent brain damage due to having been deprived of oxygen during that procedure.[40]

June Tsutsui (Amache)

The photograph of my first-born son's grave brings painfully vivid memories of his loss at birth in camp. I carried my baby full-term but the camp's inadequate medical care, including the doctor's late arrival, intensified a complex birth. A better-staffed hospital environment might have prevented the hemorrhaging aggravated by a hasty, fatal delivery on a hard flat table while I endured indescribable pain.[41]

Emi Somekawa (Nurse at Tule Lake)

We had . . . oh . . . sad cases. We had one boy there, who was in his teens, and he was epileptic. We used all kinds of girls and anybody who wanted to help in the hospital . . . . The girls would put thermometers in everybody's mouth. Well, one time, one of the girls didn't know that the boy was epileptic. Anyway, he bit the thermometer, and he got all of that mercury in him. Well, you know, the hospital records didn't say anything like that. Just that he died of natural causes . . .

These were some of the things that happened. There were a lot of unnecessary deaths in camp. You wouldn't believe it. It's just that there were not enough people to watch the patients, not enough professionals.[42]

In short, Myer's observations appear to be quite off the mark regarding medical care in the camps. Had he listened more closely to the Nisei health care-givers or the patients themselves, he might have been less enthusiastic about the state of health care.

Work   In another of the many ironies that the incarceration produced, Nisei women could usually find a job in camp, contrary to what they had found on the outside. Albeit at pauper's pay ($12, $16 and $19), work was readily available in the camp enterprises or service divisions.

[40]Tateishi, pp. 109-110.

[41]*Pacific Citizen*, December 23-30, 1988, Sec. B-11.

[42]Tateishi, p. 150.

The majority of Nisei girls, in high school, or fresh out of it, had had little work experience. Helen Murao recalled:

> I had no skills, and I did not want to work as a waitress. So I lied and said I could type, and I worked in a steno pool. Well, the fellow watched me and knew damned well I couldn't type . . . . He let me stay . . . so I had a job for which I was paid. A stenographic job was sixteen dollars a month, and I was part-time, so I got eight dollars a month.[43]

Project Directors were understandably anxious to put evacuees to work. Not only would it occupy their time (and by extension, keep them out of trouble), certain basic services had to be provided. Consumer cooperatives were established in every camp except Heart Mountain.[44]

A substantial number of Nisei girls made use of their secretarial skills in the administration offices. Others served in the hospitals as support personnel under the few nurses who had already finished their nurse's training. Still others chose work in the mess hall.

> It was really kind of fun working in the mess hall and it was nice because in camp nobody looked down on you for working as a waitress. And in between, you could always do the wash or something else . . . . What we did was set tables, pour tea and coffee for the people, and clean up after they left. It was the first job I ever had.[45]

The few women who had had two or more years of college served in such capacities as assistant teachers, nurses, or writers and artists for the camp newspaper.

Camps had few trained social workers. But Chizu Iiyama, who, fresh out of U. C. Berkeley, was initiated into that area of work at Topaz. "I didn't get any 'hard' cases," says Iiyama, "because they thought I was too young. I dealt mostly with every-day problems like neighbors' complaints, the Issei grumbling about losing control over their children, people complaining about the food and lack of winter clothing, that sort of thing."[46] Iiyama's modest assessment of her work notwithstanding, her role would have been important. Inmates in camp tended to be understandably wary of white administrators and probably would not have tendered any complaints whatever to them. The presence of a familiar Japanese face allowed them to vent their anger and frustration.

---

[43]Helen Murao in Tateishi, p. 47.

[44]Myer, p. 47.

[45]Anonymous. Personal interview.

[46]Personal interview.

Another social worker, Lillian Yuriko Iida Matsumoto, had been the first professional social worker at the Shonien Children's Home of Southern California, having received her credentials in 1933. When the Executive order came down, Matsumoto, together with her husband and representatives from other agencies, concerned about the transferral of these children to an alien environment, drove to Manzanar to view the site and make recommendations for the construction of a children's compound similar to that from which the children would be uprooted. As an upshot of this careful planning, special housing was built for the children, and a program similar to the one which had been in force at Shonien, was instituted.

Commending Matsumoto, a WRA report later stated: "Mrs. Matsumoto's training and skill, added to her intimate knowledge of each child within the group, aided in dealing with individual problems. The result of good case work services was also apparent in the good family relationships that were carefully fostered in the feeling of responsibility which the older children had for the younger ones, and the wholesome attitudes of the teenage children about their future plans."[47]

Education   Since school buildings and equipment had not been part of the original construction at the centers, students attended classes in barracks. As an example, school construction at Amache did not begin until four months after the center opened and would require four months to complete. That meant that students attended makeshift classrooms for the first school year. They sat on chairs or on the floors, had little equipment and few books. At Tule Lake, students in the typing class, lacking typewriters, drew circles on paper, lettered them, and practiced by pressing their fingers over the circles.[48]

The shortage of teachers was an ongoing problem. The center's harsh living conditions deterred many from the outside from applying. Few evacuees had teaching credentials, but they had to be recruited as teachers or teachers assistants. The quality of education was thus uneven. Students enrolled in college preparatory courses often felt short-changed:

> I recall sitting in classrooms without books and listening to the instructor talking about technical matters that we could not study in depth. The lack of qualified evacuee teachers, the shortage of trained teachers was awful. I remember having to read a chapter a week in chemistry and discovering at

---

[47]Interview for OHP.

[48]James Hirabayashi, testimony in CWRIC.

the end of a semester that we had finished one full year's course. There was a total loss of scheduling with no experiments, demonstrations or laboratory work.[49]

On the other hand, some students felt that their education, as limited as it was, had served them well. Bess Kawamura, who completed the three years of high school at Amache described her training in secretarial skills as excellent. "I knew that I wasn't going to college," she said, "because college was reserved for the four boys in our family. So I took commercial courses taught by a very capable teacher who had been in Civil Service. As soon as I graduated, I left camp for Chicago and was able to get a good job immediately at the age of eighteen. Those skills I had acquired supported me and, later on, helped support my mother."[50]

White school teachers in many camps were among the most sympathetic to the inmates' plight. Emily Light, a teacher at Tule Lake was highly regarded among the inmates. But white staff members there vilified her as "one of the schoolteachers of 'an overly sentimental missionary type' who made a special point of inviting Japanese to their homes in order to show that they had no prejudice so far as race or color is concerned."[51]

In every camp, except Tule Lake, the curriculum conformed with recognized standards of the state in which the center was located. Students could usually transfer credits to the schools outside when they left camp.

Dorothy Cragen, the superintendent of the Inyo County schools (the County in which Manzanar was located) during World War II, provides a perspective of an outsider. "I was very much opposed to the Japanese being placed in camp," she said, because most of the children were American citizens and "I had a feeling that if they could to this to the children of Japanese Americans, then they could do the same thing to me." Asked about the teachers and the schools in the camp, she replied:

> They were all Caucasian teachers. They had many helpers, however, among the Japanese who had been trained to teach. While they could not get credentials, they assisted . . . . I visited their schools many, many times, and really, I used to wonder how the children could get up and sing such patriotic songs. They would sing, "I am an American" and all the familiar

---

[49]Bruce Kaji, testimony in CWRIC, p. 171.

[50]Personal interview. Years later, Kawamura enrolled in college after her four children were grown and earned a degree in human services.

[51]Drinnon, p. 304.

songs that we sang in our schools. The teachers did everything they could to promote the idea that they were Americans. But when I would heard them sing--and they sang so beautifully--I wondered how they really felt while they were doing that.[52]

The Japanese American students evidently felt the same way that boys and girls all over America felt. Saluting the flag, singing "My country 'tis of thee, sweet land of liberty" was a part of what all Americans did. If anything, it was the Caucasian teachers who were embarrassingly conscious, as Cragen was, of the cruel paradox of children exhibiting patriotism while cooped behind barbed wire.

Recreation   To pass the time and to find relief from the monotonous routine of regimented camp life, evacuees found a wide range of diversions available to them.   The WRA encouraged recreational activities with inordinate vigor, aware of their political value in averting dissension, and of their obvious psychological value as well. A glance at notices appearing in the *Granada Pioneer* in 1942, not long after the camp opened, reveals something of the variety and character of these recreational activities.

Nov. 14. ALL GIRLS SONATINAS
"Les Sonatinas", a musical organization of 21 young women, will give a concert at Terry hall, Tuesday, Nov. 17 at 2 p.m. . . . Tickets are now on sale at the school offices in 8H. Prices will be adults 25 cents, and children 10 cents.

Nov. 21. 'GI' IS THEME OF TONITE'S HOP
New records have been obtained [for] tonight's GI dance. . . Selections include "White Christmas", "My Devotion", "Kalamazoo", and "I Left My Heart at the Stage Door Canteen".

Dec. 2. DANCERS MEET SATURDAY
Those interested in ballet and interpretive dancing are asked to attend a meeting at the 6E recreation hall at 2 p.m., Saturday.

Dec. 2. COMMUNITY SING
A community sing will be held at 11G recreation hall on Friday from 7 p.m. with Sunny Kondo in charge.

---

[52]Jessie A. Garrett and Ronald C. Larson, *Camp and Community*, (California State University at Fullerton Oral History Program 1972), pp. 159-160.

Dec. 16. GET-ACQUAINTED RALLY PLANNED

Representatives of the YWCA, Boy Scouts, YMCA, recreation department, and Buddhist and Christian churches will attend a get-acquainted rally of all youth group leaders, 6:30 tonight, 9K recreation hall.

Dec. 24. SHOW TO RUN ONE WEEK

"Pardon My Sarong" costarring Abbott and Costello will be the first regular movie to be shown in the center Jan.3. . . . Admission has been set at 5 cents for children and 10 cents for adults.

Movies were changed once a week and scheduled so that a showing could be held in each block.   Titles usually ran to the light and entertaining.   Some Issei, who had never seen an American movie, especially appreciated the easy-to-understand cowboy movies.

In addition, Nisei women formed literary and discussion groups and participated in organized sports events.

Tension, Dissension   At the same time that evacuees took part in this plethora of recreational outlets, an undercurrent of discontent drifted through the camps. Apart from the poor living conditions and food, evacuees felt understandably fearful of the future. Many of them had no economic resources to fall back on, no place to go home to. Overriding all of it was the resentment of having been forced into the wretched position of captives.

Not surprisingly, tensions flared sporadically, in some camps more than others, ignited largely by matters related to *inu* (literally, "dog"; translated, "informer").

Some evacuees, particularly the Kibei and Issei, focused their anger on JACL leaders whom they saw as superpatriots, willing to sell out their own people. In fact, some JACL members did function as informers. Reported CWRIC: "Masaoka volunteered to Myer that JACL leaders might identify the 'known agitators' at the camps so that the WRA could separate them from the rest of the evacuees."[53] Evacuees charged that these JACL members were being accorded favored treatment and the best jobs. At Manzanar, rumbling tensions exploded when a suspected *inu*, JACL leader Fred Tayama, was severely beaten.

JACL leaders, on the other hand, blamed the Kibei and Issei for camp disturbances and accused them of being "disloyal." [54]

---

[53]P. 178.
[54]*Ibid.* p. 178.

At Poston, a Kibei suspected of being an *inu*, both before and during camp, was severely beaten. The incident sparked a general strike.

Again, at Manzanar, which had more than its share of dissension, Harry Ueno organized a Kitchen Workers Union made up largely of anti-JACL, anti-administration Kibei and Issei.[55] While investigating whopping shortages of sugar and meat (rationed foods, which brought high prices on the black market), Ueno was arrested and jailed outside the center, a moved that ignited a large-scale riot. The Manzanar hospital records show that among the casualties, one man was killed instantly, another injured by inhaling tear gas. Of the nine others treated for gun shot wounds, one died from hemorrhage of the lungs.[56]

But perhaps the issue that raised the greatest controversy and ultimately did violence to the greatest number of evacuees was the issue of the "No No-Yes Yes", or loyalty question. (See "Trial by Questionnaire" in following chapter.)

Women, who had not been overtly involved in the conflicts before, found themselves inexorably drawn into this nefarious issue.

---

[55]Weglyn, 123.
[56]*Ibid*, pp. 124-125.

Nisei returning to school (UCLA), May 29, 1945. *Photo by Charles E. Mace. National Archives.*

Nisei at Day of Remembrance ceremony, San Francisco, February
19, 1989. © *Shirley Nakao*.

CHAPTER 9

Outmigration: The Third Move

Do you remember the directives we were given when we left camp? We weren't to congregate among our kind; we shouldn't speak Japanese nor be conspicuous; we were not to talk about camp. In other words, we were not to be Japanese in any way. But to the dominant society we were not only Japanese, we were "Japs." Certainly not American. So where the hell did that leave us?
                                                              ---Nisei Woman

"TRIAL" RELEASES

In the spring of 1942, when the Japanese population was being herded into camps, a group of educators, industrialists, cultural leaders and church leaders, concerned about the problem of thousands of young Japanese Americans being denied access to higher education, had set about obtaining the release of students. Through their efforts, about 250 Nisei were able to leave camp to attend colleges or universities in areas outside the military zone by the autumn of 1942. Financial aid came mainly from Christian groups, among the most prominent the American Friends Service Committee.[1] A number of girls joined this early outmigration.

About the same time, Nisei had been issued passes for short-term seasonal farm work in response to severe, wartime labor shortages. "Employers were required to furnish transportation and pay prevailing wages; evacuees could not be hired in place of available local labor." Also, State officials had to state in writing that the labor was needed and that they would guarantee the workers' safety.[2]

Not surprisingly, workers found conditions at the farms far short of requirements laid out by the WRA. "Housing" sometimes meant sleeping in a shack with no running water. Some workers met outright hostility and violence. But the pay came in handy, and workers felt a measure of satisfaction in contributing to the war effort. And although temporary, the freedom of being "outside" afforded relief.

For the most part, women did not go out on short-term leave.

---

[1]CWRIC, p. 181.
[2]*Ibid.*, p. 182.

PAROLE TO LIMITED FREEDOM

The temporary leave program proved successful, so by the end of 1942, the WRA announced "the definite recognition of relocation as the primary goal" and initiated a vigorous job-seeking program nationally.

Apart from the fact that the trial releases of students and farm laborers had been successful, other motives activated this policy for releasing and resettling evacuees. The basis for confining evacuees could not be supported legally and "military necessity" which had been used as a rationale for imprisoning the Japanese population had become ever more difficult to defend after the tide of war turned in America's favor.[3] Also, according to Director Myer, WRA officials were beginning to recognize "that loyalty could not flourish in an atmosphere of restriction and discriminatory segregation." And officials also "did not want to be responsible for fostering a new set of reservations in the United States akin to Indian reservations."[4]

Had these considerations occurred to government officials before, they might have saved taxpayers the nearly $90 million bill submitted by the Army for implementing the exclusion orders, which did not include the $160 million which the WRA was to expend ultimately.[5]

But even as the WRA encouraged and abetted inmates to resettle permanently, the latter did not have *carte blanche* to leave the camps. Like parolees, they had to show first, proof of a means of support; second, obtain FBI clearance; and third, show that their presence in a community would likely be accepted. In addition they were required to report any change of job or address to the WRA. The West Coast, of course, was still off limits.

A booklet containing guidelines for conduct was to be issued to all parolees. Mike Masaoka, who seemed to be the sole contact between government officials and the Nisei, offered suggestions to be inserted in the booklet, among them: Prospective resettler should know that they should carry on their person such identification as birth certificates, WRA ID cards, membership cards of organizations and travel permits "which shows they are legally outside the Relocation Centers."

Among the "general hints" Masaoka tendered for resettlers: "Don't speak or use Japanese in public, even though you may feel that no one will hear you. If certain hotels and restaurants refuse to serve

---

[3]The Battle of Midway, which took place in early June of 1942, is widely considered the turning point of the war with Japan. Despite this, construction of the concentration camps continued apace, and the Army continued herding the Japanese into them.

[4]Myer, p. 134. Ironically, Myer was to become the commissioner of the Bureau of Indian Affairs in May, 1950.

[5]Hosokawa, p. 351 and Myer, p.339.

you, or do so in an insolent or condescending manner, do not show your irritation or demand your rights as American citizens. . . . If you go to public places such as bowling alleys, dance halls, etc., be sure to be extra careful in the use of language and be extremely courteous to all who you many come in contact with.[6]

One notes the obsequious, non-conflictive, almost apologetic demeanor that resettlers were advised to bear, reinforcing the notion of culpability. Like parolees, they should carry special identification, avoid showing their prison stripes (deny their identity), and resist confrontation at all cost.

To the Armed Service   Meanwhile, the War Department, in another paradoxical turn, reversed its policy and reinstituted Selective Service for Japanese Americans.

At the time of Pearl Harbor, about 5000 Nisei were serving in the Army. Subsequently, induction all but ceased, with the exception of the formation of the all-Nisei 100th Infantry Battalion of Hawaii in 1942 and ongoing recruitment of students and teachers for the military language schools. The status of draft-age Nisei then remained in limbo until September, 1942, when the Selective Service officially barred them from enlisting and classified them 4C, the status of enemy aliens.

Mike Masaoka, convinced that the Nisei should serve in the armed forces to demonstrate their loyalty, prodded the JACL into passing a resolution requesting that the Selective Service be reinstated. The Nisei should "be accorded the same privilege of serving our country in the armed forces as that granted to every other American citizen," he asserted. Myer and John McCloy, Assistant Secretary of War, were equally enthusiastic over the idea.[7] And on January 28, 1943, the Army announced that an all-Nisei combat team would be recruited.

To step up recruiting in the camps, in February, the Army prepared to send out recruiting teams who would, at the same time, administer a loyalty questionnaire. Myer saw an opportunity to expedite leave-clearances and proposed that *all* inmates, aged 17 and over, complete the questionnaire. Prepared by the Army, the questionnaire provoked the stormiest period in the history of the camps.

---

[6]Letter from Masaoka to M.M.Tozier, head of WRA's Reports and Public Relations, dated October 28, 1942.

[7]It is worthwhile pointing out that McCloy, now a gung ho advocate of recruiting Nisei, was a prominent architect for the War Department in formulating the policy to imprison Japanese Americans.

The title of the document, "Application for Leave Clearance," which implied that the person filling out the form was applying for leave, "proved disturbing to many Issei and others who did not want to leave the centers," said Myer.[8] But the problem of the title paled in comparison to two items in the questionnaire which came to be known as the infamous "loyalty questions."

TRIAL BY QUESTIONNAIRE

Although no person of Japanese ancestry in the United States had been charged with espionage or sabotage, the Army and the WRA saw fit to administer the questionnaire to separate the "loyal" from the "disloyal" camp inhabitants. At the end of the long questionnaire, evacuees were to answer two questions of loyalty:

Question #27: (For men) Are you willing to serve in the Armed forces of the United States on combat duty wherever ordered?
(For women and Issei) If the opportunity presents itself and you are found qualified, would you be willing to volunteer for the Army Nurse Corps of the WAC?

Question #28: Will you swear unqualified allegiance to the United States of America and faithfully defend the United States from any or all attack by foreign or domestic forces, and forswear any form of allegiance or obedience to the Japanese emperor or to any other foreign government, power or organization?

"A bad mistake was made in the loyalty question," wrote Myer, in a masterful understatement. To begin with, Japanese American citizens were being put on trial again to prove their loyalty. Secondly, question number 27 put to the Issei was plainly idiotic, while question number 28 forced them into an outrageously untenable position. The Issei had never been allowed American citizenship, and now they were being asked to renounce allegiance to the only country of which they were citizens.

Reaction among the inmates was swift and intense, and heated debates rocked the mess halls and meeting rooms. The questionnaire had served to heighten suspicions of the Issei and Kibei who saw in question 28 a sinister trap. A "yes" could well be used as an admission of prior allegiance to the Japanese emperor, while a "no" could mean a blanket admission of disloyalty. Either way, they could be branded traitorous and deported. Belatedly noting this egregious blunder, the

[8]P. 32.

Army changed question 28 to read: "Will you swear to abide by the laws of the United States and to take no action which would in any way interfere with the war effort?"

Nisei showed their pent-up indignation at the question, yet another insult to their integrity. They had already demonstrated their loyalty by complying without complaint to the appalling exclusion orders. While in other citizens, loyalty was taken for granted, as well it should be, Nisei were badgered at every turn to demonstrate theirs.

And now the government was asking that they respond to a question that might very well cause physical as well as emotional separation from their parents. The Nisei knew that if their parents replied "no-no" to the questions, a "yes-yes" answer on their part would mean certain separation. In effect, they were being asked to choose between their country and their parents. It was "a great chess game in which the government made all the moves," aptly remarked one evacuee.

Chizu (Kitano) Iiyama's experience at Topaz, a relatively peaceful camp, testifies to the intensity of feelings that raged. Two Kibei and one Issei dominated a block meeting, loudly arguing the case for "no-no" answers to the questions. Alarmed that a mob-mentality might be developing, Iiyama stood and counseled calm, recommending that each individual be allowed to study the questions carefully and to follow their own convictions. At that, the Issei lashed out at Iiyama's father, the block manager. "That's what you get for sending your daughter to college!" he shouted, in a classic straw-man outburst. Whether block members agreed with him or not, in the charged atmosphere, they avoided the Kitano family for weeks in order to avoid appearing partisan.[9]

In the final analysis, the loyalty questions proved meaningless. Some loyal citizens answered "no" out of frustration or anger, or out of obligation to the family. On the other hand, some who had stronger allegiances with Japan than others in the population, answered "yes" to avoid trouble. In short, the answers revealed more about motives for the answers than they did about loyalty. For example:

> I answered Yes-Yes immediately and my mother agreed with me. The reason for that was my mother thought that if she answered "yes," then Dad would be returned more quickly to the family. A lot of the wives who had

---

[9]Personal interview. As a postscript to this incident, years later, the Issei in question, who had remained in the U.S., had occasion to apologize to the Kitano family for his outburst and for the pain it had caused.

an interned husband answered "yes" for that reason. The interned husbands also answered in the affirmative so that they could rejoin their families.[10]

What had long been rumored to come about in the backwash of the registration became official in May, 1943, for soon after registration was completed, Myer received orders from Secretary of War Stimson to "take immediate steps to screen out for the centers and segregate in close confinement all individuals appearing to have pro-Japanese sympathies."[11] The move had been precipitated by lawmakers, endorsed by McCloy, the WRA and the JACL, then mandated by the Senate on July 6, 1943.

Tule Lake Segregation Center   Tule Lake became the maximum security center in which all those who failed to register for the army, or who answered "no" to the loyalty question, were imprisoned. Those who had already been residing there and had answered "yes" to the question were transferred to other camps.

Carey McWilliams witnessed the departure of the segregants from some of the camps for Tule Lake and stated, ". . . it was my most fervent wish that the entire membership of the Native Sons of the Golden West might have been present to see for themselves the anguish, the grief, the bottomless sorrow that this separation occasioned . . . . In these scenes was the stuff of timeless tragedy and excellent documentation for the one immortal theme: man's inhumanity to man.[12]

Women, generally the cohesive force in families, found the segregation at Tule Lake especially onerous. They had strained to keep the family from disintegrating as they contended with the disorientating moves and the rigors of the camps. Now they found their task even more formidable. Men were being arrested for refusing to register for the draft. Husbands and brothers were being thrown into the stockade as "agitators." Tule Lake had been turned into a "seething cauldron of angry, frightened, and intimidated people," as Weglyn put it.

The Army, 1,200 men strong with eight tanks and tear gas, took charge of Tule Lake from November, 1943. A designated area of about two-thirds of an acre became the stockade, under 24-hour surveillance by soldiers armed with submachine guns.[13]   Tule Lake now had a population of over 18,000 inmates, 68 percent of whom were citizens. "Most were there because they had requested repatriation or

---

[10]Anonymous, Thomas, p. 470.

[11]Myer, p. 75.

[12]*Prejudice*, pp. 188-189.

[13]Drinnon, pp. 110-111.

expatriation (39 percent), answered the loyalty questionnaire unsatisfactorily (26 percent), or were family of someone who was segregated (31 percent)."[14]

Not surprisingly, women segregants usually fell into the third category. But reasons for making the hard decision were integrally connected, so that it was possible to be segregated for all three reasons. Such was the case with Kazue V. Matsuda, now Violet de Cristoforo.

In her moving testimony before the CWRIC, de Cristoforo stated that she had no alternative but to refuse to answer the loyalty question and later, to request expatriation because her husband and his parents had done so. Her father-in-law had owned considerable property in Japan, but in this country, his assets had been frozen, rendering him penniless. Disillusioned, but more than that, uncertain about their future in America, he and his wife declined to answer the loyalty question. De Cristoforo's husband, their only son, also a legal alien resident, who had been treated with extraordinary severity by the authorities because he had beem a Japanese school teacher and a respected leader in the Japanese community, also refused to answer the loyalty question. Thus de Cristoforo found herself caught in an inextricable dilemma:

> I was an American-born citizen, as were my three children but, as was customary in those days, I had been trained as a mother and as a housewife and had no employable skills. My husband was my sole means of support and I, too, in desperation finally decided to go to Japan with them in order to keep my family together, and because my primary loyalty was to my husband and his family. To repeat, my refusal to answer the loyalty questionnaire was not the product of free will, but was forced upon me in an effort to survive, to keep my family from disintegrating, and by the unlawful detention and humiliating and degrading conditions prevailing in the internment camps.[15]

In the ensuing years, de Cristoforo underwent a series of nightmarish events, which might have crushed a frailer soul. First, she lost her beloved mother-in-law at Tule Lake to a prolonged bout with cancer. Then she became separated (as it turned out, for good) from her husband, who was sent to the Santa Fe internment camp before being deported to Japan. By the time de Cristoforo arrived in Japan, she found that her husband had married another woman. Subsequently, her father-in-law, who had always extended aid and affection to her,

---

[14]U.S. Department of the Interior, *Evacuated People*, quoted in CWRIC, p. 209.

[15]Affidavit, "A Victim of the Evacuation and Resettlement Study," June 30, 1987.

died in Japan, still grieving over the death of his wife and despondent over the loss of his lands and property in Japan. Moreover, her own father had perished in the atomic holocaust at Hiroshima, her mother severely burned.

Alone with her children and unable to secure work that would enable her to support her three children, she finally sent the two older ones, separately, back to the United States. This move caused a breach between her and her children that was never completely mended.[16]

The decision, which had been wrested from de Cristoforo in camp, had been cruelly twisted by the winds of war, resulting in the disintegration of her family despite her arduous struggle to hold it together. Like the myriad tragic experiences at Tule Lake, hers saw its origin in the faulty and superfluous "loyalty" question.

When the war ended, to no one's surprise, the majority of Tuleans were made eligible for relocation by the Justice Department. The ones who remained had presumably been forced to return to Japan, or had made a considered choice to do so.

Taeko Okamura, testified before the CWRIC that her mother, a Nisei, married to an Issei, had written "neutral" after the loyalty questions because four of her children, who had been visiting their grandparents, were stranded in Hiroshima when the war broke out. Since communication to individuals in Japan had been abruptly cut off, Okamura's mother, whom we call Mrs. N,[17] became frantic with worry about her children.

"There was no way my mother could swear to harm her children in Japan or estrange herself from her husband," Okamura testified. Thus, when the Army found the "neutral" answer unacceptable, she was forced to write "no-no." The family was then shipped to Tule Lake.

When the war ended, the family decided that Mrs. N, along with the three children, would go to Hiroshima, while the father would remain in the U.S. to recover what he could of the financial losses he had suffered because of incarceration. And because independent civilian travel to Japan was impossible, the only way Mrs. N could soon get to Japan was to renounce her American citizenship and get on the expatriation ship.

In Hiroshima, Mrs. N. was overjoyed at finding her in-laws and children safe, but she and her children were not welcomed. "Why did you come here?" her in-laws asked, for food was pitifully scarce and eking out a living was arduous in post A-bomb Hiroshima.

---

[16]*Ibid.*

[17]So traumatized was she by this period in her life, that she still has difficulty talking about it, and declined to have her name published.

Okamura continued her testimony about her mother:

When we lived in Hollister, my father never expected my mother to work on the farm. For the first time in her life, she had to do all this manual labor, which, on a Japanese farm is very, very difficult. She literally went to town at two in the morning to sell goods in the ichi, the open market . . . all the way to Hiroshima eki (station). On her way home, she had to stop at different places to collect honey buckets (human fertilizer). To pull that wagon full of ko-e, over hills and dirt roads . . . She did it for ten years.

And for ten years she tried to get back to the U.S. My father tried. And my brother, who by this time had joined the American army and was stationed in Hokkaido, tried. And the saddest thing I watched my mother do at this time--and she did it all the time--was anytime she saw an Asian face among the throngs of occupation forces, she would go up to the person, and beg them to help her. It was so sad.[18]

By 1949, Okamura's father had re-established himself in California, enabling the two older children to return from Japan. Her mother, feeling that anything would be better for the children than staying in Japan, sent two other children to Hawaii to live with her brother's family. "Now our family was split in three ways: Japan, Hawaii, and California," says Okamura.

Finally, after a lengthy struggle, Mrs. N and the two remaining children were able to return to California with the aid of the late Senator William Knowland. Her citizenship was also eventually restored through the efforts of the noted attorney Wayne Collins. Ten, long, punishing years after the first separation, the entire family was finally united.[19]

Mrs. N. had endured the entire gamut of experience of an exiled citizen, from the temporary detention center, through the lock-up at Tule Lake, then as a "no-no, renunciant, expatriate, repatriate, strandee, and returnee," as her daughter put it. And although she prefers to remain anonymous, her story is recorded as a stark reminder of the mindless tragedies inflicted upon individuals in the hysteria of war.

PERMANENT RELEASES

Men in the Armed Service   Many Nisei left the barbed wire confines for good to serve in the armed forces. A sizable number volunteered out of the desire to prove their loyalty and in response to

---

[18]Testimony before CWRIC in *Amerasia Journal*, v.8, no.2, Fall/Winter 1981, pp. 82-89; and interview conducted for OHP, June 28, 1989.

[19]*Ibid.*

the urgings of the military and the JACL. Then, in January 1944, the draft was reinstituted for Nisei.

The paradox of men being drafted by the military out of the enclosures where they had been sent by the government in the first place because they could not be trusted as loyal citizens, has not escaped the barbs of legions of commentators. But many Nisei did volunteer, and most did comply to draft orders.

From this vantage point, it may be difficult to mine the feelings of men who enlisted, if not willingly, at least without protest. Many of these men express divided feelings. On the one hand, they were loath to enlist and leave their families in camp, or they saw the bitter injustice of being plucked out of a concentration camp to serve in the armed forces; on the other, they wanted to show their patriotism. And most simply say now: "What could you do?"

Also, despite having been treated as though they were enemies, the Nisei could not help but become caught up in the patriotic fervor that held the nation in thrall, as the following portrait of the Masuoka family strikingly illustrates:

> He was the first to volunteer for the combat unit last Monday, but the last of the four Masuoka sons to enter the armed forces of the United States.
>
> Peter Masuoka, Amache senior high's assistant physical education instructor and coach, volunteered before the registration got underway in front of the Paramount news camera.
>
> "Peter wanted to go so badly, even before Frank, who is at Camp Savage, volunteered," Mrs. Ushitada Masuoka of 6H-10B stated softly as she smiled.
>
> Besides Frank, Peter has two other brothers who have been in service for over a year. . . . On a shelf, are displayed pictures of the three Masuoka sons who are now in uniform, and in the background is a banner with three stars and the words, "In Service of Our Country."
>
> "Another star will be added soon," Mrs. Masuoka says proudly.[20]

The heroic exploits of the all-Nisei 100th Infantry Battalion and the 442nd Regimental Combat Team in the European theater came to be known world-wide. And Nisei in the Military Intelligence Service served no less importantly in the Pacific theater. More than 33,000 Nisei served in the armed forces, 6,000 of them in the Pacific theater.[21]

---

[20]*Granada Pioneer*, February 16, 1943, p. 1.

[21]*Americans of Japanese Ancestry*, p.59.

Spouses of Servicemen   Many women left camp to be with their servicemen husbands stationed in parts of the country not in the excluded zone.   A large number moved to Minneapolis, near the Military Intelligence Service base at Fort Snelling.   One woman recalled:

> My husband was drafted into the military about a year after we were married. I left Amache for Minneapolis in early 1944 by train. On the train, out in the world for the first time since I had been stuck in camp, I became very, very conscious of my Japaneseness and particularly of having been in camp. I think prisoners must feel that way when they get out, like they are tainted or something. But I had my baby son with me, and that helped. In Minneapolis, I had a job as a live-in domestic with a German couple with three kids. They had never seen a Japanese before, but they were good to us. My husband would come "home" on weekends, and sometimes the wife would baby-sit for us while we went out for a Chinese dinner.[22]

A number of servicemen's wives report similar experiences. No doubt this was in large part due to the conduct of Nisei servicemen both on the domestic scene as well as in the theaters of war. Already by the autumn of 1944, the Nisei Battalions had performed courageously in Italy and France, sustaining a significant number of casualties.

Women in the Armed Services   Largely because the recruitment of Nisei men proved successful, the Army decided to "give . . . loyal women the opportunity to serve their country along with other citizens." At about the same time that evacuees were being sorted and segregated in 1943, women volunteered to serve in the WACs. One volunteer, who had been at Heart Mountain concentration camp and had relocated to Florida to work as a domestic, provides these views:

> I felt that the Nisei had to do more than give lip service to the United States and by joining the WACs I could prove my sincerity. . . . After all, this is everybody's war and we all have to put an equal share into it. I don't know why the Nisei objected so much to my joining the WACs. . . . . Most of the Nisei girls said that they would not join because they would never be able to get married then.[23]

---

[22]Personal interview.

[23]Anonymous, Thomas, p. 319.

Contrary to the impression that "WACs would never be able to get married," many, if not most, ended up marrying.[24]   But Tak and Florence (Kodama) Kato became one of the first Nisei couple in the service, when the latter was inducted.   Both sergeants, they found Chicago a convenient place to meet, since she was stationed in Indiana, he at Camp Savage, Minnesota in 1944.

Seven WACs were ordered to Fort Snelling, Minnesota to set up a detachment of Nisei WACs in the intelligence corps.   Among them was Sue Suzuko (Ogata) Kato.   Kato had lived in Nebraska and Colorado before volunteering for the WACs in 1943 and had been assigned to Fort Devens, Massachusetts, after her basic training.   "It never occurred to us [Nisei] that we were different until the war broke out," said Kato. "The start of the war did not disrupt our lives, but I had heard about the West Coast Japanese being locked up in camps."   Her family did not suffer the humiliation of the concentration camps.

"I joined the WACs--and this may sound like flag-waving--to prove my Americanism," she stated.   After her training at Fort Snelling, Kato was sent to Washington, D.C. to help translate Japanese documents. Most WACs who trained there did similar work since they were not used as interpreters or interrogators.   Kato, who served three years, believes that there were about 100 Nisei WACs, all told.[25]

According to a booklet prepared by the 6th Annual Veteran's Reunion (July 1-July 6, 1970) and an article from the "MISLS Album," Nisei WACs served at various bases all over the country, in medical detachments, in the Public Information Office, in Military Intelligence School and as typists, clerks and researchers in occupied Germany and Japan.   Teiko Harata, Yaye and Yoshiye Togasaki, Margaret Ugai and Masako Mary Yamada were among a dozen or so medical personnel, commissioned as second lieutenants in the Army and sent overseas.

And when the U.S. Cadet Nursing Corps opened its doors at the same time as the WACs, more than 200 Nisei women enlisted.

In other war-related work, Nisei women participated in federal broadcasting and communications.   Some served up their talents as "Kimi," contributing to the morale of American servicemen stationed in Kauai by singing and with light patter.

---

[24]In a letter sent on August 1971 to members of a reunion of WACs which had taken place earlier, a considerable number of those listed had married surnames.

[25]Correspondence with Sue Kato; "Souvenir Booklet," prepared for the 6th National Nisei Veteran's Reunion, July, 1970, p. 87 and "Niseiweek 1988" booklet.

Out to Work   "To go 'outside' was considered extremely hazardous," reported a government publication.[26] At first, only those who had high employment potential and who had no immediate family responsibilities ventured out.   But by the middle of 1943, the outmigration had steadily increased with inmates now being able to obtain indefinite leave clearance from the project director instead of having to go through Washington.

But a thorny question plagued the public: If Japanese Americans were too dangerous to be permitted on the West Coast, weren't they dangerous here in the East and Midwest where vital defense work was going on? For, according to law, the individual was innocent until proved guilty, and many found it difficult to allow that there had been no individual charge or proof of guilt as a basis for the exclusion.

Thus the WRA launched an extensive public information campaign, establishing regional offices in major resettlement sites like Denver, Chicago, Salt Lake City and New York.   Enlisting the cooperation of churches and civic organizations, it succeeded admirably in allaying the fears of the public and setting up programs to meet the needs of the exiled Americans.

A booklet issued by the Congregational Church entitled "70,000 Refugees: Made in USA," serves as an example of the kind of information disseminated. After presenting a historical sketch of the exclusion as well as positive statements about the Japanese quoted from various government officials, it ended with suggestions about what congregations could do:

> The task of resettlement . . . must be done locally or it will not be done at all. Your church will be missing a supreme opportunity for enlightened Christian action if it does not take definite steps toward finding jobs and preparing your community for the reception of these uprooted fellow-citizens. If your church has a vigorous Committee for Social Action, encourage it to take the initiative in this matter. *Call attention to this source of employees when your friends talk about the manpower shortage.* Tell them of the variety of skills available, and offer to put them in touch with the Committee for Work with Japanese Evacuees.[27]

Church groups also set up hostels in Chicago, Cleveland, Cincinnati and Des Moines by mid-1943. Their work, performed at a time when being

---

[26].S. Department of the Interior, *People in Motion*, (U.S. Government Printing Office, 1949), p. 6.

[27]Truman Douglas, Citizens Committee for Resettlement of the Congregational Christian Committee for Work with Japanese Evacuees, (Saint Louis, Mo., 1943), p. 15.

sympathetic to the Japanese in America made them vulnerable to attack and criticism, proved invaluable to the Nisei.

Job offers like the following sample which appeared in the April 21, 1943 issue of the *Granada Pioneer* began flowing into the camps:

- Three tray girls for hospital, $60 a month plus room and board at Rockford, Ill.
- Ten to 12 girls for power sewing machine operators, wages vary, Chicago.
- First-class bookkeeper, $35 to $40 a week, Chicago.
- Four graduate nurses, $100 per month plus meals and laundry, Chicago.

These were among a mere 11 job listings included in the issue; by the end of the month, the list grew to two dozen. In succeeding months, an ever greater number and variety of job opportunities became available.

Calls for domestic workers were among the most frequent. And women often took domestic work as a base for finding more suitable work and housing.

Newlywed Judy (Karakane Yawata) Rudder headed eastward out of camp to Minnesota with no particular job in mind when she left with her husband in December, 1943. By then, restrictions for leaving had eased and, while her husband had a job, the couple reached their destination without housing.

"I found the place amazingly friendly and warm," says Rudder, who had lived all of her life in Los Angeles. She had many job offers and soon found an apartment as well.[28]

Like Rudder, persons outmigrating eastward generally found the climate measurably more hospitable than that of the West Coast. Minneapolis is often cited by Nisei as one of the most congenial hosts during that period.

But Elmer L. Shirrell, midwest director of WRA touted Chicago as "the nation's warmest and most generous host to thousands of American citizens of Japanese ancestry." He noted that already, in July 1943, 2500 Japanese Americans had found work and homes in the Chicago area. Said he: "Almost without fail each Japanese American asks only three things: a job directly helping the war effort, money enough to live on and help out the older folks in the relocation center, and enough left over to buy war bonds . . . . The newcomers are ideal tenants who pay their bills before they are due."[29]

---

[28]Personal interview.

[29]*Granada Pioneer*, July 14, 1943, p. 3.

Myer reported during the same period that "the demands for manpower were so great that from the Chicago area alone we had 10,000 requests for evacuees which could not be filled. The demand increased as the evacuee relocatees demonstrated their efficiency as workers, and as general acceptance of them spread into dozens of communities across the country."[30]

Bess Kawamura left Amache for Chicago, fresh out of high school. Wearing a "homemade" suit and shoes whose soles had been lined with cardboard to cover the holes, she made the long train trip alone. Looking back, Kawamura says:

> I don't know where I got the nerve. I was only eighteen and had never been away from home before. And here I was, going to this strange city, without even a place to stay. But being young has its own pluses. I don't remember being afraid. And as soon as I got to Chicago, I connected with a friend, who let me stay with her. I already had a job with the WRA, so everything worked out well. In about a year, my brother (who was there by then) and I were able to send for our mother.[31]

As in Kawamura's case, by 1944, the movement out of camps began to include those family members who had been left behind. Parents joined their Nisei children who had gone out earlier, wives and children joined their husbands. Occasionally, a whole family left at the same time.

Hannah Yasuda's husband left camp on short-term leave only one month after he arrived at Amache. A serious, hard-working man, a successful farmer before the war, he had difficulty enduring the confinement of camp and moved in and out of camp on work leaves. At one juncture, he traveled as far as Cleveland, looking for work that would sustain him, his wife, and one child. But the couple, wanting a more stable home life, decided to leave camp permanently to accept an offer share-cropping with an Italian family in Colorado. "They were nice enough," recalls Yasuda, "but apparently didn't know much about farming, so we lost everything. Everything. John had sent for a cultivator, and we even lost that."

Then came a succession of moves in which Hannah's husband engaged in another share-cropping venture that turned sour, became a truck-driver on a farm and worked at whatever other jobs available to keep his growing family afloat. Along the line, the couple and their two children shared with a brother a one-bedroom hovel with bare floors.

---

[30]P. 140.

[31]Personal interview.

"Those were the most traumatic years of my life," says Yasuda, recalling the bone-chilling winters. "I kept getting pregnant, and we were always destitute. I remember when I had my third baby, we had to leave the two other children with people who were practically strangers and travel to Denver to have the baby delivered. We had to borrow the money for it. When I returned after a week and saw the faces of the two forlorn little girls, I just broke down and cried.[32]

Students   For women without family responsibilities, resettlement presented an excellent opportunity to pursue an education. A substantial number of women took advantage of the scholarships offered by colleges and universities throughout the Midwest and East. Others relied on their family resources. The June 21, 1943 issue of *Time* carried a story about the education of the former evacuees, noting that already over 1000 Nisei were enrolled in about 125 colleges in 37 states. Mentioned in the article were Setsuko Matsunaga, a USC Phi Beta Kappa, who was studying at Washington University in St. Louis and twins Eva and Hannah Sakamoto, UC Berkeley students, who had entered the University of Colorado to study for a career in nursing.

Since nurses were in great demand, many Nisei women prepared for that profession. Kiyo Sato was released from camp to attend Hilton College in Michigan on a scholarship.

> I didn't have shoes. They were all worn out. So Mrs. Crawford, the camp director's wife drove me to Parker to buy a pair of shoes and a small suitcase, a cardboard suitcase. That's all I had, plus some old clothes--hand-me-downs . . .
>
> WRA wrote a letter saying, "You are one of the first students being relocated to the state of Michigan and upon your deportment depends the release of others students from camp." It was a heavy burden, and I took it very seriously. They wanted me to make speeches to the churches, in the community . . . a scared 19-year-old. It was hard.

Sato graduated with a B.S. in biology, and applied to the best schools for further education in nursing. "Mayo, John Hopkins, and Western Reserve--they all turned me down without considering my application," she recalls. "But I'm never going to forgive Mayo for this: I passed the medical, which cost $10, big money for me at the time. Then, they wrote

---

[32]Personal interview.

me saying I had passed my requirements, but they had this policy, that they couldn't have anyone of my ancestry . . .[33]

Sato's experience typifies that of other Nisei women who left camp to go to school. In camp, their Issei parents urged them to take advantage of the opportunity afforded them. The cost was sometimes great, financial and otherwise. Secondly, the students encountered hostility in differing degrees of harshness on the "outside" and endured severe financial strains. But, on the positive side, in plunging into this unfamiliar environment, most appeared to be strengthened by learning to deal with the outside world without the cushion of a supporting community and the comfort of friends and family. Also, afterwards, none appeared to regret the chance they had taken to leap outside of their confined lives into the mainstream of American life, however delimiting their movement in it was to be.

END OF THE EXCLUSION

By the end of 1944, the exclusion of the Japanese from the West Coast had just about spent its specious rationale. Some 36,000 former inmates of the camps, already settled into various parts of the nation, had been found loyal, industrious, law-abiding. The remarkable performance of the Nisei troops had gone a long way towards promoting community acceptance. The Allied offensive in the Pacific was going well, and victory appeared imminent so that even the "A Jap's a Jap" justification for the exclusion seemed now redundant. And if treachery and sabotage by the Japanese in America had been a real concern, that concern had been acutely mitigated at the expense of those who had been locked in at Tule Lake.

Thus in the spring of 1944, the War Department proposed to the President that the exclusion be ended. After extensive discussion and correspondence between the President and the War and Justice Departments, General DeWitt's mass exclusion order was rescinded on December 17, 1944, two years and nine months after it had been handed down.

In the ensuing months and years, most of the exiled Japanese would tread the long return road westward to the places from which they had come.

Mitsuye Endo On December 18, significantly the day after the rescission orders were issued, the Supreme Court ruled in cases

---

[33]Interview for OHP, May 7, 1989. Later, out of her work testing school children for visual acuity, Sato developed a testing kit called Blackbird Vision Screening System, now enjoying limited use in every state.

involving two Nisei: *Korematsu v. United States* and *Ex parte Endo*. In both cases they sidestepped the issue of the constitutionality of the exclusion. In *Korematsu*, the Court upheld the conviction of Fred Korematsu for failing to report to a detention upon the order of the exclusion.[34] In *Ex parte Endo*, the Court ruled that Mitsuye Endo, held in Topaz, was "entitled to an unconditional release by the War Relocation authority . . . and [that] necessarily implies 'the right to pass freely from state to state,' including the right to move freely into California."

Mitsuye Endo had been employed by the state of California as a typist, when she was fired in the wake of the Pearl Harbor bombing. Concerned about such racially-motivated dismissals, Saburo Kido, a JACL leader, asked attorney James Purcell to see what he could do to prevent further terminations.

Meanwhile, the exclusion was ordered. Appalled, Purcell launched a course to seek the freedom of the Nisei and selected Mitsuye Endo for his test case. While Endo would have preferred that he select someone else, she believes Purcell selected her because "I had the best background: my brother was in the Army, and my parents never went back to Japan. They felt that I represented a symbolic, 'loyal' American . . . ." She agreed to do it, finally, "because they said it's for the good of everybody."[35] In her petition for freedom, Endo declared that she was a loyal, law-abiding citizen, that no charges had been filed against her and that she was being illegally detained against her will in the Relocation Center under guard.

While in Topaz, she was advised to refuse to apply for "indefinite leave" because of the restrictive conditions attached to it. Thereupon, Attorney Purcell sought a writ of *habeas corpus* on her behalf in July, 1942 in the U.S. District Court. An entire year passed before the petition was denied. Purcell than appealed the case to the Ninth Circuit Court of Appeals. This led to certification of the case before the Supreme Court, which, in turn, rendered its landmark decision.

Mitsuye Endo became something of an abstraction, a figure embraced in a principle throughout the long period it took to have her case adjudicated. It was a difficult position for a shy, young woman, incxperienced in the ways of the world. "While this was going on, it seemed like a dream. It just didn't seem like it was happening to me."[36]

---

[34]In 1983, the federal district court of San Francisco vacated Korematsu's original conviction for refusing to obey the exclusion orders.

[35]Tateishi, pp. 60-61.

[36]*Ibid*.

Endo left camp for Chicago in June of 1945, three years after she had first stepped into the confines of Walarga Assembly Center. "I could have left earlier," she said, "but Purcell needed me to be in camp." As it turned out, all Japanese Americans needed her to be there.

The "Residue"   Thomas makes the point that seven out of ten persons who left camp permanently were young people between the ages of 15 and 35. And "while young men were the pioneers in the migration from Japan to America,. . . appreciable proportions of young women migrated, alone or with their husbands or their brothers, from camps to the "outside world."[37]

At the same time, closer examination of the figures provides some interesting details about those who remained in camp, what Thomas calls "the residue."[38]   Excluding approximately 18,000 evacuees who were detained at Tule Lake, slightly over 60,000 persons remained in camp as of January 1945.

Females and males, who remained in camp, numbered about the same in the 0 to 20 and the 40 to 60 age brackets. But significantly, in the 20 to 40 category, females outnumbered men by a margin of 8,320 to 4,787. These women were, of course, mainly married Nisei, and the figures confirm what many women have testified: they stayed in camp to tend to the children, to see to the care of their parents or see to the needs of the sick. Among the elderly, the 60 plus age group, males outnumbered females by a whopping 6 to 1 margin, many of them bachelors, but many of them ailing. Their wives or daughters had seen to their care.

Mitsuyo Amano had entered the Amache camp with her husband and two-year-old daughter in September, 1942. Apart from them, her only "family" was a brother and his wife, who were put into the same camp. Her parents, along with a sister, had been caught in Japan when the war broke out.

While in camp, Amano bore another daughter. Then, unexpectedly, her husband was drafted, as was her brother, and they were ordered overseas, he to Europe, her brother to the Pacific. Her sister-in-law had gone east to be with her family.

Alone, then, with virtually no place to go, she found herself in the unlikely position of being trapped in a place whose gates were now open, a place where she had been imprisoned three years before.

---

[37]P. 115.
[38]*Ibid.*, p. 616.

Meanwhile, the WRA was urging people to relocate. In early 1945, Myer visited each of the centers to announce that the camps would be closed by the end of the year.[39]

In August of the same year, the U. S. dropped atomic bombs on Hiroshima and Nagasaki. Japan formally surrendered in September.

With the revocation of the exclusion order, nothing would seem to impede the movement of Japanese Americans to their West Coast homes. But thousands of people like Mitsuyo Amano had no homes and meager funds. Finding housing outside was a major problem.

Through the WRA, Amano learned of a public housing opening in the small town of Rodeo in northern California. Although far away from her pre-exclusion home in Los Angeles, and though hostility in California was still rampant, she had little choice but to take it. So, packing up her belongings, she boarded the train for California with two other women and seven children, including her two daughters. At a stop-off in Fresno, California, they were refused service in a restaurant. "No, we didn't make a fuss," Amano says. "There were the children to consider, so we just bought some sandwiches and ate."

Amano and her family spent two years in the public housing apartments before they could establish themselves in their own house. She and her husband raised four children, all successful in their separate fields.

Heroines   It is worthwhile pausing a moment to reflect on women like the Mitsuyo Amanos and the Hannah Yasudas, as representative of hundreds of other Nisei women. Unassuming, out of the public eye, they would be astonished at being called heroines. But, in the tradition of their mothers before them, they *are* heroines in the best sense: it was largely through their strength and tenacity that the family survived, and yes, ultimately thrived.

This would seem something of a cliche, a repeat of the story of women the world over but for the fact that Nisei women traversed the perilous ground of racism and experienced the ultimate debasement of their selfhood in their imprisonment. Many women liken their experience during World War II to the ravage of rape. They had been forced to submit, and, as if they were somehow at fault, they carried around a nameless guilt that would prevent them from talking about it for years. But the healing would come, and with it, the renewal.

---

[39]The exception was Tule Lake, which had come under the jurisdiction of the Justice Department. It was closed on March 20, 1946.

CHAPTER 10
Nisei Women in Wartime Japan

*But I do think that not having a country of our own is the tragedy of us
Nisei. We try to become Americanized overnight. We do not realize the
reservoir of culture and tradition that is in our race.*
                    ---Mary Kimoto Tomita (Japan, October 17, 1946)

A surprising number of Japanese Americans (approximately 10,000) were living in Japan during the war. Some were students, some visitors, some expatriates, some young children of Issei repatriates. The ordeals that the Nisei endured in wartime Japan easily rivaled those of their counterparts in U.S. camps.

STUDENT
Mary Tomita had arrived in Japan in June, 1939 to study at the Waseda International Institute in Tokyo. She stayed with the Nagata family, a family of seven, in moderately comfortable circumstances. Some of her brightest moments were spent with the eldest son, Iza-chan (for Isaiah), a student at the Tokyo Institute of Technology, with whom she could carry on lively discussions and enjoy the sights of the city.

In a series of letters to a friend in Japan, Tomita recorded the gamut of her feelings from the joys of discovering Japan and friendships to utter despair in wartime. We present excerpts from those letters.

January 7, 1940
> He [Iza-chan] asks me why I want to go back to America. He says that Americans will always be prejudiced against the Japanese. As long as we have yellow faces, the Nisei will be discriminated against. I answer that America is my country, and I am going back to fight the prejudice. Iza-chan says that is futile. We are people without a country. In the end we will become just like the Negroes. We will intermarry and lose our identity altogether. Maybe there is some truth in what he says, but I hope not.

May 6, 1940
> I never realized before how the Japanese hate the United States and know about the racist laws discriminating against them, such as those that prohibit

owning land, becoming naturalized citizens and . . . immigration. Moreover, it is well known how racist the South is toward the Negroes. Mr. Nagata travelled all over the United States. He sat in a Jim Crow car in the South and the conductor told him to go to the white section, but he refused. The lynchings receive widespread publicity, and people do not believe that I have never witnessed one . . . .

Do you think there will be a war? Mother's letters are optimistic. She says we will not have war, and even if we should, she is sure that they will be treated fairly. She tells me to stay here and study a little longer. In one month it will be a year since I have come to Japan. I might as well stay another year since I will graduate next spring.

Tomita's decision to stay another year proved fateful. In November, 1941, Tomita's parents, alarmed at the ominous signs of war, cabled her to return on the next boat. But it was too late. By the time she got her papers in order and boarded the ship, the date was December 1. The ship she had boarded, turned and headed back to Japan after a week at sea.

In wartime Japan, Tomita found her life drastically changed. Deprived of the comfort of the Nagata home, she was now totally on her own in a country where she did not belong. Some friends now became distant, as if they saw her as a burden. Basic survival--food in her stomach, clothes on her back and escaping the horror of bomb raids-- became all-absorbing. "I was so hungry that I could only think of appeasing my hunger," Tomita said, "my basic needs, what I was going to do when my shoes wore out." At one point, she was forced to add her name to the family register in order to obtain a meager wartime ration of food.[1] This act was to become an obstacle in her efforts to return to the United States.

Shortly after the outbreak of war, Tomita moved into the home of a Mrs. Sakai, where she had earlier been a paid boarder. Now, however, helping out with housework for her keep, Tomita found circumstances vastly changed.

January 20, 1942

. . . What a slave I am. She [Mrs. Sakai] rules me with an iron hand, and I have to bow meekly to her since I have no alternative. How can she be so malicious? She gloats to me over the success of the Japanese army and navy

---

[1]Before the war, placing a Nisei's name in the family registry in Japan was tantamount to conferring dual citizenship on the individual. During wartime, however, this act could have been seen as a shift in allegiance.

as though she won these victories herself. She despises me as an American who is her helpless victim. Is it my fault that I am stranded here?

After nearly three years of unremitting struggle, she wrote in despair: "I don't know what has happened to me. I have never been so weak and sickly . . . as during the last few years. I guess I have lost incentive to live. The future looks so hopeless. War drags on interminably. Was there ever a world at peace?"

Then the "interminable" war ended. More than anything, Tomita yearned to return to the United States and her family. As an American in Japan, she had heard of the imprisonment of Japanese Americans back home, and had heard rumors that the occupation forces would "sterilize all the Jap men, just as they did the Nisei men in the concentration camps." On the other hand, she had also witnessed the racism and cruelty that pervaded wartime Japan. But because she had put her name in the family registry, her citizenship was in question.

January 20, 1946

. . . If I ever get back to America, I am determined never to live in poverty again. Having gone hungry, I never will again. And I will never be cold again--so cold that I cannot sleep all night and get up in the morning still shivering. No human being should have to go hungry and cold. I am determined that even if I have to steal or beg, I never again will be deprived of the necessities of life.

I have been thinking . . . that our morals have been made by the haves, and not by the have-nots. "Thou shalt not steal" was decreed by someone who owned property that he did not want others to take. But is it right that some people should have everything, and others nothing? I think that is a worse sin than stealing. My whole concept of right and wrong has been revised during these years of struggle and deprivation in Japan, and I hope I now have empathy with the poor and oppressed.

More than a year after war's end, Tomita was finally able to return to the United States. After raising a family, she earned three master's degrees and became a librarian. She also made good her vow to herself and to Iza-chan to combat prejudice and social injustice by becoming politically active through her church.[2]

---

[2]"Letters to Keiko" manuscript in progress, by permission of Mary Tomita; and interview for OHP.

ATOMIC BOMB SURVIVOR

Close to 700 Japanese Americans survived the atomic holocausts of August, 1945. The majority of them returned to the U.S. eventually. Of those survivors who incurred, or developed, problems, the overwhelming number were women, according to Dr. Thomas L. Robertson, associate director for research at the U.S. Public Health Hospital, where survivors were examined.

Judy Enseki, a native Californian, was attending Bakersfield Junior College, when the war broke out. Along with thousands of other Nisei, she was sent to a concentration camp. There, at the bidding of her husband and family, Enseki expatriated to Japan. She had never been there and had not wanted to go, she said, but looking on the bright side, "it got me out of camp." As fate would have it, she was in store for a greater calamity. On August 6, 1945, she was in Hiroshima:

> We heard the noise above us and I saw that mushroom cloud you see in pictures. The cloud was red like fire and there was a whirlwind around us. Somehow I managed to get my son and other relatives to an air raid shelter. We saw people with the radiation fever. They wanted water, but when they drank it they would vomit yellowish matter. After about a week, we were able to take baths. Some relatives lost their hair. We found later that it was a common side effect.

Enseki returned to the U.S. with her son after the war. Her husband had been taken prisoner of war, and she never saw him again.

Like so many other atomic bomb victims, Enseki developed anemia, a classic symptom of radiation sickness, and stress-related hypertension. In 1980, cancer invaded her body and claimed her life.[3]

Before her death, she and other female survivors of the deadly bomb, became subjects of a remarkable film, *Survivors*, made by Steven Okazaki. Along with tracing the horrors that the bomb produced, the film revealed the quandary in which Japanese American survivors found themselves: while bomb victims in Japan received free care from the government, U.S. survivors had to pay for their own. In many cases, they were loath to reveal their condition. But under the leadership of Kanji Kuramoto, himself a victim of the Hiroshima blast, the Japanese American community was mobilized to obtain treatment for survivors, gathering funds to secure the services of medical teams from Japan and working towards legislation that would provide free and adequate care in the United States.

---

[3]From Steven Okazaki's film *The Survivors*, and report by Joan Voight, The News-Herald, July 29-August 4, 1981.

IVA TOGURI: VICTIM OF A LEGEND

Like Mary Tomita, Iva Ikuko Toguri, a native Californian, had missed the last chance to return home to America before the war. In Japan, she came to serve as the embodiment of the infamous "Tokyo Rose."

According to a document published by The National Committee for Iva Toguri,[4] this Nisei's dramatic story began in July, 1941, when she was sent to Japan as the family's representative to care for her sick aunt. A graduate of UCLA, Toguri found herself ill-at-ease with the Japanese language and culture and wanted to make certain she could return to the U.S. Due to the emergency nature of her trip, Toguri had left for Japan with a State Certificate of Identification and instructions to obtain her American passport at the U.S. Consulate in Japan. Thus in August, she followed those instructions, presenting her birth certificate along with the Certificate of Identification, but, as revealed later, her application was ignored. By October, she had not yet received her passport. Nonetheless, when she got an urgent cable to return to the U.S. from her father, who had become alarmed over foreboding signs of war, Toguri tried frantically to board a ship leaving on December 1, but was thwarted by Japanese authorities because she lacked a passport.

In subsequent months, Toguri found herself caught in a maelstrom of harassment, suspicion, and privation. Because she refused to give up her American citizenship, she was hounded by the Kempeitai (Army Thought-Control Police) and the Internal Security. Officials also restricted her movements and denied her wartime food rations. Moreover, her aunt and uncle asked her to leave their home because neighbors taunted them for harboring an enemy. Without income and food rations or a supportive family, she faced a grim future. Authorities even denied her request to be imprisoned, like other Americans.

In February, 1942, Toguri applied for repatriation at the neutral Swiss legation through whose offices a Japan-U.S. repatriation agreement had been negotiated. But her application was denied again because she lacked a passport. (Later that year, she would receive notification that the last repatriation ship was leaving, and while she thought her chances good of boarding that ship, she would not be able to raise the $425 required for passage.)

---

[4]"Iva Toguri (D'Aquino)," booklet prepared by The National Committee for Iva Toguri, 2nd ed., May 1976. The Committee had been formed by a group in San Francisco and had been sanctioned by the JACL to campaign to restore Toguri's citizenship. It published this informational booklet as a starting point. The booklet and an interview with Clifford Uyeda, who spearheaded the campaign, served as the sources for the entire account presented here.

Meanwhile, a desperate search for a livelihood brought her a short stint as a typist and piano teacher at a cultural school. Then she landed a part-time job typing and monitoring English language shortwave broadcasts at the Domei News Agency. There she met Felipe J. d'Aquino, a Portuguese citizen of Japanese ancestry, who became her friend and supporter, and later, her husband.

By the middle of 1943, Toguri suffered from malnutrition and beriberi. But nursed back to health by d'Aquino, she took a second part-time job as a typist in the business office of Radio Tokyo to supplement the meager salary she was earning at Domei. There, she met and befriended three prisoners of war, all experienced radio broadcasters who had been assigned to work on the English language "Zero Hour" program since March of that year.

In November, Japanese authorities decided to add a female voice to the "Zero Hour" program. The POWs persuaded the Japanese to select Iva Toguri. [They] needed a trustworthy companion because they were covertly burlesquing the Japanese program intent. When informed of her new duties, Iva Toguri refused. She was then ordered to broadcast by Japanese authorities and was reminded she had "no choice" in the matter since she was an enemy alien without any rights. Refusal in militaristic wartime Japan usually resulted in severe punishment, including starvation, beatings, even execution. Although she was not explicitly threatened with bodily harm, she was well aware of what happened to others who had refused and was conscious of the non-direct manner in which the Japanese spoke. Moreover, Major Cousens [one of the captives] took her aside, confided their scheme, and assured her that she would not harm and might possibly help the American war effort. Cousens' confidence won her over, and she read her first POW-written script over the air on November 10 or 11, 1943.

In January 1944, Iva Toguri found full-time employment at the Danish legation, and continued to report to Radio Tokyo to host a program of music, humor, nostalgia, and news. It is important to note that the female voice heard on "Zero Hour" was not always hers: at least thirteen other English-speaking women of various nationalities, including American, replaced her in her frequent absences.

A series of unfortunate events thereafter led to Toguri's downfall as the infamous "Tokyo Rose." But some background information is essential to an understanding of this climactic event.

At the outset of hostilities in 1941, English language programs had drifted over the airwaves, featuring women's voices, the latest American pop music, war news and propaganda. The collective voices had become distilled into a single entity by servicemen and referred to as

"Tokyo Rose." The propaganda was so laughingly obvious that Navy Director of Welfare, Captain T.J. O'Brien, issued a tongue-in-cheek citation to this entity for "meritorious service contributing greatly to the morale of the U.S. Armed Forces in the Pacific . . . by persistently entertaining them during those long nights in fox-holes and on aboard ship, by bringing them excellent state-side music, laughter and news about home." However facetious the comment, it signified that a sizable number of servicemen listened to the broadcasts.

By the end of the war, "Tokyo Rose" had grown larger than life. Now, American newshounds converged on Japan, frantically tracking her down. Through a series of turns, involving media rivalry, a newspaperman at *Domei* who more or less pointed the pursuers toward Toguri, and her own naivete (considering herself a heroine of sorts, she gave interviews and autographs freely), Toguri virtually *became* "Tokyo Rose."

In September, she was interviewed by two writers, Harry Brundidge and Clark Lee, who submitted the manuscript to *Cosmopolitan*. The editors rejected it, declaring that it glorified a traitor. A few days later, Toguri was arrested, then inexplicably released the next day. Investigators later suspected that Brundidge and Lee had engineered the arrest to prevent other journalists from interviewing her.

> She was rearrested on October 17 [1945] and held at a Yokohama prison for one month; then she was transferred to Sugamo Prison in Tokyo, where she remained for another eleven months.[5] During her 12 months imprisonment, she was never informed of the charges against her, was denied legal counsel, was denied a speedy trial, and was prohibited from sending or receiving mail. She was held incommunicado for over two months until a Christmas visit from her husband was allowed.

When Toguri was released after U.S. government authorities found insufficient evidence to bring charges, she settled in Tokyo with her husband and became pregnant in 1947, satisfied that her ordeal was over.

But it was not. Anxious for her child to be born an American citizen, and longing to see her family, Toguri applied once again for a passport to the United States. The government, then, for reasons of its own, issued a statement to the press that "Tokyo Rose" had applied to return. As might be expected, that opened up a Pandora's box of

---

[5]Sugamo was the prison in which Japanese leaders accused of war crimes had been confined. Prime Minister Tojo and six other high officials were executed there in 1948.

protest from right-wing organizations as well as powerful voices like that of Walter Winchell. Her child died at birth amidst this turmoil.

On shaky grounds, Iva Toguri was again arrested on August 26, 1948 and charged with treason. Brought the United States, she was indicted by a grand jury, tried and convicted on what must now surely be regarded as equivocal evidence and unfortunate timing, heavily weighted in favor of the prosecution. She was convicted on one count out of eight "overt acts . . . with treasonable intent" with which she had been charged, pronounced guilty for allegedly reading over the air, shortly after the Battle of Leyte Gulf, the words: "Orphans of the Pacific. You really are orphans now. How will you get home, now that all your ships are sunk?"

The Committee's comment on the conviction: "The incongruous fact is that the Battle of Leyte Gulf was a resounding victory for the United states, and it is difficult to imagine how American troops could have been demoralized by such words. If anything, it must have sounded like hilarious comedy."

After the trial, Toguri's husband, who had attended the trial, was sent back to occupied Japan, after signing a statement that he would never try to enter the United States.

Iva Toguri ended up serving six years and two months in the Alderson Federal Reformatory for Women.

Meanwhile, the noted civil rights attorney Wayne M. Collins, who, together with Theodore Tamba and George Olshausen, had represented Toguri without fee at her trial, convinced of her innocence, filed petitions for executive clemency (pardons) for her, in 1954 and 1968, but their petitions went unanswered.

Then in 1974, under the auspices of the JACL, the National Committee launched an informational campaign and enlisted support from some legislators to secure the pardon for Toguri. With that public support, attorney Wayne Collins, son of one of the late attorney, who had earlier represented Toguri, filed a formal request for pardon. On January 19, 1977, President Ford granted full pardon to Iva Toguri d'Aquino.

She presently lives quietly in Chicago, where she operates a gift store, once owned by her father.

The stories of women like those presented here, strikingly point up the untenable position in which Nisei found themselves in wartime: "aliens" in their own country, aliens in the land of their ancestors.

CHAPTER 11

After the War: The Final Move

The horror-filled war between the United States and Japan ended on September 2, 1945 with Japan's formal surrender. By the end of the same year, all permanent detention camps, with the exception of Tule Lake, were closed.[1] Evacuees had dispersed largely in urban centers throughout the United States.

Return to the West Coast   The majority of these sojourners, along with those from the camps, made their way back to the West Coast, beginning with a trickle in 1945. By 1949, over 57,000 persons had already returned to California, Oregon and Washington.[2]

Because of the critical housing shortage on the West Coast, returnees moved into temporary quarters like tents, public housing, hostels, and make-shift quarters. One woman reported living in a two-bedroom house in Los Angeles which held thirteen relatives, all told. "It's hard for me to remember how we managed, especially with three small children and one baby in the house . . . and only one bathroom, " she said. "But after camp, I guess you could take anything."

Housing was not the only problem. The returnees faced hostility and outright violence. In Placer County, California, for example, terrorists tried to scare off a returning evacuee by attempting to dynamite and burn his fruit packing shed. About thirty other incidents occurred, mostly shots fired into the homes of returnees.[3] Harassment, such as signs announcing 'No Japs allowed, no Japs welcome,' was widespread. Retailers attempted to discourage evacuees from returning or tried to drive them out by refusing them goods and services.

But again, a core of compassionate, humanitarian souls, which has always been present in America to counter destructive forces, presented themselves to aid the returnees. Mobilized by the WRA,

---

[1]Tule Lake closed on March 26, 1946, after Wayne Collins, indefatigable friend of the Nisei, engineered the release of thousands of renunciants on grounds that their decisions to expatriate to Japan were not free acts.

[2]*People in Motion*, p. 1

[3]Myer, p. 198.

groups such as the Council of Civic Unity, numerous churches, civic organizations and individuals denounced racist activities, and helped those who were returning by locating housing and jobs.

1945-1950

Circumstances had changed substantially for the Nisei woman upon her return. At the time of exclusion, she had been in her late teens, single, and, as one woman put it, "flighty." Now, three years later, she was apt to be married, or would be soon, anxious to establish her own household. Or, she might even have gained a college education.[4]

Although the Nisei woman would likely deny it then, her experience in exile had been devastating to her sense of self. She refused to discuss it, to dwell on it, wanting above all to get on with her life. This attitude became even more resolute when children began to arrive.

Post-War Employment   Note was made earlier of the shifting relationships between Nisei and Issei in camp. Now those changes become increasingly fixed: more often than not, Nisei were making the major decisions in the household: where to live, how the family would subsist and the management of income. While the number of Issei and Nisei men in the work force was about equal immediately upon their return, Issei numbers dwindled gradually. And many Issei, in their late fifties or sixties, never reestablished themselves in their pre-war occupations. Some, like farmers and owners of businesses, who had the most before the war, also lost most:

> With their financial reserves gone or depleted by the time they were released, many had little or no capital with which to reestablish independent enterprise, particularly with the postwar rise in prices. Most were forced to accept whatever jobs they could find, often menial; others went into businesses that required little start-up capital, such as contract gardening.[5]

Farm ownership by the Japanese had been reduced to about one fourth of its prewar holdings. The future of Japanese agriculture on the west coast would be in the hands of the Nisei because the Issei were fast

---

[4]*People in Motion*, p. 105, notes that no accurate estimate of college-educated Nisei who had returned to the formerly excluded area had been made, but if those in Los Angeles were any measure, the number was "not very large."

[5]CWRIC, p. 296.

becoming of advanced age and lacked knowledge of modern technology, said an Interior Department report.[6]
It also found that

> The people [Japanese Americans on the the West Coast] are working excessively hard . . . . Everything is secondary to work. The people are driven by insecurity and a sense of urgency. They must make up their losses, prepare for future uncertainties, and get ready to take advantage of opportunities that may come along. And these things must be done now while jobs are abundant and wages high.

In Los Angeles, said the same report, more than 3,000 gardeners earned from $400 to $600 a month, compared to approximately 2,000 who averaged $120 a month before the war. Professionals, like doctors, lawyers, dentists and optometrists, set up practices and thrived, serving the Japanese population as well as the wider community. But by far the greatest number (approximately 5,000 Nisei and Issei owners and employers) worked in the produce markets controlled by Japanese, scattered throughout Los Angeles County. Patronage came largely from the general community.[7]

Dry cleaning shops, food stores, hotels, florists and nurseries sprang up as soon as the Japanese could muster the start-up money.

The economy in the Japanese community had shifted from one that was basically controlled by the community itself to one that depended on employment to be found in the general community, as earlier noted. Another contrast between pre-war and post-war economic patterns was the sharply increased number of Japanese American women who now joined the work force. While Nisei men were still finding discrimination in white collar work, Nisei women were in great demand. In Seattle, for example, young women employed as typists, stenographers, and office clerks were now reportedly making more than they ever did before at rates between $150 to $185 per month. Large numbers of them took various civil service positions, but in addition several were employed by private businesses."[8]

Nisei women were also being sought as garment factory workers and as domestics. Employment agencies often hesitated to place Nisei as domestics, however, aware that most of them viewed the work as temporary. One employment agency manager's remarked,

---

[6]*People in Motion*, p. 70.

[7]Pp. 94, 83, 99.

[8]*Ibid.*, p. 128.

The Issei and Kibei girls may be fitted [for domestic work], but the Nisei, brought up in this country where they are independent, don't last. The Englishman can serve as a butler, the German can serve as a house-woman and be happy because of their training. But anyone brought up in this country just can't fit into that type of work. So even if there are good domestic jobs open, I don't place the Nisei.[9]

College-educated women had not yet returned to the West Coast in great numbers, but those who were college-trained began to find employment as teachers, social workers and executive secretaries, work that had previously been unavailable to them.

Marriage   Typically, the Nisei woman was married by 1950. Unlike her mother, she had most likely chosen her mate, although older Nisei women (born before 1920) often accepted arranged marriages.

The overwhelming majority married Nisei men. For one thing, many states, including California, still had anti-miscegenation laws on the books in 1948, prohibiting marriages between whites and Asians.[10] But importantly, for Nisei, marriage within their own race was no doubt also a consequence of tradition as well as having been largely excluded from social interaction with the outer society. However, attesting to rapidly changing attitudes both within and outside the Japaneseo community, a few interracial marriages did occur during this period.

The fact that all Nisei were "in the same boat" most of the time suggests that socio-economic class was not a significant consideration in marriage. But there are indications that one who attended college, more often than not, married someone who had had some college experience. However, it appears that the factor most apt to spark romance and marriage was propinquity: living in the same neighborhood, working at the same same place, or going to the same school.

These marriages usually lasted but, as will be discussed in a later chapter, there is considerable range of opinion as to how satisfying they were.

Interracial Marriage   However rare, interracial marriages did occur.

Elaine Ishikawa Hayes married Ralph Hayes, an African American in 1950 in Seattle. Hayes had met her husband in Chicago while both

---

[9]*Ibid.*

[10]Sixteen states still had anti-miscegenation laws in effect as late as 1967: Alabama, Arkansas, Delaware, Florida, Georgia, Kentucky, Louisiana, Mississippi, Missouri, North Carolina, Oklahoma, South Carolina, Tennessee, Texas, Virginia, and West Virginia.

were working for agencies that were spearheading studies and practices in the burgeoning field of race relations.   She had relocated to Milwaukee to attend college, then moved on to Chicago.

Hayes describes her successful marriage as being relatively free of the kind of problems that an interracial marriage might have aroused at that particular time:

> My mother was one of those unusual Issei women. She had taken over my father's insurance business when he became ill in 1935, which required that she learn to drive a car [most Issei women never learned to drive], and that she learn English, particularly the nomenclature of the insurance business. She also made it a point to attend some non-Japanese functions. So, because she had this rather broad perspective of the world, she had no problem with Ralph. And Ralph's family was great: they had no problem with me.

Asked if her mother was not sensitive to "what the neighbors might think," as other Issei would likely be, Hayes laughingly recalled that her mother had once confided to her that a friend had asked rather jealously, "Do you think a black person is better than my son?"

Besides supportive families, the Hayeses moved about in what could be called a liberal environment, their social lives more or less dictated by their professional lives. She had worked for the American Friends Service Committee, the University District Branch of the YMCA and the Family Life Department of the Seattle Public Schools. Later, she became director of the Head Start Child Care program, then worked for the Model Cities program. She retired in 1986 after ten years of implementing health services for childcare through Seattle-King County Public Health.

Her husband gained attention as one of the few African Americans to be hired as a teacher in the Seattle high school system in 1955. Having earned his master's degree in political science, he taught history for thirty years. Now retired, he has written a book on the history of African American pioneers in Washington state and continues work on a three-volume history and research on Blacks in the Pacific Northwest.

The Hayeses raised four children, one of whom married a native Japanese woman and travels to Japan in connection with his work in a lumber-exporting business. "I think they all have a universal outlook," said Hayes, "and pretty much fit in comfortably wherever they choose."

She herself attends Japanese American functions on occasion and counts many Nisei among her close friends. "Marrying Ralph," she says, "gave me insight into two worlds, for which I am grateful. I think we Asians need to broaden our horizons. We need to be much more active in the area of human rights, not just for ourselves, but for everyone. And we need to get out of social self-segregation, now that most of us are socio-economically able to do so."

Motherhood   Typically, women stayed at home until their children reached their teens, often until they finished high school. As might be expected, education retained a revered place in the scheme of Nisei values. This motivated many women to take a giant leap and cross into the unexplored area of community service, taking part in PTA, Scouts and Camp Fire Girls, and other organizations which related to the welfare of their children. Said one Nisei woman, speaking of her office as Secretary of the PTA. "I have to laugh about it when I look back. But my only experience at doing anything like that was at church. So I used to write the minutes over and over again to make sure they were right. I was always nervous when I had to read them in front of all those people."

Nisei mothers tended to be more permissive in their child-rearing than their mothers had been. Says Harry Kitano: "The Issei view of child rearing is more 'old fashioned'--children are viewed as dependent, quiet, and unequal, and to be raised with strictness. In contrast, the Nisei view is more 'modern' and more American--children are viewed as comrades with a subsequent sharing of experiences; they are encouraged to ask questions, and they are permitted a higher degree of sexual exploration."[11]   Nisei family activities also tended to be more child-centered.

Apart from cultural predilection, the mood of the whole population had moved towards more liberal child-rearing methods since the publication of Dr. Benjamin Spock's seminal work *The Book of Baby and Child Care* in 1946. The views advanced in the book exerted enormous influence on Nisei parents, who were anxious that their children be brought up the "American way."

Housing   Practicing the frugality their parents had taught them, Nisei began buying their own houses largely in depressed and middle-class neighborhoods. For most, it would be a first move. Successive moves would see them buying "up," until perhaps they were in their fifties, when most would secure for themselves a comfortable, but not luxurious home.

While the Supreme Court had ruled in 1948 that race-restrictive housing covenants were unenforceable, many deeds did contain those restrictions. Real estate agents tacitly abided by those restrictions and

[11]*Japanese Americans*, p. 110.

more often than not would only show houses to minorities in areas that were known to be "open." Some Nisei purposely avoided moving into so-called restricted neighborhoods. They wanted to feel comfortable in their homes and were reluctant to expose their children to racial taunts or isolation.

One woman described her house-hunting experience in 1949:

> We wanted a place in San Leandro [California] to be close to my husband's work, and when we tried to rent, the real estate agent could only show us one house that we could rent, and it was a dump. Then, he showed us houses in a couple of areas where several Japanese had already bought, but we couldn't find a house that we liked.
>
> Then, we happened to see a "For Sale" sign on a little stucco house that seemed like something we could afford. The owner was selling the house himself, so we went there with our two small kids, after phoning him. When he saw us, I think he was really surprised that we were Japanese. Our name sounds Italian to some hakujin. Then he kind of stammered something about this thing on the deed. We didn't know about such things then, but it turned out to be that the deed barred the owner from selling the house to anybody who wasn't white. But he was a very nice man and he showed us around the place anyway. Then, at one point, he looked at us and the kids and said, "Listen, I'm not supposed to sell this house to you. It's in a restricted neighborhood, and the neighbors are liable to raise hell, but if you don't care, I don't either!" And he sold the house to us.[12]

Why did they move into the house? For one thing, she said, they were just beginning to feel that they ought to be able to choose where they wanted to live. "But the flip side of that is," she said, "that the children were sometimes called names like 'Japs' or 'Chinks' at school. I guess all Asian children went through something like that, but when you're the only ones in the school, it's hard."

Total integration in housing, however, was still a long time coming. Despite adequate incomes, many Japanese Americans and other minorities could not buy or rent housing freely on the open market as late as in the sixties. Real estate agencies often colluded with homeowners to create ghetto neighborhoods as well as large zones designated as "restricted." In California, a practice known as "block-busting" paid handsome profits for some owners and realtors. Here, a minority family moved into an all-white neighborhood, (either by chance or with the help of a real estate agent). Real estate agents then swooped into the area and persuaded homeowners to sell, forecasting

---

[12]Personal interview.

calamity to the value of their homes with the invasion of non-whites into the neighborhood. Homeowners would then sell at inflated prices to minorities anxious to buy in a "good" neighborhood. The rapid turnover of homes in this scheme reaped whopping benefits to all but the buyer.

Alien Land Law Repealed   Meanwhile, California's alien land law, which prohibited Asian aliens from owning land, was finally ruled "untenable and unenforceable" in 1948. But because the issue remained on the statute books, it was put to the test of voters. In 1956, Proposition 15 appeared on the California ballot to strengthen the existing alien land law and was roundly defeated. "The JACL's Anti-Discrimination Committee spearheaded the attack against Proposition 15," wrote Bill Hosokawa, "and that effort marked the successful beginning of effective political involvement by the *Nisei*."[13]

In Washington state, alien land laws were not repealed until a decade later.

1950-1970

Shifting Temper of the Nation   Directly after the war, the role of the Federal Government had changed from one of relative non-interference in the area of civil rights to one of active involvement. President Harry S. Truman had issued executive orders ending segregation in the armed forces and barring discrimination in federal employment and work done under government contract. In rapid succession, such civil rights triumphs as the *Brown v. Board of Education* decision handed down by the Supreme Court in 1954,[14] and the successful year-long boycott of buses in Montgomery, Alabama in 1955 to prohibit segregation on buses.[15] took place, followed by the integration of the Little Rock schools in 1958. Meanwhile, a cluster of civil rights legislation was enacted beginning in 1957. For the first time, a Civil Rights Commission was created to recommend Federal Government action in the fields of voting, education and housing.

African Americans thrust themselves in the front lines of this civil-rights revolution to crush the barriers which had long separated whites from non-whites, the haves from the have-nots. They marched through the streets, staged sit-ins, forced themselves into segregated schools,

---

[13]*Nisei*, P.45.

[14]The decision held that in the field of public education the doctrine of "separate but equal" had no place and that separate educational facilities were inherently unequal.

[15]The boycott was ignited by Rosa Sparks, a seamstress, who refused to give up her seat to a white man and was arrested and fined $10.

often at risk to their lives. Indeed, it might be said that this milestone in American history was carried on the backs of black Americans.

Women Participate in Politics   Buoyed by the shifting tide of the nation's temper, Japanese Americans decided to grapple with the issue of citizenship for the Issei, which had long galled their sense of justice. Thus in 1950, JACL launched a campaign to eliminate race as a consideration for naturalization. Headed by the indefatigable Mike Masaoka, the campaign traversed a tangled course, but culminated in the passage of the Walter-McCarran Immigration and Naturalization Act of 1952. The Act, passed over the veto of President Truman,[16] not only entitled the Issei to become naturalized citizens, but granted token immigration quotas to Japan and other Asian nations.

Not everyone was happy with the Act. Apart from the token quota provision, it included parts of Title II of the 1950 Internal Security Act, which had been promulgated during the fierce, anti-communist McCarthy era. Among other things, Title II authorized, without proof, the detention of persons believed to be engaged in "acts of espionage or sabotage" and provided for detention camps to hold them. In effect, it validated the wholesale incarceration of Japanese Americans.

Anxious to prevent a repeat of such an egregious violation of human rights, the Nisei mounted a campaign to repeal Title II of the Act. In the early 1970's, they succeeded.

Nisei women, just beginning to feel their way into the political arena, played an integral part in the campaign, disseminating information, leading workshops and writing letters to legislators.

---

[16]Truman vetoed the act because he felt it contained flaws, one being the quota system it prescribed which weighed heavily in favor of some European nations.

ABOVE: Student Relocation Council office, Philadelphia, January 1944. *National Archives.*

BELOW:Working at Home Public Market, Denver, March 2, 1945. *Photo by Bud Aoyama. National Archives.*

CHAPTER 12

Widening Horizons

People! Listen! This alone you must believe
All of the sleeping women
Will awake now and move!
                    ---Yosano Akiko (1911)

RIGHTS FOR WOMEN: THE 1970'S and 1980'S

One of the more significant effects of the civil-rights movement of the 1960s was its affirmation of the validity and importance of different cultures.   African-American, Asian American and Chicano studies proliferated in the colleges. Symbolic of this pride, African Americans donned dashikis, sported "afro" hair-styles and traveled to Africa for the first time. Japanese Americans began studying the Japanese language again and even invited non-Japanese to their homes for a meal to be eaten with chopsticks.

Not surprisingly, the revolution in civil rights also infused new vigor into the struggle for women's rights.   New women's rights organizations had mushroomed in the 1960s, the most prominent among them, The National Organization of Women, founded by writer Betty Friedan. On the 50th anniversary of winning the right to vote, women worked for the passage of the Equal Rights Amendment in 1970, which provided that "equality under the law shall not be denied or abridged by the United States or by any state on account of sex." Although the Amendment did not pass, the effort had galvanized the troops nation-wide. Women fought institutionalized sexism, demanding equal job opportunities and equal pay; some women's groups even advanced the radical notion of ending the practice of monogamous marriages. Others struggled for liberalized abortion laws.

In the domiciles around the country, women also reassessed their roles vis-a-vis their spouses, and concluded that the unequal load they carried needed remedy. They, too, needed the freedom to develop their careers, or any other aspirations, they asserted. But transformation was slow; the pattern of male privilege was not to be uprooted overnight.

Nisei Women and "Liberation"   If women in the society-at-large had difficulty advancing their program of liberation, Nisei women found it doubly hard. Like their mothers, they had found a large measure of contentment in their roles of wife and mother. To a large extent, too, they had lived for, and through, their children.   Their children's successes or failures became their own.

But as the Bob Dylan ballad proclaimed "the times they are a-changin'," and the militant mood of women in the society resonated, if faintly, in Nisei households. Nisei women were beginning to wonder if they weren't missing something. When their children were married and gone, would it be enough for them to sit back and bask in their children's successes as their mothers had done?

The answer, at least for many women, was no. Like Ibsen's Nora Helmer, they began to look at themselves in relation to society in a "different light," an emerging realization that being a wife and a mother was not enough. While those were "sacred duties," they also had a duty to themselves. They lived in a different world than did their mothers, one in which, if they were to participate as equals, they needed to seek equality. They would continue to support their children in every way, but they also recognized the necessity to expand their horizons.

Moreover, now that their children were in school, Nisei women had joined the work force by the thousands, primarily to finance their children's college expenses, but also to put their own training and talents to use. An unprecedented range of occupations had opened up to them since the civil-rights movement.   Women found work as stenographers, bookkeepers, teachers, social workers, department store clerks, dental hygienists, and in all manner of employment that had been previously denied them. This exposure to the workplace, the locus which had driven the struggle for women's rights in many ways, energized women's search for an ever more satisfying sense of selfhood, a desire to exploit their talents and to explore their inner selves.

But working outside, added to the myriad responsibilities of a household, provided little time and energy to pursue personal interests. This often caused strain in their marital relationships.

In an interesting study, Teri L. Scott sought to discover how Japanese American women handled dual careers in the household and how, if in any way, "Japaneseness" affected their attitudes and behavior. Although her sample was not large, the study yielded important insights.[1]

---

[1]"Japaneseness: How Does It Affect Dual Career Mothers?" Unpublished, 1978. Scott based her study on questionnaires and in-depth interviews of thirteen professional women

Scott found that most women married to Japanese American men had not always worked, while most of those married to Caucasians had. "This suggests," she says, "that the closer one remains to Japanese culture, vis-a-vis spouse, the more likely one is to maintain a certain degree of traditionalism in relation to the concept that the women's place is in the home . . ."

Are the roles of wife and mother of primary importance? "Yes," answered both the Japanese women, not surprisingly, while slightly more than half of the Japanese American women agreed. Nearly all agreed that their primary obligation was to their families. Both Japanese women agreed that the children were *their* primary responsibility and 70% of the Japanese Americans also agreed. As for feelings of familial obligation toward the husband's family, 80% of women married to Caucasians did not feel any such obligation, while 71% of those married to Japanese Americans did.

The most noteworthy responses came with the question of whether family interests should take priority over individual fulfillment: 82% of the Japanese American women remained neutral, or disagreed, and only two women agreed. Along with this, only two women agreed that the husband should act as the head of the household.

These findings lend credence to some evidence that, while women's feelings regarding their obligation to their children and families remained strong, it was not at all clear how much energy they were willing to devote to them at the expense of their own growth and fulfillment. It also suggests that they were questing for equality on the domestic front. This departed significantly from that of their mothers, who had been willing to sacrifice all and no doubt caused tension in the marriage.

For, not surprisingly, when the radical notion arose in the 1970s that husbands should share in the work of the household, Nisei men hardly budged. While some tended to share more of the work if the spouse brought income to the household, gender roles remained largely defined along traditional lines of inside/outside work. A glimpse at a large family gathering would still find the women doing the cooking, serving and cleaning up afterwards. As part of this "inside work" telephone calls had been made, the shopping done, the house cleaned. The husband, meanwhile, had mowed the lawn, and now, with the other

---

who were mothers: two Japanese, seven Nisei, one Sansei, one Nisei-Sansei. Five were married to white Americans, one to a Chinese American, and the remaining seven married to Japanese American men. Because the sampling was purposive, the researcher's findings might have been skewed toward a more assertive female than was likely to be found in a random sampling of Japanese American women.

men, entertained himself watching a game on television. Or, he engaged in some backyard sport with the children outside. He might also cook the entree on the barbecue, if that were on the menu. This pattern of rigidly demarcated, outside/inside work persisted until the men retired from their jobs, typically in the 1980s. At that time, many, but by no means, the majority, of men began to share household responsibilities more or less equally.

In the late 1970s, often an Issei, most likely the elderly, widowed Issei mother, came to live in the Nisei home. "The Nisei uniformly agree that co-residence with one's parents after marriage is a burden to be avoided if possible," wrote anthropologist Sylvia Junko Yanagisako. In spite of that, she states, certain circumstances required it. If, for instance, parents could not be supported in a separate household, or if parents required physical care. "Few Nisei place elderly parents in nursing homes or other institutionalized care centers," says Yanagisako, "if they can care for them at home, especially since those available are managed by Whites and are considered "foreign" environments for their parents.[2]

In the event of illness or prolonged debilitation of the Issei, the care-taking was usually done by the daughter or daughter-in-law, the daughter being preferred, following the tradition of the Japanese household.

In short, while Nisei women were fulfilling many of the traditional expectations, they were also in a state of transition, easing out of some of the constraining aspects of the traditional mold.

Nisei Women in the Public Arena   During the latter half of the 1970s, Nisei women began to exercise increasing independence, what with their children moving out and with the net income of the household rising. They often enrolled in classes for self-improvement or to learn the arts typically associated with the Japanese. Many plunged into volunteer work, particularly in the Senior Centers, which burgeoned in the latter half of the 1970s. Scores of women began to travel with their spouses, with female friends, or alone. One woman recalls that on her first trip to Japan, she and four other women travelled without their husbands. "We had a lot of fun," she remarks. "And it taught me a lot about handling tickets, baggage and tips. I stopped being intimidated by those things after that."

Nisei women took tentative steps into the political arena too. Already, some had taken part in effecting the repeal of Title II of the

---

[2]"Two Processes of Change in Japanese-American Kinship" *Journal of Anthropological Research*, V. 31, (1975), p. 210.

Internal Security Act. A few had been active roles in the protest against the Vietnam War in the late 1960s. They marched alongside their daughters and sons and opened their pocketbooks for the cause.

This growing consciousness of their responsibilities as members of the society-at-large, motivated numerous women to walk the streets for political candidates, local and national, and to support issues, such as housing laws, nuclear disarmament and planned parenthood.

But they themselves did not generally run for political office (outside of school boards and the like, and Japanese American organizations). Their past experiences and their present ages (most were in the fifties and sixties) bore against it. A notable exception was Patsy Takemoto Mink of Hawaii, the first Nisei woman to be elected to the U. S. House of Representatives in 1964, just five years after Hawaii became the fiftieth state. Later, from the same state, Jean Sakako King and Patricia F. Saiki also secured legislative offices.

The decade of the 1980s had been pronounced "the decade of women in politics" by no less than the redoubtable Dan Rather of CBS. While Nisei women, as a rule, were not visible in the politcal arena in any notable degree, they began to to assert themselves in large numbers in Japanese American organizations, especially the JACL.

Nisei Women and JACL   As a microcosm of middle-class Japanese American society, the JACL had always been top-heavy with males formulating policy and occupying the leadership chairs. Women had been relegated to carrying out their decisions, or pouring tea, both literally and figuratively.

But by now, JACL had become a nationally recognized civil rights organization, having successfully propelled substantial pieces of legislation through Congress including the Walter-McCarran Immigration and Naturalization Act. And by the end of the 1980s, it had taken on a different configuration, having been prodded by a few women and having been infused with new blood, participation by younger, more liberal-minded Sansei. Numerous females as well as Sansei attained key positions within the organization. In the northern California district, for example, Mollie Fujioka became the first woman to assume the position of governor, after having served as her chapter's first female president. Countless women were seated as presidents of their local chapters. The Golden Gate Chapter in California even elected an all-woman list of officers.

This impressive influx of women taking active part in the organization proved to be propitious, for in the most important political task the JACL had set for itself, women were to play an integral part. That task would be the campaign for redress from the government for abrogating the constitutional rights of Japanese Americans during World War II.

THE REDRESS MOVEMENT

The JACL had taken the first step towards redress right on the heels of the civil rights movement. Spearheaded by the late Edison Uno, a progressive visionary, the JACL adopted its first resolution in 1970 to seek congressional legislation to compensate all former internees. Not much action resulted. There followed three more resolutions in 1972, 1974 and 1976, each one more specific in its demands and strategy for action.

In the meantime, Michi Weglyn's remarkable book *Years of Infamy* had appeared on the scene in 1976. Painstakingly researched, utilizing primary documents, the work compellingly pointed up government callousness and downright deceit in the imprisonment of the Japanese. Often acclaimed as the best work to tell the story of this shameful period in history, it was also seen as an instrument to promote "a decent retribution . . . to the heirs of those made to suffer."[3]   The work no doubt gave substantial impetus to the movement for redress and contributed toward its ultimate passage.

In 1978, JACL became more specific and passed a resolution to seek $25,000 compensation for each person incarcerated. With that, they formulated a strategy to achieve it. It would be ten years almost to the day before the Redress Bill, by then called the Civil Liberties Act of 1988, would reach President Ronald Reagan's desk to be signed.

Perhaps the event that served more than anything else to galvanize the Japanese American population for this campaign was the government Commission hearings. At the suggestion of Senator Daniel Inouye of Hawaii, JACL had changed its legislative strategy from aiming directly for redress to support for a government study commission that would investigate the facts of the internment and recommend appropriate remedies. John Tateishi, then chairperson of JACL's National Committee for Redress, articulated the reason for the JACL's new strategy: ". . . any direct approach [for redress] would not stand the chance of seeing the light of day. Any type of legislation other than the commission . . . would never get beyond some sub-committee or committee of Congress."[4]

---

[3]Testimony, Dr. William Petersen, Robert Lazarus Professor Social Demography, Ohio State University.

[4]Quoted in William Minoru Hohri, *Repairing America*, (Washington State University Press 1984), p. 45 .

The Commission   The idea of a study commission was apparently amenable to Congress, for even Senator S. I. Hayakawa of California, an adamant opponent of redress, endorsed the idea. Thus a commission was established in 1980 when President Jimmy Carter signed the bill to create the Commission on Wartime Relocation and Internment of Civilians (CWRIC).[5] The Commission held 20 days of hearings in sites across the country, particularly on the West Coast. Over 750 former internees gave testimony, some speaking for the first time about their camp experience.

"It's important to understand," said a member of a team videotaping the testimonies of Jewish survivors of concentration camps, "that giving testimony is not a healing process. It hurts. Survivors are doing a service for us, not we for them." Indeed, rather than confer catharsis and release to the testifiers at the Commission hearing, the act of giving testimony appeared to rekindle bitter memories and fire the participants' determination to require that the government tender an apology and monetary redress so that such an injustice might never happen again. In the process, they hoped that the public would become more than perfunctorily informed of this wretched event in American history.

Hundreds of women testified. Many of their testimonies have already been cited in previous chapters. But, attesting to how the act of testifying affected them, Tsuyako Sox Kitashima reported that her growth as an activist and community volunteer began at the hearings.

> I really didn't know the impact of internment until I went to the hearing and saw the number of people in attendance. I saw a group of students with their notebooks so intent on learning about this . . . . It made me very emotional . . . And seeing that commission of nine well-qualified people sitting up there listening to our stories . . . I got really generated after I was there.[6]

The Commission issued its findings in 1982, concluding, among other things, that

> The promulgation of Executive Order 9066 was not justified by military necessity, and the decisions which followed from it--detention, ending

---

[5]Serving on the Commission were Joan Bernstein (chairperson), former Senators Edward Brooke and Hugh Mitchell, Representative Daniel Lundgren, former Supreme Court Justice Arthur Goldberg, Judge William Marutani, Arthur Flemming, Father Robert F. Drinan and Father Ismael Gromoff.

[6]*Asian Week*, June 9, 1989, p. 9.

detention and ending exclusion--were not driven by analysis of military conditions. The broad historical causes which shaped these decisions were race prejudice, war hysteria and a failure of political leadership.

Civil Liberties Act of 1988   A Redress Bill, then, was first introduced in the House of Representatives by Majority Leader Jim Wright and in the Senate by Senator Spark Matsunaga in 1983. But it was not until 1988 that the bill was finally signed into law, after years of lobbying, letter-writing and disseminating information.   The law required payment of $20,000 to eligible Japanese Americans interned during World War II, as had been recommended by the CWRIC.   In addition, the government would acknowledge, and apologize for, the fundamental injustice of the evacuation, relocation, and internment and establish a fund for a public educational program to prevent the recurrence of any similar event in the future.

Japanese Americans were jubilant.   Though the payment could never compensate for their three years in exile and the scars that the incarceration had inflicted on their psyches, as a symbolic act, it gave them a sense of redemption, and an affirmation of their faith in America's system of justice.

NCJAR   The triumph had not been achieved by JACL alone. In 1979, the National Council for Japanese American Redress (NCJAR) had been formed under the leadership of William Hohri. Skeptical of the study-commission route the JACL had taken, which seemed to them a temporizing method of gaining redress objectives, the group decided to mount a separate campaign for direct redress legislation.   It thus provided an alternative to JACL through which hundreds of Japanese Americans could support a drive for redress.

The NCJAR began its offensive by taking the legislative route, but veered mid-course to attempt remedy through the courts. In 1983, it filed a class action suit against the United States. As Hohri, NCJAR's national chairperson put it:

> For the first time in the history of mass exclusion and detention of Japanese-Americans and their aftermath, the defendant is identified and the plaintiffs defined. For the first time in this history, we, the plaintiffs, spell out our injuries from our perspective, as the injured parties.[7]

It was a bold move, its intentions admirable. In the end, however, the suit was dismissed. But the protracted ten-year struggle of the

---

[7]*Repairing America*, p. 192.

group had produced vital new information and had engaged the interest and involvement of many who would never have otherwise participated in this historic crusade.

NCRR   Another group concerned with the issue of redress was the National Coalition for Redress and Reparations (NCRR). Formed in 1980 largely by Sansei, the organization put emphasis on educating the public about the removal and imprisonment. They were primarily responsible for instituting the Day of Remembrance in or around February 19th, a day when Americans could reflect upon the infamous order for removal and take renewed vows to help protect the rights of all citizens.[8] The NCRR sponsors candlelight ceremonies and marches on that memorial day.

The organization also sent representatives to Washington to lobby for redress and organized a successful campaign to obtain redress from Alameda County, California for workers who had been fired shortly after Pearl Harbor. Their present work entails monitoring the redress payment process and ongoing public education.

Women in the Redress Effort   Aiko Yoshinaga-Herzig had early been recruited by William Hohri as a lobbyist for the NCJAR.   In conjunction with that duty and her work as an "amateur" researcher by her own admission, she uncovered what one writer called "a bombshell".

Herzig began digging through the records of the internment at the National Archives out of curiosity.   Intrigued by what she had discovered in her own record, she continued to sift through copious documents concerning the removal and detention of Japanese Americans.

Because of this experience, Herzig secured a position as a research associate with the CWRIC, the government study commission, and began earnestly culling through material that might cast light. Working into the night, even on weekends, she hit the jackpot in 1982. She had, by accident come upon a rough copy of a report by Lt. Gen. John L. DeWitt, who had headed the Western Defense Command. The report had earlier been altered and all copies of the original were thought to have been destroyed. Part of original report read:

> It was impossible to establish the identity of the loyal and the disloyal with any degree of safety. It was not that there was insufficient time in which to make such a determination; it was simply a matter of facing the realities that

---

[8]On this day in 1942, President Roosevelt issued Executive Order 9066. On the same day in 1976, President Ford rescinded the order.

a positive determination could not be made, that an exact separation of the 'sheep from the goats' was unfeasible.[9]

To Herzig, it was now clear that DeWitt did not believe that time was of the essence in carrying out the internment; rather, he harbored the racist notion that all Japanese Americans couldn't be trusted.

Herzig ferreted out other documents which became part of the Commission files. Says Hohri:

> This collection of documents had great impact. [They] demolished the doctrine of military necessity, which was the main rationale for exclusion and detention. They revealed the presidential politics involved in extending the exclusion program twenty-one months beyond the cessation of "military necessity," such as it was. They revealed the suppression of evidence and other unethical conduct by the U.S. government which compromised the Supreme Court decisions in the Yasui, Hirabayashi, Korematsu, and Endo cases.[10]

Aiko Yoshinaga Herzig, with her modesty and dedication, was, as one writer put it, an "unsung hero" of the redress effort.

Countless other women worked unstintingly in the struggle for redress, writing letters, conducting informational seminars, speaking and lobbying.

Among the more prominent was Grayce Uyehara, who became the executive director of JACL's Legislative Education Committee (LEC). In her capacity, Uyehara organized major letter-writing campaigns at the grassroots level and helped shepherd the redress bill through Congress. Often cited for her energy and astuteness in matters pertaining to congressional politics, Uyehara lobbied Congress and effectively kept the troops informed of all developments. The ultimate passage of the redress bill was not a little due to the tenacity and will of this woman, who had devoted three years to the campaign.

Despite having passed the bill, Congress had difficulty appropriating funds to implement it for the years 1988 and 1989.[11] It was experiencing severe fiscal restraints imposed by the Gramm-Rudman Bill, which had mandated a zero deficit by 1992. It also had to consider funding for new priority items like the drug enforcement program. The grim prospect appeared ahead that no monies would be

---

[9]Josh Getlin, "Redress: One Made a Difference," *Los Angeles Times*, June 2, 1988.

[10]P. 88.

[11]The Bill required that payments be made within 10 years, not more than $500 million to be appropriated within one fiscal year.

provided for the fiscal year 1990 and whatever sums allocated in the years following would likely be stretched out thinly. Meanwhile, many of the now remaining 60,000 survivors (approximately one half of the original number of those imprisoned) were dying daily.

Entitlement Program and Redemption Considering these circumstances, Senator Daniel K. Inouye (D-Hawaii), who had figured prominently in driving redress legislation through Congress, made the innovative proposal that redress payments become a permanent federal entitlement program, the monies to be included in the appropriations bill for the Departments of State, Justice and Commerce. The proposal was approved by a Senate-House conference committee on October 19, 1989.

President George Bush signed the appropiations bill containing the redress payment provision on November 21. Under the terms of the entitlement program, redress payments would begin in the fiscal year 1991 with $500 million, the same sum to be paid in 1992, and up to $250 million in 1993, thus retiring the obligation.

Representative Robert Matsui (D-California), who, with his colleague Representative Norman Mineta (D-California), had worked resolutely for the redress cause from the beginning, perhaps expressed best the collective sentiments of Japanese Americans:

> November 21, 1989, is a day of redemption and healing for the American system because now we know without reservation that redress payments will be made. A wrong has been made right and the national honor has been restored.
>
> Happily, this chapter ends constructively with a reaffirmation of the values this country was built on. This is the end of the long ordeal, an arduous national march toward redemption.[12]

It *had* been a long ordeal. Now nearly fifty years after the incarceration, Japanese Americans, and indeed all Americans, could reflect upon that folly and vow never to allow such an egregious breach of citizens' rights to happen again.

---

[12]*Nichi Bei Times*, November 23, 1989.

COMING OF AGE

By 1980, 716,331 persons of Japanese ancestry lived in the United States, compared to approximately 120,000 in 1940.[13] According to the census, females, whose median age was 35.9, constituted 54% of this population.

Japanese Americans, reported *Asian Week*, appeared "most assimilated" of the various Asian/Pacific Islander groups.[14] The finding was based on language ability, income and education, the Japanese scoring among the highest in all three categories.[15]

Nisei women were feeling as good about themselves as they ever had. Finally, it was all right to be a Japanese. Finally, it was all right to be a woman. Most were now in the sixties and seventies, and had retired from their paid work by the end of the decade. And with pensions and social security, the majority would enjoy comfortable, if modest, economic conditions the remainder of their lives.

"It's Never Too Late"   This new-found sense of having secured for themselves a place in society, caused them to enlarge the activities they had begun in the 1970s.   Now, women talked with other women, organized conferences and workshops for self-discovery, self-recovery and self-improvement.

Women also plunged into the arts, painting, potting, sculpting, making jewelry and becoming award-winners of the art of flower arrangement. They also ventured into unexplored territory.

Tomo Shoji of Seattle had shown an independent spirit early on, but she began to take up acting at age 74, after having become a grandmother. In 1987 she wrote and staged a one-woman show "Born Too Soon, It's Never Too Late," about growing up Japanese-American and female.   She first performed the show at the Northwest Asian American Theater in Seattle where it was a hit.   There followed performances at other stages on the West Coast. Later, she did another show, "Nisei Love Story," regarding her marriage. She was working on yet another show centered on her Issei mother, but died before it was finished. Shoji inspired her granddaughter to write: "When I grow old, gray and wrinkled, I want to be something like my grandmother Tomo."

---

[13]Current figures presented here are taken from the 1980 Census, cited by the *Pacific Citizen*. Included in the present census is the large Hawaiian population, not counted in the 1940 census.

[14]July 28, 1989, p. 14.

[15]One should note, however, that the median income for Japanese American women was $7410, less than half that garnered by Japanese American men.

Alice Hager, another Nisei, performed the astonishing feat of sailing solo to Kagoshima, Japan in 1984 at age 63. Hager, a nurse, had sometime before decided on this adventure. "There were multiple reasons that I was ready to do it," she says. "but it started around 1977 with my search for the meaning of life and culminated after seven years of night duty in a surgical-medical-trauma, intensive care unit, and upon the unexpected death of my spouse. Now, the time was right. Nursing no longer held its original attraction. My three children were young adults. I was free to give to myself--I had paid my dues. Why Japan? It only seemed natural to seek the people of my parents and the country of their birth, to experience life among the gentle people of my ancestors." Having had no previous experience, she read voluminously about the subject, then bought a boat and practiced for a year. In 1983, she set sail for a successful practice run to Hawaii. This was followed by the remarkable voyage to Japan.[16]

Along with their quest for self-fulfillment, Nisei women were realizing that they needed to change their relationship with the world, to modify culturally-set expectations of themselves. They would otherwise continue to be locked into the prison of a wife-mother-worker-sex object identity.

Dr. Florence Uyeda-Miyahara appears to have understood this well. She became the first woman commander of American Legion Nisei Post 185 in Denver in 1988. Having served in the Air Force Nurse Corps after the war, Miyahara received her medical degree in Denver, and practiced pediatrics there. She had joined the all-male Legion Post in 1980, primarily because it afforded an opportunity to give service to children, her particular area of interest.

If problems relating to her gender didn't emerge in her role as commander, it was no doubt due to Miyahara's matter-of-fact attitude. A recent incident typifies that attitude. She had received a call from one of the members asking her to bring rice balls to the annual Post picnic. Miyahara shot back: "Listen, I'm commander of the post. Doesn't the auxiliary do that kind of thing?" When the man answered "yes," she said, "Well, then, call my husband." And he did. And her husband brought the rice balls.[17]

Perhaps the greatest burst of expression exploded in the area of writing. I have already cited many of these writers, including those published in the 1970s: Michi Weglyn (*Years of Infamy*), Monica Sone (*Nisei Daughter*) Akemi Kikumura (*Through Harsh Winters*), Evelyn Nakano Glenn (*Issei, Nisei War Bride*) and Nikki Sawada and her

[16]Personal interview.

[17]*Medical Staff News*, (Children's Hospital, Denver CO, Fall 1988).

spirited short stories.   *Farewell to Manzanar*, written by Jeanne Wakatsuki Houston with her husband was also published in the 1970s. Yoshiko Uchida, who had for years published versions of Japanese folk tales, wrote novels informed by her own experience in the 1970s and 80s (*Desert Exile, Journey to Topaz, Picture Bride*).   Hisaye Yamamoto, whose finely-wrought short stories had long been enjoyed by readers of the language press and literary journals, were finally brought together in a book in 1988 (*Seventeen Syllables*)   And from Hawaii, Patsy Sumie Saiki rendered *Sachie, Daughter of Hawaii* and more recently, *Japanese Women in Hawaii.*   Wakako Yamauchi, among the few Nisei playwrights, had her poignant *And the Soul Shall Dance* produced and aired by public television.   This is by no means an exhaustive list. Others have written short stories, plays and poetry in anthologies, and articles and essays for the language press.

THE LEGACY

In their latter years, Nisei women were thus able to take advantage of the sundry opportunities opened to them. Unlike their mothers, who had set for themselves no greater aspiration than that their children succeed in America, Nisei women could seek growth and expression in a range of activities, including paid work.

At the same time, Issei women had in a sense been cushioned from the outside world, and were thus able to find meaning and a sense of wholeness in their selfhood in spite of their circumscribed lives. Conversely, the Nisei woman had been required to face the hostile world head-on at school, at play, at work. To be rejected, even hated and abused because of her face, had cut deeply into her psyche.

But the changing character of the American political scene had allowed healing, renewal, growth. And Nisei women had held onto the legacy of a strong sense of family as well as other positive cultural values, which had helped sustain them. It seems self-evident that they would have passed many of these values on to their children, despite the competing values imposed by the society-at-large.

In the contemporary society, which seems increasingly motivated by greed, one in which individuals are more and more influenced by outside forces like television, the family (whatever that unit might comprise) may yet be the bulwark against the shattering of all that is good and valuable in our lives.

PART IV

The Sansei

Sansei attorney of San Francisco Human Rights Commission participating as panelist at the Asian American Law Students Association conference, San Francisco, November 11, 1989. © *Shirley Nakao*.

Sansei dancer with the Asian American Dance Collective, San Francisco, 1987. *Photo courtesy Marty Sohl.*

CHAPTER 13

Too Good To Be True

Must they inevitably melt into the pot and become like the rest of us--variously great and small, good and bad, but mostly that passable, fallible, likeable, middling creature beloved to his fellows as The Average American?

---R. B. Read.

"Meet the third generation Japanese Americans, who face a problem without precedent," proclaimed the heading of a news magazine article, "They're too good to be true,"[1] Indeed by conventional standards, the Sansei were a collective "success story," at the top of the heap for scholastic achievement, at the bottom for delinquency and crime.

These were of course outward signs. Beneath the surface lay complex questions relating to identity, prejudice and, as one woman put it, "cultural baggage." Yet twenty years after Read's article appeared, it is clear that the auspicious beginnings of the Sansei have translated into unprecedented achievement for a third-generation minority group.

The question is well-posed: Have they indeed melted into the pot and become that "middling creature," The Average American? Research sociologist Darrel Montero, who had completed a decade-long study of three generations of Japanese-Americans, funded by the JACL, the Carnegie Corporation and the National Institute of Mental Health found that

> . . . the demise of Japanese-American ethnic values may serve to bring about the leveling off of the Nisei and Sansei's socioeconomic achievement.
>
> As their values become more congruent with the rest of American society, they will quite likely begin to mirror the lower achievement patterns of American society in general.

---

[1]R. B. Read, "The Sansei," *S. F. Examiner and Chronicle*, CALIFORNIA LIVING, (August 14, 1966), p. 20.

By replacing the traditional Japanese dedication to community and family with the individualistic outlook that is more prevalent in American society, it is quite possible that Japanese-Americans might lose those very advantages that this cohesive ethnic community has afforded them.[2]

The vast amount of studies completed on the Sansei occurred between 1965 and 1975 and dealt primarily with persons 18 years and older. No doubt these studies were prompted by curiosity as to why the Sansei appeared to be faring so well. They do not suffice to serve our purposes completely here, since they examined only relatively older Sansei, but they nevertheless yield important insights into the Sansei character and the difficulties they faced in the process of assimilation.

Here we review those studies in discussing the earlier years of the Sansei. We then proceed to a more contemporary discussion of this remarkable and diverse group. For the major part of the discussion, we rely on experiential and impressionistic evidence.

GROWING UP

The majority of Sansei were born approximately between the years 1940 and 1960.[3] Older Sansei, that is, those born before, say, 1950, tended to hold closer to the values and behavior of the Nisei, while younger Sansei leaned more towards the behavioral norms of the contemporary society.

Most Sansei grew up in urban or suburban areas. As noted in the Nisei section, up to or about the middle of the 1950s, minorities tended to congregate in certain areas of the cities and towns where they could buy homes. Sansei (most likely older Sansei) who were raised in these ghetto-like communities, socialized to a great extent with other Sansei. Although they belonged to organizations like the Bluebirds or Girl Scouts, or later, college sororities, the membership was liable to be Sansei.

One Sansei female who lived in Gardena, California, where a sizable Japanese American population had congregated after the war, recalls being totally immersed in that society until she graduated

---

[2]"For Japanese-Americans, Erosion," *The New York Times*, December 4, 1978, p. A21.

[3]The dates are approximate, since census data does not reveal Sansei birth rates. I have inferred these dates from calculating the childbearing years of the Nisei. As with the Nisei, I refer here exclusively to the Sansei in the continental U.S. Those born in Hawaii tend to have a much wider age spread.

from high school. And even when she went on to UCLA, her close friends were Sansei. She married a Sansei.

Another woman who grew up in a mixed neighborhood but who socialized almost exclusively with Japanese Americans in her childhood, presents what she deemed a resultant problem:

> Up to the time I was in high school, I never had a real good white friend, the kind who invited you to a slumber party, for instance. My extended family was very close, especially my mother's family, so we spent a lot of time with them. Also we went to a Japanese church and most of my good friends came out of that. But I think that kind of life . . . the way we were sort of enclosed wasn't real. So I had a hard time in high school and college, not academically, but socially. I didn't go out of my way to cultivate white friends, and so I felt out of it.[4]

One Sansei appeared to fault her parents for her rather insular life:

> All the activities I did was with the family, with the family . . . I was overly involved with the family. Like it was, we lived in an apartment building that a relative owned, and my father's sister owned another share. . . and everything was, you know dinners . . . I suppose I made friends in school, but it was really hard, because the obligation was always to the family first . . .[5]

Growing up in an all-white suburb, on the other hand, produced difficulties of its own. A Sansei who had been raised in such an environment, commented:

> When I went to UCLA as a freshman [1973], I was really confused. I didn't know how the social dynamics worked. But I learned soon enough that you had to choose whether you wanted to hang out with Japanese or with hakujins [Caucasians]. If you went on a date with a hakujin, the Japanese guys wouldn't ask you and vice versa. It was bizarre, like there was a stupid agreement, or something.[6]

---

[4]Anonymous. Survey of Sansei women, primarily on the West Coast, conducted by Mei Nakano (hereafter Survey), August, 1989.

[5]Mark Joshua Gehrie, "Sansei: An Ethnography of Experience," Diss. Evanston, Ill. 1973, p. 28.

[6]Personal interview. Comments from former UCLA students create the impression that, at least in the 1970s, Sansei students tended to socialize among themselves at that university.

A number of Sansei had white friends at school, but not outside of school. At the same time, they felt alienated from Japanese Americans:

> I felt an uneasiness . . . I had very few Oriental friends and it was largely the Japanese kids that were cliqueish. As an outsider I could see that . . . [I felt] isolated, an outsider coming in and trying to play because I'm Japanese too.[7]

But the majority of Sansei appeared to have white friends during their high school years and beyond. Like many other Sansei, Mariko Abe said, "My best friends were non-Japanese." And like others whose friends were mainly non-Japanese, she married a non-Japanese.[8]

Family Life   Sansei women appeared on the whole to have a satisfying family life in their growing years. Some even felt that they had been indulged and spoiled with material things. But as Nikki Omi says laconically, "Positives always outweighed negatives, plenty of both," Sansei were likely to have experienced more positives than negatives. A sample of their statements serves to amplify:[9]

Joyce Emiko Kawasaki (Sales, investments and insurance):
> Strong family ties, our parents' dedication to us gave us a sense of confidence and of possibilities they never had. Through their efforts they made it possible to develop the attitudes, the expectations, the values, the character to go on for whatever we wanted.

Janice L. Shimizu (Public sector development):
> Positives [in growing up years]: Strong family unit, parental support for positive self-image; mother's assertiveness.

Jennifer M. Kawamura (Law student)
> In my opinion, although Japanese parents are exceptional in terms of the time, effort and money they expend on behalf of their children, we would probably be better off if more emphasis was placed on independence and surviving on our own.

---

[7]Gehrie, p. 48.

[8]Interview for Oral History Project, Japanese American Women's Exhibit (hereafter "Interview for OHP"), National Japanese American Historical Society, June, 1989.

[9]All ensuing statements from "Survey".

Patti Iiyama (Political activist):

My parents gave me love, warmth, the knowledge that I was loved unconditionally . . . . This gave me self-confidence and a feeling of self-worth. They also taught me my values: that material things are not the most important, that other people should be given the chance to develop to their full potential, that we can change people and society.

Wendy C. Horikoshi (Youth educator):

There were so many of us (5 girls) that parents did not have time to be overbearing. We were fortunate to have Mom at home until the youngest went to extended school day (4th grade). Dad was in and out due to the farm, and grandparents lived next door. Being raised on a farm we learned how to work hard and together as a unit. Father did not do a great deal of parenting, although we now see with grandkids that he played a lot with us as infants.

Diane Fukami (Television news producer):

When my mother and father realized I was not a traditional Sansei (didn't play basketball, and went to speech contests), they encouraged me to go after whatever I wanted and instilled confidence that I'd achieve whatever I sought.

Gayle T. Nishikawa (General manager, Asian American Dance Collective):

There was a strong emphasis on family relationships. I was connected to people and important to people simply by being born into the family.

Lea Haratani (Environmental biologist):

What strikes me about my family most in retrospect is the lack of real communication between members, the lack of romantic love between parents, the confusion that resulted from being "subtle" and "indirect" in a very direct, real, larger world.

Ann Lew (Teacher):

I'm glad for the discipline and the sense of aesthetics which I picked up during my childhood. What was most difficult was always trying to figure out what was being said between the lines.

In sum, the majority of respondents gave only positive statements about their early family lives, a few offered both positive and negative, two emphasized the negative and three declined to answer the question.

Education "If the Nisei pursued higher education vigorously," reported one study, "the Sansei have done so relentlessly."[10] In 1973, 88% of the Sansei had completed some college training. As for careers they aspired to, research conducted at U.C. Berkeley revealed that Japanese-American males entered the physical sciences (math, chemistry, engineering) more frequently than other students and "appeared more interested in occupations comprising the skilled-technical trades (farmer, aviator, carpenter, printer, . . .) and less interested in sales . . . and verbal-linguistic occupations (advertising man, lawyer, author-journalist)." They also tended to be more interested in business fields and less interested in the aesthetic-cultural fields such as music and the visual arts.[11]

Asian-American females, the researchers found, exhibited roughly similar interests to their male counterparts. Put another way:

> The college professor, giving a seminar to Sansei, will notice that, while these students are not as reticent as Nisei, they are still somewhat subdued and conforming. Their education is job-oriented; they enter "secure" professions. The fierce desire for upward mobility is occasionally frightening, and is more typical, perhaps, of an aspiring rather than a fully acculturated middle-class American.[12]

Motivation for a college education was spurred by Nisei parents. Elizabeth Uno, for example, felt that part of hers came from her mothers' "frustrations." While she never heard her mother say "You should go to college because I never got a chance to," she perceived a clear message that she should utilize the opportunities that were offered her. She adds:

> There was sort of a pattern that we were supposed to go through. I don't know whose idea it was. We were supposed to go to high school. We were supposed to get really good grades . . . . We were supposed to go to either S.F. State and become a teacher or we're all supposed to go

---

[10]Gene N. Levine and Darrel M. Montero, "Socioeconomic Mobility Among Three Generations of Japanese Americans," *Journal of Social Issues,* V. 29, No.2, (1973, p. 45.

[11]Derald Wing Sue, "Ethnic Identity: The Impact of Two Cultures on the Psychological Development of Asians in America," *Asian Americans: Psychological Perspectives,* eds. Stanley Sue and Nathaniel N. Wagner, (Science and Behavior Books, Palo Alto, CA 1973), pp. 145-146.

[12]Harry H.L. Kitano, *Japanese Americans: The Evolution of a Subculture,* (Prentice-Hall, Inc., Englewood Cliffs, N.J. 1969), p. 142.

to UC Berkeley and then . . . become a teacher or become a pharmacist.[13]

Cultural Identity   Since Japanese was not spoken at home, few Sansei spoke Japanese with any fluency.   Only about 2% had a functional knowledge of the language, according to the estimate of one researcher.   With the loss of the language, many of the cultural values that inhere in it were bound to be lost.

Wrote a Sansei: "I am not embarrassed that I cannot speak for more than a minute of coherent Japanese. . . . The third generation of all immigrant groups stands to lose the use of their grandparents' tongue."   At the same time, he conceded that "for the Sansei, . . . the value of speaking Japanese is immense."   He then set a course for himself to study the language and something of the culture and history.[14]

Jane Muramoto Yung provides an important insight into the matter of cultural identity for Japanese Americans:

> As for customs and practices, New Years has always been big for me, more so than Christmas. It's a time when I feel very Japanese. As a kid we'd always go to Bachan's [Grandma's] for family and Japanese "soul food."   Now we always go to my folks.   We didn't celebrate other Japanese holidays or speak Japanese because my grandparents died early.   I know the camp experience made my folks minimize Japanese customs in our house.   My dad told us we probably would have gone to Japanese school to speak Japanese if it weren't for camp.   It got ingrained in them to raise their children 100% American.[15]

If the stigma attached to their race induced Nisei to strive to be "100% American," the searing experience of the concentration camp no doubt caused them avoid even more assiduously their connection to things Japanese in the years directly following World War II. Thus, in their most formative years, their children, were likely not to have been exposed to any great extent to features of their Japanese heritage.   Nor were they likely to hear about their parents' imprisonment. This pattern of denial on the part of their parents up until the late sixties was certain to make its imprint.   As one Sansei woman candidly remarked:

---

[13]Interview for OHP, July, 1989.

[14]Todd Endo, "How Japanese Am I," *Pacific Citizen*, July 16, 1965.

[15]Interview for OHP, July 1989.

As far as being Japanese, I don't believe that I was raised to value it. I do regret not having been cultured in the language, foods and customs. I once entertained the idea of making a button to wear which says, "100% Made in the U.S.A." Just last week, someone assumed that I made my own egg rolls.[16]

Another Sansei woman's statement captures the Sansei's rather ambiguous sense of their ethnicity in their early years:

I always knew I wasn't white, but I'm not really sure when I knew I was Japanese American. I know I was terribly embarrassed at being called a "Jap" or a "Chink", and I still am! . . . . I remember the first time I had a Sansei boy in my class. It was right after the 6th grade in summer school. I was very self-conscious and very much aware of our "sameness."[17]

What seemed to be required was a new ethnic identity, one that had evolved from the Sansei's separate and distinctive experience, uncluttered by tired stereotypical images. But the process was difficult:

I guess that one of the most difficult things for me to understand is how to relate to my boyfriend who is white. Sometimes I flash back on all the ideas my parents taught me such as the idea that to marry a white man was to sort of degrade myself, and it's really hard to know how to deal with these kinds of feelings.

I once read this poem by an Asian woman where she said that after looking into blue eyes for so long she forgot hers were black. I really feel this, and it's hard to understand: I identify so strongly with this man I love and that's inevitably tied up somewhat to the way he looks, which conflicts with me and my background and the way I look.[18]

One can read Masaoka's "boyfriend" as metaphor for "white Americans" and discern the dilemma that beset many Sansei women. How much of their selfhood, their Japaneseness, if you will, would they be willing to cede to the demands of becoming fully integrated in American society?

---

[16]Anonymous, Survey, August 1989.

[17]Jane Muramoto Yung, interview for OHP, July, 1989.

[18]Jan Masaoka, "I Forgot My Eyes Were Black," *Asian Women*, University of Berkeley, 1971, pp. 57-58.

Portents   As Sansei reached maturity and the socio-political climate changed measurably, many appeared to become increasingly interested in their cultural identity. And unlike their parents, who were in many ways locked into their Japaneseness by forces outside their control, Sansei would possess the freedom to choose the elements in it that they wished to preserve and those they wished to cast off.

Thus, wrote Minako Maykovich, "One characteristic of the Sansei group is their heterogeneity in comparison with the relatively homogeneous Issei and Nisei generations." The Sansei, she concluded, "no longer believe nor behave uniformly. Although the majority of them still seem to be conformists, there are others who are trying to bring forth evolutionary or revolutionary changes to society. Yet underlying all these heterogeneous Sansei behaviors is found their common search for a new ethnic identity."[19]

The Sansei, then, even more than their parents, are in a process of evolution. No longer are they the Sansei of the 1970s who were scrutinized so zealously. In the following chapters, we present them in a more contemporary light.

---

[19]"Political Activation of Japanese American Youth," *Journal of Social Issues*, v. 29, Number 2, 1973, p. 183.

CHAPTER 14

Melting in the Pot?

Assimilation is a minority response likely to occur only when the dominant group accepts the idea, and the minority, for whatever reason, concurs.
                                                                    ---Minako Kurokawa

During the mid-1960s, sociologist Mamoru Iga completed a study of to determine the degree of assimilation of the Sansei to middle-class American culture. Reporting on the study, Alan Kumamoto, said it suggested that

"1) the differences between Japanese Americans and Caucasians facilitate rather than hinder the Oriental adjusting to American culture, and

2) the third generation return theory is untenable with reference to the Sansei]."[1]

Kumamoto reported further:

> It is believed that the Sansei desire to be assimilated appears to be so complete and their knowledge of Japanese culture so marginal that we cannot anticipate their return to traditional Japanese cultural interests. The only factor which prevents them from complete assimilation seems to be a combination of their physical visibility as well as any racial prejudice on the part of the dominant group.

Now, some 25 years later, Iga's prediction appears on the brink of fulfillment. Sansei have taken giant steps toward assimilation by absorbing various values and practices of the majority culture. Yet, at this juncture, they do not appear to be rushing headlong toward making their assimilation complete. Some thoughtful reflection appears to be taking place.

How assimilated are they? Measuring the assimilation of the Sansei is complicated by varying factors peculiar to the Japanese American society (as in the case of religion), but the process itself entailed stages similar to that undergone by most minority groups.

---

[1]"An Assimilated Generation," *Pacific Citizen*, September 2, 1966, p.1.

Acquiring the language, characteristic attitudes, habits and modes of behavior of the larger society took place inexorably, often unconsciously, step by step or in great strides, depending on the necessity. Where prejudice existed, assimilation was even a conscious, aggressive act, a strategy to acquire greater mobility in the dominant society. In this case, assimilation was seen as a positive evolutionary step, a leg up to increasing empowerment.

Conversely, assimilation acquired a negative color when one began to perceive it as assuming Anglo superiority, involving the denial of one's own cultural heritage, or to paraphrase Jan Masaoka, a state of mind that caused one to forget one's eyes were black.

Japanese Americans were feeling less and less pressed to shed their Japaneseness and to become Americanized as the lessening of institutional discrimination was struck down and prejudicial practices abated. Now, some Sansei appear determined to provide a counterforce to the tide of assimilation in order to avert culture extinction and total immersion into the "melting pot." They are working towards preserving the integrity of the culture, attempting to retain its positive features so that those can be added to a mix that would constitute a truly pluralistic society rather than one in which Anglo values maintain dominance.

These Sansei serve the Japanese community and are putting to work their education and their considerable talents in the Japanese community--in the centers for the elderly, at community festivals, Asian legal and political organizations, the arts and the like. "There comes a point in the lives of Asian women who pursue professional careers," says Jennifer Kawamura, a law student, "where they either choose to become totally assimilated in the white, yuppie culture or they consciously decide to maintain and foster their Asian identity. I hope that I can follow the latter course."[2]

But these workers and thinkers appear to be but a small minority. Have the others, in fact, leaped into the pot?

Here, it is useful to refer to Milton Gordon's work on assimilation.[3] As a means of measuring assimilation, Gordon identified roughly four types: cultural, structural, marital and identificational. To facilitate our discussion on Sansei assimilation, we took Gordon's identificational and cultural categories and lumped them together. Then we added a category on the family, since the family occupied such an important place in Japanese American society. An examination of structural as well as marital assimilation rounds out the discussion.

---

[2]Survey.

[3]*Assimilation in American Life: The Role of Race, Religion, and National Origins,* (Oxford University Press 1964).

The Survey   To get some indication of the assimilation of Sansei women, sixty survey forms were mailed to Sansei women, fifty-one (or 85%) of which were returned. The forms contained statements and questions relating to the family, cultural identity and work. Additional space was alloted for free-ranging comments that pertained to the subject of "being a Japanese American woman," some comments of which have already been cited in this book.

The purpose of the survey was no more ambitious than to sample opinions and attitudes of the women to suggest their degree of assimilation. Because of the particular mailing list from which names were chosen, it is quite possible that a bias exists in favor of professional and semi-professional women (all of the women worked, and only 5 did not identify themselves as professionals). At the same time, it should be borne in mind that upwards of 88% of Sansei are college graduates, so that the sampling may not be quite as skewed as it appears. No other population was surveyed for purposes of comparison.

Attitudes Toward Traditional Families   The image of the ideal traditional American family tends toward the one created by the popular 1950s television family of Ozzie and Harriet Nelson. Mom was always at home, very often with an apron neatly cinched around her waist, ever loving, ever warm and understanding. Pop also managed to be a ubiquitous presence around the home, involved in whatever problems that emerged in such a household. And the children enjoyed a great deal of freedom and independence. But the salient feature of this family was the free exchange of conversation between adults and children, whether in the form of praise, criticism or comment.

This American ideal contrasted most sharply with the traditional Japanese family, or *ie* (see Chapter 2) in the independence and freedom it accorded the child and in its non-hierarchical arrangement of family members.

For the section in our survey pertaining to family, a list of statements was presented, modeled after one designed by Professor John W. Connor of Sacramento State University.[4] In his excellent discussion, Connor compared the relative "Americanization" of three generations of Japanese Americans. We were only interested in that of the Sansei. On a scale of 0 to 10, respondents were asked to respond to five statements on the basis of least to most true. The statements and their mean scores follow.

---

[4]"Acculturation and Family Continuities in Three Generations of Japanese Americans," *Journal of Marriage and the Family*, February 1974, p. 162.

1. Parents can never be repaid for what they have done for their children. (6.89)

2. In times of need it is best to rely on your own family for aid rather than to
   seek help from others or to depend entirely upon yourself. (5.23)

3. The best way to train children is to train them to be quiet and obedient. (2.58)

4. The greatest satisfaction comes from being with one's own family. (5.54)

5. The strongest emotional bond is between a mother and a child. (5.93)

While Connor found Issei and Nisei responses strongly positive in Items 1, 2, 4 which, he says are "family items directly related to the preservation of the ideal," our survey showed the same strong positive indication only on Item 1. The respondents remained neutral on other Japanese values like Items 2 and 5, the dependency measures and on 4, an indicator of the family's tendency towards insularity, but they appeared to retain the Japanese cultural value of a fairly strong sense of obligation toward their parents as reflected in Item 1.   Our conversations and interviews with Sansei bear this out. For example:

> Listening to my folk's stories about growing up, about camp, what they went through in addition to raising five kids, makes me feel so very pampered, self-indulgent. By the time my mom was my age, she had gone through camp, the Indian Reservation, had five children and now was raising all of us by herself while my dad was away in the army . . . . My folks didn't have time to philosophize or head trip like yours truly: they were too busy surviving. In reflecting more deeply, I see that we Sansei can freely choose to do and be whomever we want to be because of what our grandparents and parents endured.[5]

In one round table discussion of five Sansei women, the word "guilt" surfaced a number of times. "I think I often do something out of fear that if I don't do it I'll feel guilty," said one woman, accompanied by a chorus of "yes, yes." This onus of having to perform according to expectations, often refers to parental expectations. Because of the knowledge that their parents and grandparents "endured," as Yung noted, their feelings of obligation "to do right" is even stronger than might be expected otherwise. Said Gayle Nishikawa: "There is much guilt and responsibility built into me that comes from family upbringing.

---

[5]Jane Muramoto Yung, Interview for OHP, July, 1989.

This can lead to sticking to only "acceptable" modes of thinking. [There is] also stress in always having to do the right thing."[6]

This heavy sense of responsibility together with the cultural value invoking shame, compellingly move the Sansei to perform well in school and behave in socially acceptable ways.

On the other end of the scale, respondents' strong negative score on Item 3 suggests that they prefer the more democratic household arrangement of the traditional American family to the authoritative one of the Japanese family. Sansei women themselves enjoyed much more freedom and flexibility in being reared than did their parents, and they appear to be raising their children, the Yonsei (fourth generation), in like manner.

The New Family   In the larger scheme of things, Sansei women face a host of issues about family which did not exist in the earlier generations. Family structures are changing, and with it, new challenges have emerged.

A nationwide survey showed that the Ozzie and Harriet type of family occurred in only one out of ten families, representing approximately a 72 percent decrease from just twenty years ago. Single-parent families make up 15 percent of American families, up from 11 percent a decade ago. Two-thirds of all first marriages are expected to end in separation or divorce, according to the survey.[7]

The divorce rate of Sansei women is not a matter of record at this writing. But most Japanese Americans know of a considerable number of single-parent households. These single parents have few models in the Issei and Nisei generations from which to take their cues. But many of them say, not surprisingly, that they receive financial support from their Nisei parents as well as help in the form of child care.

The dual-career family appears to be the standard of Sansei households today. Women want to be with their children; on the other hand, they feel a need to pursue their careers or are forced to work for the needed income.

Paula Shimizu provides a good-humored account of motherhood in her dual-career family:

> I could tell Erma Bombeck a story or two. As a working mom, I feel my life is precariously balanced between the best of both private and professional worlds.

---

[6]Survey.

[7]Pat Schroeder, "Letters to Editor," *Press Democrat*, July, 18, 1989.

After my daughter was born, I stayed at home for a year and breast fed. I should have been thankful: for the first time in my life, I had a bustline.

... [With] my husband's 12-hour commute [to work], the closest I came to carrying on a conversation in complete sentences was asking the checkout clerk at Safeway what day it was. The gray matter in my head was turning to strained peas, and the pail of dirty diapers had more self esteem than I did. I needed help and found it in a support group for moms . . . . I repeated the "Parenting Your Baby" course three times. A donation to the California parenting Institute came out of my first paycheck.

I am currently in hospital personnel management, and my daughter is in daycare . . . Now that [my husband] has started a home-based consulting business, it allows him to take Angela to daycare and pick her up three days a week. This shared responsibility on [his] part is the only way I make it day to day as a working mom. My only hesitation in extolling his virtues as a participative parent is that he may find out that not all fathers do diapers or dishes.[8]

Shimizu's comments point up two significant factors: one, that Sansei husbands appear to be taking much more responsibility in the household than did their fathers and, two, that many dual-career families are seeking ways to strengthen family bonds by making home a work location.

Another family issue that is fairly new to this generation is spousal abuse. If this occurred in prior generations, the fact was never made public, nor is it today. But at least in one city, San Francisco, an Asian women's shelter has been established, again, largely by third generation Asian women. The need is obvious by the very existence of the agency.

There seems to be no question that family concerns remain high on the agenda of Sansei women. But they will need support, not only from their own families but from the government as well.

Culture and Identity   To elicit indications of the cultural and identificational assimilation of the Sansei, the survey posed five questions. Responses follow:

1. How often do you eat Japanese food? Rarely 5.5% Sometimes 52.8% Often 41.7%

2. Have you attended a Japanese American play? Yes 64% No 36%

3. Do you favor Japanese art? Not particularly 14% Depends 37% Yes 49%

---

[8]Survey.

4. Do you feel obligated to return a favor for a favor, a gift for a gift? Not necessarily 19% Most of the time 58% Always 23%

5. Do you think of your "Japaneseness?" Rarely 22%; Sometimes 58% Often 20%

According to one research paper, in the matter of cultural assimilation, "the minority group changes its behavioral patterns to conform with those of the host society."[9] These researchers used fluency in Japanese as an indicator of assimilation: if the respondent had no ability to speak the language, this indicated a movement away from traditional cultural practices and toward greater assimilation. By that indicator, Sansei would seem to have reached almost total cultural assimilation.

Yet by other, more subtle touchstones, that remains in question. Take for instance the responses to Question 4. Gift-giving is almost a moral obligation in Japanese society. In no other society does there seem to be such an abundance, almost a ritual, of give and take, whether it be gifts, favors or appearances at special occasions such as funerals or weddings. A Japanese business manager knows full well that when he attends the wedding of one of his employees, the employee will feel the obligation to return the favor in some form. Suppose then that the employee puts in extra hours to "repay" the manager. The latter is now likely obliged to do another good turn and so on.

We see in the responses to this question how deeply ingrained this practice appears to be. Many Sansei complain about the obligatory nature of exchanging gifts and favors which they seemed to have "inherited." It takes the joy out of "voluntary" giving or voluntary service, they say, but they participate in it anyway. Others see it as valuable in fostering ties.

Responses to Question 5 indicate that most Sansei women are not intensely conscious of their Japaneseness, as were their mothers. "I don't even think of my Japaneseness," one woman said, in response to a question asked about how she regarded her position as the only Japanese American woman employed in a firm. "I am more conscious of myself as a woman." According to comments on the surveys, this view seems fairly predominant.

"Yes, I eat *chazuke* [rice immersed in tea] and *tsukemono* [pickled vegetables]," says Delphine Hirasuna, "but that's about the extent of my

---

[9]Darrel Montero and Ronald Tsukashima, "Assimilation and Educational Achievement: The Case of the Second Generation Japanese-American," *The Sociological Quarterly* 18, Autumn 1977: 400-503.

Japaneseness lately. I have Sansei friends, but we don't sit around discussing Japanese topics either--mostly what movies we've seen and what we think of the Alaska oil spill, etc. I can go through entire weeks without talking about anything Japanese."[10]

On the other hand, it is quite possible that some Sansei do not think of their Japaneseness as a rule, but every now and then experience a kind of epiphany:

Joyce Emiko Kawasaki:

> Being Japanese, I have absorbed the trait of looking out for others as much as I do for myself, which I just learned is not what most Americans do . . . I'm amazed it's taken me this long to realize it! I feel lucky being bi-cultural: it enhances a multi-cultural global perspective, which is rapidly [becoming] the current business trend.[11]

Paula Shimizu:

> I led a pretty sheltered childhood in Mill Valley, California. All my friends were hakujin, which was probably the biggest contributing factor to my identity crisis. I really didn't know I was Japanese American until college when I became involved with the Japanese American Citizen's League.
>
> I spent eight formative years wearing a plaid woolen uniform in school. The bumper sticker "I Survived Catholic School" probably sums it up best. To this day, one of the main factors of motivation in my life is guilt. Hell, there are times when I feel guilty for not feeling guilty.[12]

Questions 1, 2 and 3 on culture and identity are rather superficial gauges of one's appreciation of the culture. Yet, in the case of the Sansei, they seemed important to pose as indications of a desire for affinity with the culture. The strongly positive responses affirm that desire, as can be noted in Hirasuna's comments above.

Structural Assimilation   In spite of reservations about cultural assimilation, no minority group disputes the necessity of structural assimilation in order to acquire broad options about careers and housing and opportunities for advancement. Montero and Tsukashima employed four measures of structural assimilation: ethnicity of the respondent's neighborhood, co-workers, two closest friends, and

---

[10]"Kaleidoscope," *Hokubei Mainichi*, April 27, 1989.

[11]Survey.

[12]*Ibid.*

favorite affiliate organization.[13] We asked the following questions, and received these responses:

1. Do you belong to any Japanese American organizations? 57% of respondents belonged to an average of 2.05 Japanese American organizations. The other 43% belonged to none.

2. How many Japanese Americans live in your neighborhood? None 39% A few 47% Fair amount and many 14%

3. Approximately how much time of your social life is spent with Japanese Americans? None 14% Very little 42% Some 22% Most 22%

These responses suggest that Sansei women have attained a fairly high degree of structural assimilation. Most live in neighborhoods where few or no other Japanese Americans reside. More often than not, they spend their leisure time with persons other than Japanese Americans.

On the other hand, one notes that the majority of those surveryed belong to one or another of the Japanese American organizations that proliferate throughout the urban areas. Nearly all of these groups perform services to the community, but many of them exist for the purpose of advancing the interests of Asians and Pacific Islanders (APIs). API law caucuses, political and civil rights organizations exist in every city with a sizable API population. The need for these organizations suggests that Asian Pacifics have not yet gained entry into the highest political (or corporate) levels, a reliable test of structural assimilation.

That is not to say that great strides have not been made. Many Sansei women have made dramatic inroads into previously off-limits occupations and have established themselves in careers with higher levels of salary, responsibility and influence. Georgette Imura, for example, has worked in the California State Capitol for years. Now serving as an Asian American liaison person for state Senators as well as a political consultant, she says:

It took many years before I was taken seriously by males in the political, legislative arena. I am a typical JA woman physically, small and younger looking than my age, so I was always treated like a little girl. Therefore, I had to be twice as good and twice as tough in order to get ahead . . . . When I got my first promotion to a professional position, there were almost no

---

[13]"Assimilation and Educational Achievement . . .", p. 496.

women consultants, let alone Japanese American women consultants. It was very lonely in those days.[14]

Irene Takahashi is a municipal court judge. Having traversed the demanding course over which many judges have traveled, as defense attorney, federal prosecutor and serving in the District Attorney's office, she was appointed to her position by the Governor of California. Asked to comment on her Japanese heritage she said: "I think it helped me because of the Japanese [cultural] values passed on to me--being respectful towards others, being thoughtful, placing a high value on education, and having parental support in every way. My Japanese heritage is something I'm very proud of, and I didn't have anything to do with it: it was there before I was born.[15]

Diane Fukami, a news director for a major network affiliate in San Francisco, is sensitive to her womanhood as well as her Japaneseness:

I feel fortunate to be a Japanese American woman, especially in my profession. There are so few Asians in my business, especially in management, so that I am highly visible in the industry. Many things that contributed to my success belie traditional Japanese American women stereotypes. I am assertive to the point of sometimes being aggressive; I am outspoken and an extrovert; I care about things passionately and show that easily. On the other hand, some things are part of my culture: I worked hard to prove myself, I have a lot of pride, my family is very important and I am hard to read by those who don't know me well.[16]

If evidence of structural assimilation is tantamount to having gained entree into the highest corporate levels and positions of political power, Sansei women apparently have a long way to go. On the other hand, that may not be their highest priority. "Japanese American women may be more likely to view child-rearing as important, and may view time spent with family as more significant than putting in the hours necessary to advance their careers," says Jennifer Kawamura, typifying the comments of many others. A number of women also wrote that Japanese American women are likely not moved up the fast track for top executive positions because of the stereotypical image held of them as passive and non-assertive.

---

[14]Survey.

[15]Interview for OHP conducted by Chizu Iiyama.

[16]Survey.

Marital Assimilation   Our final attempt at measuring the assimilation of Sansei women is with the rate of marriages of Sansei to persons outside their ethnic group. We asked the questions, "Are you married? If yes, is your spouse Japanese American?" Out of those who answered the question, 74% were married, 22% were not; the rest were, as one respondent put it, "sort of."

Of those married, 60% said they were married to Japanese Americans, while 40% said they were not. This rate of outmarriage is roughly the converse of what sociologists are finding in recent preliminary studies.

This reflects a dramatic rise in the rate of outmarriages. In 1959, roughly ten years after anti-miscegenation laws were struck down, fewer than three out of ten Japanese Americans had outmarried.[17] By 1972, the rate of Japanese Americans was reported at 49%.[18] In 1989, Harry Kitano estimated their rate of outmarriage as high as 60%, higher than any other ethnic group.[19] Increasingly greater social contact with other groups through schools, places of residence and work, undoubtedly contribute toward these rising rates. Also the more favorable images of the Japanese both in Japan and in the United States may be a contributing factor.

Before 1960, Asian females outmarried a higher rate than males, say researchers. Several reasons have been advanced for this phenomenon. For one, a marriage between a white male and an Asian female was more readily accepted by the society, it being assumed that the male made the choice, which he had every right to do, according to this line of thinking. But when Asian males and males of other colored minorities made the choice to marry white women, they were not accorded that same sanction. Secondly, marriage to a white male in the dominant society increased a female's chance for upward mobility, presumably because the white male had greater opportunities for upward mobility than the Asian male in the larger society. However, since 1960, it appears that the rate of Asian males and females outmarrying is balancing out, possibly due to increasingly favorable images and financial circumstances of the Asian male.

Sansei women marry "out" for other reasons. Some are attracted by the more egalitarian attitudes of white men regarding marriage roles.

---

[17]John N. Tinker, "Intermarriage and Ethnic Boundaries," *Journal of Social Issues*, v. 29, Number 2, 1973, p. 53.

[18]Akemi Kikumura and Harry H. L. Kitano, "Interracial Marriage: A Picture of the Japanese Americans," *Journal of Social Issues*, V. 29, Number 2, 1973.

[19]"Interracial Marriage Rate Jumps in Each Generation," *Asian Week*, March 24, 1989, p. 15.

One study showed more Japanese-American males held attitudes of male-dominance in marriage roles than did Japanese American females or white females and males.[20] Interestingly enough, one woman said in a personal interview with the author:

> I married [a white male] because he allows me to be Japanese. Unlike the other guys [Japanese Americans] I've been out with, he encourages me to be connected with my Japaneseness. He keeps tabs on what is going on in the Japanese community, and he likes to go to Japanese cultural things. Oh yes, he likes Japanese food and is learning to cook it.

Nik Omi was earlier married to a white male, now to a Sansei. While finding differences in them which could be attributed to race, she could not single out anything really significant. "The only noteworthy difference I perceived," she said, "was in the way the parents accepted the marriage. It was instant acceptance on the part of both sets of parents in my second marriage."

Whatever the case, the rate of marital assimilation is high and appears to be rising, along with the other factors of assimilation. Whether this cultural "erosion" will cause the decline in the value Japanese Americans place on the family remains to be seen. At this point, there seems to be little indication that such is the case.

Children of Intermarriages   Intermarriage produces a relatively new phenomenon in Japanese American society: children of mixed heritage. Not until the Sansei began outmarrying in great numbers did social scientists become interested in children from interracial marriages.

A seminar on this very subject was held at UCLA in late 1989, according to a report in *Asian Week* (October 27, 1989, p. 12). Panelists included researcher Amy Iwasaki Mass and a number of young adults of dual-heritage. Mass reported that her study showed the majority of those persons with only one Asian American parent possessed the same level of self-esteem as their counterparts whose parents were both Asian American. But the study also showed that they tended to have a weaker sense of cultural identity than the others.

Overall, the panelists expressed satisfaction with their mixed heritage. Said one: "I feel that I belong to both cultures. We don't have to look at ourselves as half-and half, we are doubles!"

---

[20]A. Arkoff etal. "Attitudes of Japanese-American and Caucasian- American Students toward Marriage Roles," *Journal of Social Psychology* 59, 1963, pp. 11-15.

Enigma of Assimilation   In sum, Sansei are becoming increasingly concerned over what Montero had called "the demise of Japanese American values," and are attempting to stave off the rather dismal scenario he predicted by laboring to preserve Japanese culture. But in the overwhelming drift towards material acquisitiveness and outward show of success prevalent in the 1980s in America, assimilation may have seemed more urgent. And moving up into the citadels of prestige and power may not be possible without the cost of forfeiting one's cultural heritage.

There is, of course, subtle racism built into that proposition, a fall back to the old slogan, "you gotta be white to be right." How much more profitable it would be to American society if the positive characteristics of each culture were to be valued and incorporated into it intact. This would go a long way toward precluding the desire, or the necessity, of minorities to dissolve in the melting pot.

Sansei anti-war activist and Socialist Workers Party candidate for Secretary of State, Los Angeles, 1970. *Photo by John Gray. Courtesy Patricia Iiyama.*

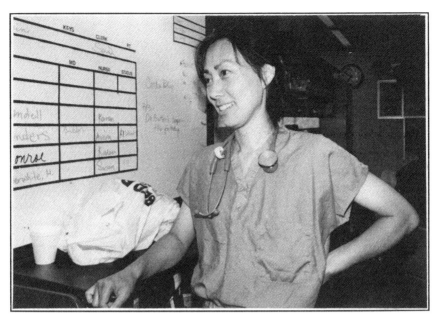

ABOVE: Sansei RN at Intensive Care Unit of Highland Hospital, Oakland, CA. © *Shirley Nakao*.

BELOW: Mother and daughter preparing food for Cherry Blossom Festival, Christ Church, San Francisco, April 22, 1989. © *Shirley Nakao*.

CHAPTER 15

Diversity

But the 1990s ought to be a good decade for American working women. We could even see a female president before the turn of the century. Now there's a rash prediction for you.

---Marianne Means

While Sansei women are not yet entertaining thoughts of becoming president, they have attained goals to which their mothers would never even have aspired. As earlier mentioned, the vast majority of Sansei are college graduates, allowing them a wide range of choices in their work. Our survey shows women dentists, consultants in government and finance, personnel managers, attorneys, editors, writers, doctors and a myriad other occupations. But we heard from secretaries, women in blue collar work, women who have been used and abused, ordinary women.

On the face of it, the diversity of their lives appear to parallel that of the contemporary lives of women around the nation. But there is a difference. Listening to them, one hears resonances of their cultural background, often a consciousness of the pull between the demands of being an American woman and one of Japanese ancestry.

Here, we represent something of the variety and dimension of their lives with fragments from stories, speeches, interviews, a poem and their appended statements in the surveys.

VOICES OF THE 80S

The major turning point in Barbara Morita's life, as in the lives of numerous other Sansei women, came with the Third World Strike in 1968 at U.C. Berkeley. She switched from pre-med courses to political science and sociology courses and became involved in the movement to establish ethnic courses on campus. Said Morita: "While my parents disapproved [of my actions], and they might yell at me, but as Japanese Americans, they would never abandon me. They would not disown me."

Jill Obrochta (Law Student):

My social life has been average American middle-class. Most of my Japanese American friends' parents wanted them to marry Japanese. My parents never did that. I think many Japanese Americans were afraid they would lose their culture, lose the blood line, which are good reasons. But I think you can keep the culture going by marrying a white person. My husband is very much into the culture. . . .

There's an inner strength that Isseis and Niseis have. I hope it's not lost among the Sanseis . . . . It's hard to explain what it is exactly, but I think it can be taught to our children if we teach them the way our parents brought us up.[1]

Renee Tajima, together with Christine Choy, produced the remarkable documentary *Who Killed Vincent Chin?* about the man who was mistakenly taken for Japanese and savagely clubbed to death by two disgruntled Detroit auto workers. When the film was nominated for an Oscar, Tajima said: "I think this recognition says a lot about Asian Americans, that they are part of this country. Their problems are very real problems. In a sense that's what this film is all about."[2]

Linda Jofuku (Carpenter, Coordinator for 1990 Census for Asian Pacific Islander population)

[About carpentry:] You would be working with hot wires and they [the men] would take water and douse you to see your wet tee shirt. Now they'd think it was funny. Or you'd get comments like "Hey, it's Wendy Tokuda!" I don't think I look anything like Wendy Tokuda, not even close. But that's how they relate to you.

[About work for the Census Bureau:] Throughout all my life I've always felt there was not an accurate representation of Asian Pacific Islanders or any other culturally diverse population. People really didn't know who and what we were, and we ourselves didn't speak up . . . . [The problem] really does stem from numbers and how people depict us or how we culturally identify ourselves. That's where the census comes in. There has traditionally been an under-representation of culturally diverse people throughout the years, and how we identified ourselves really makes a difference. One, it creates the false perception that we [Asian and Pacific Islanders] are all the same . . . . We are one of the fastest growing populations percentage-wise, and that . . . creates fear of too many of us coming in and too many of us in the schools.[3]

---

[1] Interview for OHP.

[2] "Stars Turn Out for 'Asian Oscars'," *Asian Week*, p. 18.

[3] Interview for OHP.

Susan Hayase (San Jose Taiko Group drummer)
Because of the media hype of the successes of Japanese multinational corporations, there has been a lot of fetishization of Japanese culture. There are "sashimi experts," calendars with twelve months worth of pictures of sushi, ninja classes, ad nauseum. Some of these people, --I call them Japanophiliacs--think that . . . American taiko groups are a part of this trend. But they couldn't be more wrong; that's not where American taiko comes from . . . . For one thing, the movement for justice and equality for all people, against assimilation and racist violence, for pride and a new Nikkei identity and culture, are what give American taiko its strong appeal, its power to inspire.[4]

Judy Narita, wrote, staged and acted in a one-woman show *Coming Into Passion, Song for a Sansei*, which won the Los Angeles Drama Critics' Circle Award, Drama-Logue Award and the "Jimmie" award from the Association of Asian/Pacific Artists. The show, a series of vignettes exploring stereotypes and truths about Asian women, includes depictions of a Vietnamese hooker, a punked out, teen-age Sansei, and a Filipina mail-order bride. What she ardently attempts to skewer is the stereotype of the Asian woman as "sexual, submissive and willing." Said she to a reviewer: "Did you see *Year of the Dragon*? The Asian model takes this garbage spewed at her and sleeps with the man. She's this passive *thing*. Appalling. And worse for me because she was an Asian because the perception of Asian women in this country is based on experiences with women in a country [Vietnam] where prostitution was not a matter of choice, but of survival."[5]

Anonymous:
Up until two summers ago, I had the sense that if I did my utmost to be a good human being, no harm would come to me. Two summers ago I was in a Japanese neighborhood when I was assaulted by a young Asian-American with a buck knife who said that if I continued to scream he would leave some interesting scars on my face and body. I believed him . . . . He proceeded to take my money, my car keys and then out of pure spite he decided to do to me what he believed the world had done to him many times over.

[At the hospital] I was embarrassed and ashamed. What would my family think? What if everyone found out? The headlines in Rafu [an ethnic newspaper] would blare out: "DAUGHTER OF UPSTANDING JA

---

[4]"Taiko," *East Wind*, Winter/Spring 1985, pp. 46-47.

[5]Janice Arkatov, "Narita's 'Song' Looks at Roles of Asian Women," *Los Angeles Times*, August 16, 1987.

FAMILY VIOLATED . . . (and besides, she probably asked for it)." So there I was, a couple of blocks from family and friends and yet they were the last people on earth I would want to know what had happened to me.[6]

Janice Mirikitani (Pres., Glide Memorial Foundation; Prog. Director, Glide; Poet):

Soul Food
for Cecil

We prepare
the meal together.
I complain,
hurt, reduced to fury
again by their
subtle insults
insinuations
because I am married to you
Impossible autonomy, no mind
of my own.

You like your fish
crisp, coated with cornmeal,
fried deep,
sliced mangos to sweeten
the tang of lemons.
My fish is raw,
on shredded lettuce,
lemon slices thin as skin,
wasabe burning like green fire.
You bake the cornbread flat
and dip it in
the thick soup
I've brewed from
turkey carcass, rice gruel,
sesame oil and chervil.

6"Rape: My Ordeal," *Nikkei-Sentinel*, n.d., p.8.

We laugh over watermelon
and bubbling cobbler.
You say,
there are few men
who can stand
to have a woman equal
upright.

This meal,
unsurpassed.[7]

Janice Shimizu (Public Sector Development)

In my opinion and experience, generally Japanese American women do not suffer significant economic/class oppression, as compared with other minority women in this country. Because JA women are not threatening to the racist and sexist, white-dominated culture, if we choose to play out the stereotype and remain within acceptable boundaries of behavior, we are allowed a certain measure of acceptance in society (even desirability) that other minority women and JA males are prohibited. It is this "advantage" that makes me feel that we have a personal and collective responsibility to take an active role and strong position in the struggle for equality among all people of color and to insist on equality within our own community.[8]

Dede Ogami (Partner, *Communicart*, Typesetting and Printing):

I started this business when I was fairly young, 23, with Ken Azebu who is now my husband. At first, I felt that I had many strikes against me, being a woman, being a minority, being young. Those factors did, I am sure, play some part in our struggle. But looking back, they were probably more of a mental handicap than an actual one. . . . I had to consciously separate myself from being docile and eager to please as I had been raised to be, and shift gears to a more direct and demanding persona. That's still hard for me at times. I often rely on Ken to help me determine which "me" I need to be to get things done. I'm embarrassed to admit that when I just can't face an unpleasant task, I coax him to do it for me. But I think as time passes I get a little better at it. I guess a cultural makeover is not an overnight process.[9]

Harriet Ishimoto (Partner, Kiyomura-Ishimoto Associates, Consultants):

---

[7]By permission, Janice Mirikitani, *Shedding Silence*, (Celestial Arts, Berkeley 1987), pp. 55-56.

[8]Survey.

[9]*Ibid.*

Being Japanese American is the deepest part of me. It gives a unique dimension to being a woman. It's an inescapable part of me. Without it, I am not whole . . .

Being Japanese American is not a disadvantage. America needs alternatives to traditional western know-how to stay competitive and maintain its stature as a world power. America needs what our heritage has to offer.[10]

To sum up the experience of Sansei women: their earlier ambivalent feelings about themselves as Japanese Americans seems to have settled into something touching on pride and, as a whole, they appear to hold a sense of high self-esteem. Our interviews and surveys tell us that this can largely be attributed to the nurturing home environment they enjoyed in their natal families, along with the lessening of prejudicial attitudes against them by members of the dominant society.

They acknowledge their strong feelings about family and their inclination to emphasize the importance of education, priorities handed down from their predecessors. And they appear to want to pass these values on to their children.

And while they have reached the penultimate stages of integration into American society, that is, they can obtain housing commensurate with income and status, they have acquired education for a broad spectrum of activity, have gained entry into status private clubs, to some degree, and have intermarried, they have yet to break down barriers to full participation. Sansei women have still to gain entry into high level executive positions in large business, industry and government, they have still to exert measurable political influence, and they have not gained entry into highest status organizations.

They have, however, not yet hit their peak years. And as they continue to push the boundaries of their former limits, something will have to give. For their progeny and for society as a whole, one hopes that it will not be the values that have sustained them and the generations before them.

---

[10]*Ibid.*

Bibliography

Arkatov, Janice. "Narita's 'Song' Looks at Roles of Asian Women." *Los Angeles Times*, August 17, 1987.

Arkoff A., etal. "Attitudes of Japanese American and Caucasian American Students Toward Marriage Roles." *Journal of Social Psychology* 59 (1963), pp. 11-15.

Befu, Harumi. "Patterns of Descent." In *Japanese Culture*, p.34. Chicago: Aldine Publishing Co., 1962.

Bridges, Noriko Sawada. "Papa Takes a Bride." *Harper's.* (December 1980), pp. 58-64.

Broom, Leonard and Ruth Reimer. *Removal and Return.* Berkeley: University of California Press, 1949.

Connor, John W. "Acculturation and Family Continuities in Three Generations of Japanese Americans." *Journal of Marriage and the Family.* February, 1974, p. 162.

Daniels, Roger. *Asian America.* Seattle and London: University of Washington Press, 1988.

Drinnon, Richard. *Keeper of Concentration Camps.* Berkeley and Los Angeles: University of California Press 1987.

East Bay Japanese For Action Presents "Our Recollections." Berkeley: EBJA Inc., 1986.

Garrett, Jessie A. and Ronald C. Larson. *Camp and Community.* Fullerton: California State University, 1972.

Gehrie, Mark Joshua. "Sansei: An Ethnography of Experience." Ph.D. Dissertation, Evanston, Ill., 1973.

Getlin, Josh, "Redress: One Made a Difference," *Los Angeles Times* (June 6, 1988).

Glenn, Evelyn Nakano. *Issei, Nisei, War Bride.* Philadelphia: Temple University Press, 1986.

Gordon, Milton. *Assimilation in American Life: The Role of Race, Religion and National Origins.* London: Oxford University Press, 1964.

Grodzins, Morton. *Americans Betrayed.* Chicago: University of Chicago Press, 1949.

Hayashi, Susan. "Taiko." *East Wind.* Winter/Spring 1985, pp. 46-47.

Hohri, William Minoru. *Repairing America.* Seattle and London: Washington State University Press, 1984.

Hosokawa, Bill. *Nisei, the Quiet Americans.* New York: William Morrow and Co., 1969.

Ichihashi, Yamato. *Japanese in the United States.* Palo Alto: Stanford University Press, 1932.

Ichioka, Yuji. *The Issei.* New York: Free Press, Macmillan, 1988.

Ito, Kazuo. *Issei, A History of Japanese Immigrants in North America.* Seattle: Executive Committee for Publications, 1973.

Kikumura, Akemi and Harry H.L. Kitano. "Interracial Marriage: A Picture of Japanese Americans." *Journal of Social Issues.* v. 29, No. 2, 1973.

Kikumura, Akemi. *Through Harsh Winters.* Novato: Chandler & Sharp Publishers, 1981.

Kitagawa, Daisuke. *Issei and Nisei.* New York: Seabury Press, 1967.

Kitano, Harry H.L. *Japanese Americans, The Evolution of a Subculture.* Englewood Cliffs, N.J.: Prentice Hall, 1969.

Kumamoto, Alan. "An Assimilated Generation." *Pacific Citizen*, 2 September 1966, p. 1.

Leighton, Alexander. *The Governing of Men.* Princeton: Princeton University Press, 1968.

Levine, Gene N. and Darrel M. Montero, "Socioeconomic Mobiity Among Three Generations of Japanese Americans." *Journal of Social Issues*, 29, No. 2 (1973), p. 45.

Masaoka, Jan. "I Forgot My Eyes Were Black." In *Asian Women*. Berkeley: 1971.

Maykovich, Minako. "Political Activism of Japanese American Youth." *Journal of Social Issues,* 29. No. 2., p. 183.

McWilliams, Carey. *Prejudice*. Boston: Little Brown and Co., 1944.

Mirikitani, Janice. *Shedding Silence.* Berkeley: Celestial Arts, 1987.

Montero, Darrel and Ronald Tsukashima. "Assimilation and Educational Achievement:The Case of Second Generation Japanese Americans. *Sociological Quarterly*, 18 (Autumn 1977), pp. 400-503.

Montero, Darrel, "For Japanese Americans, Erosion," *The New York Times*, (December 4, 1978), p. A21.

Myer, Dillon S. *Uprooted Americans*. Tucson: University of Arizona Press, 1971.

National Committee for Iva Toguri, "Iva Toguri D'Aquino.," San Francisco, 1976.

National Japanese American Historical Society. *Americans of Japanese Ancestry*. San Francisco: NJAHS, 1987.

Okamura, Taeko. Testimony in *Amerasia Journal*, v.8, no.2 (Fall/Winter, 1981), pp. 82-89.

Okubo, Mine. *Citizen 13600*. Seattle and London: University of Washington Press, 1983

Read, R.B., "The Sansei." *San Francisco Examiner and Chronicle* (August 14, 1966), p. 20.

Commission on Wartime Relocation and Internment of Civilians. *Personal Justice Denied.* Washington D.C.: U.S. Government Printing Office, 1982.

Sarasohn, Eileen Sunada, ed. *The Issei: Portrait of a Pioneer*. Palo Alto, CA: Pacific Books, 1983.

Smith, Bradford. *Americans from Japan*. New York: Lippincott, 1948.

Sone, Monica. *Nisei Daughter*. Seattle and London: University of Washington Press, 1953.

Sue, Derald Wing."Ethnic Identity: The Impact of Two Cultures on the Psychological Development of Asians in America." In *Asian Americans: Psychological Perspective*. ed. by Stanley Sue and Nathaniel N. Wagner.

Takaya, Junsuke. "Sei Wo Shiru Musume." *Colorado Times*, (January 1928).

Taketa, Henry. "Mayflower of the Pacific," *Pacific Citizen*, (December 1966) Sec. 3-B.

Tateishi, John. *And Justice for All*. New York: Random House, 1984.

tenBroek, Jacobus, Edward N. Barnhart and Floyd M. Matson. *Prejudice, War and the Constitution.* Berkeley and Los Angeles: University of California Press, 1954.

Thomas, Dorothy Swaine. *The Salvage.* Berkeley and Los Angeles: Univ. of California Press, 1952.

Tinker, John N. "Intermarriage and Ethnic Boundaries." *Journal of Social Issues*, v. 29. No. 2, 1973.

U.S. Department of the Interior. *People in Motion*. Washington D.C.: U.S. Government Printing Office, 1949.

Weglyn, Michi. *Years of Infamy*. New York: William Morrow and Company, 1976.

Yanagisako, Sylvia Junko. "Two Processes of Change in Japanese American Kinship." *Journal of Anthropological Research*, 31 (1975), pp. 201-202.

Index